D1246168

To Jim & Barbara
with Great JOY

Ken
(Kid brother)

2003

JACOB & *the* PRODIGAL

How

Jesus

Retold

Israel's

Story

KENNETH E. BAILEY

InterVarsity Press
Downers Grove, Illinois

InterVarsity Press
P.O. Box 1400, Downers Grove, IL 60515-1426
World Wide Web: www.ivpress.com
E-mail: mail@ivpress.com

InterVarsity Press® is the book-publishing division of InterVarsity Christian Fellowship/USA®, a student movement active on campus at hundreds of universities, colleges and schools of nursing in the United States of America, and a member movement of the International Fellowship of Evangelical Students. For information about local and regional activities, write Public Relations Dept., InterVarsity Christian Fellowship/USA, 6400 Schroeder Rd., P.O. Box 7895, Madison, WI 53707-7895, or visit the IVCF website at <www.ivcf.org>.

Scripture quotations, unless otherwise noted, are from the Revised Standard Version of the Bible, *copyright 1946, 1952, 1971 by the Division of Christian Education of the National Council of the Churches of Christ in the U.S.A., and are used by permission.*

Cover design: Kathleen Lay Burrows

Cover and interior images: The Meeting of Esau and Jacob: The Jewish Museum, NY/Art Resource, NY; Return of the Prodigal Son: Alinaii/Art Resource, NY

ISBN 0-8308-2727-7

Printed in the United States of America ∞

Library of Congress Cataloging-in-Publication Data

Bailey, Kenneth E.
  Jacob and the prodigal: how Jesus retold Israel's story/
Kenneth E. Bailey.
     p. cm.
Includes bibliographical references and index.
  ISBN 0-8308-2727-7 (pbk.: alk. paper)
  1. Prodigal son (Parable) 2. Jacob (Biblical patriarch) 3. Bible.
N.T. Luke XV, 11-32—Relation to Genesis. 4. Bible. O.T. Genesis
XXVII, 1-XXXVI, 8—Relation to Luke. 5. Bible. N.T. Luke
XV—Criticism, interpretation, etc. I. Title.
  BT378.P8B25 2003
  226.8'06—dc21

                                                                                    2003001545

P 17   16   15   14   13   12   11   10   9   8   7   6   5   4   3   2   1

Y 15   14   13   12   11   10   09   08   07   06   05   04   03

To

S ARA J AN B AILEY

in gratitude for her living faith

her courage in adversity

her compassion for all who suffer

her tenderness toward every living creature

and her deep love for her family and friends

CONTENTS

III. THE PARABLE OF THE PRODIGAL SON IN LUKE 15 COMPARED WITH THE SAGA OF JACOB IN GENESIS 27—35: *The Saga and the Parable: Comparisons and Contrasts*

FIGURES

PREFACE

Inasmuch as many have undertaken to" interpret the parables, "it seemed good to me also, having followed all things closely for some time past, to write an orderly account" (Lk 1:1, 3) of what I have learned about Luke 15 and of how the parable of the prodigal son is a new story patterned after the saga of Jacob.

For sixty years, from 1935 to 1995, my home was in the Middle East, first as a child and then as an adult. As an adult, teaching in Arabic Christian circles, reading Arabic and Syriac Christian literature from the early centuries, and trying to glean as much as possible from the extensive writings of the early rabbis, it has been my privilege to study the New Testament in the light of the cultural world of the Middle East. It is out of that background that I approach this topic.

For hundreds of years the Latin tradition has called this parable *Evangelium in Evangelio* (the gospel within the gospel), and so it is. But to discover its depths one must turn a number of corners in the mind while, at the same time, wrestling with a series of critical problems that the text presents even to a casual reader.

Jesus appears in the Gospels as a theologian who begins with a mastery of the tradition and then reshapes it by offering a new vision centered on his own person. This book will attempt to trace the movement of Jesus' mind along one critical stage of that vision. It is my intention to examine carefully the way in which Jesus takes the great saga of Jacob and reflects it in a new story composed with himself at its center. Jesus walks on stage not as a different Jacob but, rather, as a transformed figure of the father (Isaac). Reaching this conclusion has required some patient "digging."

Biblical exegesis is much like Middle Eastern archeology. The archeologist often returns, season after season, to the same tell, each year penetrating a deeper level of the ancient site in the hope of making a new and significant discovery. There is always the tantalizing possibility that the next dig *may* uncover a mosaic floor, a stone inscription or even a library.

For decades, the fifteenth chapter of Luke has been the center of my study of the New Testament.[1] Until recently, I was confident that I had considered at least all the major interpretive options available. Then, after extended intense focus on this "tell," I almost tripped over an ancient inscribed "mosaic floor" whose existence I had completely missed. For seven years, the British archeologist Howard Carter deliberately searched for the tomb of Tutankhamen and finally found it. I cannot take credit for such an intentional search because I chanced onto a treasure without even looking for it.

A gnawing hint of a connection between Luke 15 and the Jacob saga has lingered at the back of my mind for decades. This possible parallel was reawakened in my consciousness by a brief footnote in N. T. Wright's book *Jesus and the Victory of God.*[2] Wright observes that both Esau and the father "run, fall on the neck and kiss" a wayward younger son who is returning from a far country. This connection, along with the various "older brother" versus "younger brother" contrasts in the Old Testament, as they relate to the parable of the prodigal, has already been observed.[3]

But, to my knowledge, a full comparison between the prodigal and Jacob has not been pursued. In my personal study, a list of fifty-one points of comparison and contrast have gradually emerged. Because the fifty-one are interwoven, any discussion of them inevitably produces some overlapping.[4] Furthermore, the full significance of these parallels cannot be captured in a

---

[1]Cf. K. E. Bailey, *The Cross and the Prodigal; Finding the Lost: Cultural Keys to Luke 15;* "Exegesis of Luke 15," pp. 142-206; "Jacob and the Prodigal: A New Identity and a New Vision of Atonement," pp. 54-72; "Psalm 23 and Luke 15: A Vision Expanded," pp. 54-71; "Jacob and the Prodigal Son: A New Identity Story," pp. 23-24; "The Pursuing Father," pp. 34-40.

[2]N. T. Wright, *Jesus and the Victory of God,* p. 127, n. 10.

[3]I. Abrahams, *Studies in Pharisaism and the Gospels,* p. 11; J. D. M. Derrett, "Law in the New Testament: The Parable of the Prodigal Son," p. 68; B. B. Scott, *Hear Then the Parable,* p. 112.

[4]I have developed a threefold classification of these fifty-one points of comparison and contrast, which is reflected in the labels (A), (B) and (C) found in the table of contents and in the subheadings of chapters 11-14. A full explanation of the categories is given on pages 132-33 and in the appendix (pp. 216-18).

single brief volume. Instead, I intend here to display the unearthed artifacts (as it were), with a few preliminary reflections on what they may mean.

Some of these parallels are heavily freighted with theological significance. Others appear to function only as threads that help bind the two stories together. Multiple examples of each type appear below. It will be argued that in Luke 15:4-32, Jesus of Nazareth addresses the scribes and Pharisees and through them speaks to the entire nation. He deliberately creates a new story patterned after the Jacob story and offers his people a revised identity story with himself at its center. As Wright says, "Most historical characters worth studying are so because they held mindsets that formed significant variations on the parent worldview."[5] These "variations on the parent worldview" are the subject of this monograph.

Another way to look at this task is to view the parable of the prodigal son as a story with three settings like three zoom-lens photographs of a single scene. Imagine being shown a photograph of a happy child on a swing. The picture has its own integrity and is a joy to behold. Then the photographer places a second picture beside the first; the second is the same scene but has been taken with a wider lens. Now it is possible to see the mother pushing the child on the swing and observe that the swing is suspended from the branch of a cherry tree in full bloom. The smile on the child's face takes on new meaning, and the larger picture provides the viewer with additional delights. Finally, the photographer presents a third picture, which is still of the same scene. Only this time the shot is even wider, and it is evident that the cherry tree with its swing is growing in a zoo and that the child is looking at a baby elephant being cuddled by its mother. Once again the yet larger scene adds new and important meaning to the other two.

In like manner, the parable of the prodigal son can be studied on its own. Such a "close-up" is certainly valid. A wider "lens" shows the parable of the prodigal as part of the three lost-and-found stories in Luke 15.[6] This is like looking at the child on the swing with the mother and the cherry tree in view. The third shot depicts how the parable of the compassionate father and the two lost sons, as I prefer to call it, is a reshaping of the saga of Jacob. This is akin to the third picture that shows the child on the swing in the zoo looking at the elephants. Examining the third picture is the major task of this book. It

---

[5]N. T. Wright, *Jesus and the Victory of God,* p. 139.
[6]In my publications listed in footnote one, I use these first two lenses.

will be necessary to reflect briefly on the "close-ups" before getting to the "widest lens," and perhaps a good starting place for the whole endeavor is to note a few unsuspected problems that the entire chapter presents.

The parable of the prodigal son appears to have no savior. The prodigal (representing one type of sinner) "came to himself" in the far country. Traditionally, this has been understood to mean: He repented. The prodigal eventually discovers that he can not be successful on his own feeding pigs and only then starts for home, where his father welcomes him. For centuries the father has been seen as a symbol for God. It seems, therefore, that God waits for us to return home and then welcomes us but does not go after us. The story appears to have no incarnation, no "word that becomes flesh," no cross, no crown, no suffering, no death, no resurrection and no mediator between God and human beings. How can this be "the gospel within the gospel" when the gospel, as known throughout the New Testament, is apparently missing? But there is more.

The first two stories appear to be in conflict with the third. In the first two the "finder" does all the work. The good shepherd leaves his flock and goes after the lost sheep, "until he finds it." The poor sheep cannot find its own way home. My Middle Eastern shepherd acquaintances tell me that a lost sheep becomes disoriented quickly and crawls under the nearest bush awaiting rescue. The good woman lights a lamp, sweeps the house and "searches diligently" until she finds her coin. The coin does not flip up out of a crack between the flagstones of the rough floor and land on the table. The woman must find it. Yet, *on his own,* the prodigal *goes home* from the far country. Is Jesus confused? These and other problems of interpretation will be examined carefully as we proceed.

But, as stated, the central thrust of this modest effort is to identify and reflect on the relationship between the saga of Jacob (Gen 27:1—36:8) and the parable of the father and the two lost sons. As observed, some have noted the phrase, "run, fall on the neck and kiss," and others have identified the younger brother/older brother conflict that appears in both stories.[7] This study will examine many additional observed points of comparison and contrast between these two great stories. The question of the importance of this inter-

---

[7] B. B. Scott, *Hear Then the Parable,* pp. 112-13; I. Abrahams, *Studies in Pharisaism and the Gospels,* p. 11; N. T. Wright, *Jesus and the Victory of God,* p. 127; R. Q. Ford, *The Parables of Jesus,* pp. 134-39.

connectedness for understanding Jesus as a theologian and for comprehending his theology will be addressed. As N. T. Wright has written, "He [Jesus] was telling the story of Israel, giving it a drastic new twist, and inviting his hearers to make it their own, to heed his warnings and follow his invitation."[8]

I hasten to add that this book will make no attempt at source criticism of the Jacob saga. Nor will it wrestle with the question of when the book of Genesis came together in its final form. Contemporary scholarship on the biblical account of Jacob is important but not for this subject. The focus here will strictly be on Genesis 27—35 as a story read by Jesus and his contemporaries in the first century. From the author of *Jubilees* (c. 150 B.C.) through to Josephus (c. A.D. 90) it is clear that first-century Jews knew the Jacob saga as a continuous narrative. The scribes and Pharisees who composed Jesus' audience also saw it as a single story. Exactly how they interpreted it cannot be fully recovered, nor does it matter for the purposes of this study. What Josephus, Philo and the pre-Christian Jewish author of *Jubilees* did with Jacob's story will be noted briefly. The fourth-century rabbinic commentary *Genesis Rabbah* will enter into the discussion. These works will provide a quick overview of other Jews, before and after Jesus, who also interacted with the Jacob story. It is my intention to narrow the subject to an examination of that which Luke records from Jesus in the parable of the prodigal son and how it compares and contrasts with Genesis 27—36:8.

Twentieth-century publications on the parables of Jesus are extensive. Craig L. Blomberg and others have ably reviewed the various authors and methodologies that have developed.[9] I will not attempt a similar survey. And it is not my intention to debate with those who have disagreed with my published work on Luke 15. This brief study will explore uncharted territory rather than defend the past. As mentioned, current scholarship on the parables does not discuss this topic. It is my hope that the new ground broken here will be of use for the worldwide church, both East and West. The peoples of the Two-Thirds World, where the majority of Christians now live, easily understand extended family sagas and they, better than we, may be able to articulate yet deeper understandings of both these stories.

---

[8]N. T. Wright, *Jesus and the Victory of God*, p. 173.
[9]For a thorough, detailed review of this literature, cf. C. L. Blomberg, *Interpreting the Parables*, pp. 13-167. A shorter discussion is offered by B. B. Scott, *Hear Then the Parable*, pp. 3-73.

Luke 15 contains well-known "classical" tales. I have chosen the RSV as my text of choice because its style is more formal than many recent translations. On rare occasions I have made my own translations from the Greek text, and these will be identified as such.

Sincere thanks go to thousands of Arabic-speaking Christians across the Middle East with whom I have studied the parables for decades. My debt to them and to the rich Arabic Christian exegetical heritage can never be adequately expressed or paid. I am also deeply grateful to Tom Cousins, Harris and Susan Cummings, Eastminster Presbyterian Church, the Loch Raven Presbyterian Church, and Richard and Beverly Spaan for making possible the acquiring of special resources, and securing critical secretarial help needed for the research and writing of this manuscript. To all of them I offer my thanks. My gratitude must also be expressed to my editor, Andrew Le Peau of InterVarsity Press, for his vision, insight, patience and encouragement. My dear wife of fifty years, Ethel, has put up with more hours of discussion and lecture on Luke 15 than anyone should have to endure. Without her never failing help and encouragement this book would not have been written.

I invite you, gentle reader, to join me in pondering first the girl on the swing and then to look more intently to see her with her mother. The climax of the study will be an attempt to present the entire scene complete with the elephants in full view.

I

Introduction:
What Does It Mean to
Call Jesus a Theologian?

1

Jesus as a Metaphorical Theologian and the Rabbinic World

What is theology, and what does it mean to be a theologian? Is theological meaning created by linking ideas together with reason/logic, ideas that may or may not have illustrations attached to them for clarity? In such a world, the illustration is sometimes useful but, in reality, nonessential and can be discarded once the concept is clearly grasped. The illustration becomes a delivery system for an idea. The creator of meaning who uses this method probably will not add an illustration if the concept is clear to the reader/listener without one.[1] The idea matters. The illustration introduced to clarify or communicate that idea does not. This is a time-honored way to "do theology" and will continue to be important.

There is, however, another way to create and communicate meaning. It involves the use of word pictures, dramatic actions, metaphors and stories. This latter method of "doing theology" shines through the pages of Scripture. Dale Allison has written, "Meaning is like water: it is shaped by the container it fills."[2]

The biblical writers and reciters make extensive use of metaphors, parables and dramatic actions. Jesus does not say, "God's love is boundless." Instead, he tells the story of the prodigal son. He does not say, "Your

---

[1]Dietrich Bonhoeffer is capable of creating profound meaning relying strictly on concepts. He can pen entire essays or sermons without a single illustration. He doesn't need them (cf. D. Bonhoeffer, *Meditations on the Cross*).

[2]Dale Allison, "Books and the Book," installation address by Dr. Dale C. Allison Jr., 2001, p. 16.

benevolence must reach beyond your own kith and kin." Rather, he tells the story of the good Samaritan. He does not say, "Try to influence the community around you for good." But he does state,

> You are the light of the world. A city set (by men) on a hill cannot be hid. Nor do they (i.e., the women) light a lamp and put it under a bushel, but on a lamp stand, and it gives light to all in the house. (Mt 5:14-16; author's translation)

Thomas Aquinas created meaning with the masterful use of philosophical and theological language. Saint Francis affected the church and the world with powerful dramatic actions that have resonated for more than seven hundred years. It is easy to claim that Saint Thomas was a theologian while Saint Francis was a simple man who went about doing good. But such an equation is not adequate to the reality of the significance of these two theological giants. Both men created and communicated meaning, but in different ways, and each method is valid.

Jesus, as noted, was clearly a "metaphorical theologian" whose primary style of creating meaning was the skillful use of metaphor, parable and dramatic action.[3] But is it accurate to refer to Jesus as a theologian at all? Theologians are known for changing their minds. They publish second editions of their works and describe themselves as "birds in flight." Yet Jesus, reason some, was different. Being who he was, he understood the things of God instinctively and did not need to wrestle, like others, with how to understand or express divine truth. He was neither puzzled nor uncertain about the deep things of God.

The christological convictions that prompt the above reservations are important, and I share those convictions. But do we have the right to confine Jesus to the category of "simple carpenter"? Would not the "divine word made flesh" be the first to reflect deeply on the significance and meaning of that word? Could Jesus' indescribable impact on history have been possible were he not a profound thinker?

The answers to these questions are clear. Jesus was indeed a craftsman. In Mark 6:3 he is referred to as a *tektōn.*[4] This word is usually translated "carpenter," but it can also mean a carpenter/builder or artisan. Traditional village culture in the Middle East uses little furniture. The Gospels rarely mention home

---

[3]For a more complete discussion of this chapter's topic, cf. K. E. Bailey, *Finding,* pp. 15-28.
[4]The only other use of this Greek word is in Matthew 13:55, which identifies Joseph as a *tektōn.*

furnishings.[5] In short, a cabinetmaker would find little to do in a small village like Nazareth. But doors and roof beams are necessary in every house, and they require a woodworker's skills.[6] Jesus tells a number of parables that refer to the building trade (Mt 5:14-15, noted above; Lk 6:46-49 and parallel Mt 7:24-27). While he was growing up in Nazareth, the provincial capital Sepphoris was being constructed by Herod Antipas.[7] Joseph may well have moved to Nazareth because there was work for a carpenter/builder in Sepphoris four miles away. But, carpenter/builders are generally known to be practical, non-intellectual types. Is it possible to envision a carpenter/builder as a theologian?

In the world of the rabbis, a scholar was expected to earn his keep by engaging in a secular profession. The Mishnah tractate *Avot* reads:

> Make them [the words of the Law] not a crown wherewith to magnify thyself or a spade wherewith to dig. And thus used Hillel to say: He that makes worldly use of the crown shall perish. Thus thou mayest learn that he that makes profit out of the words of the Law removes his life from the world.[8]

From this severe stricture it is easy to understand that rabbis in Jesus' day were expected to support themselves with secular professions. Engaging stories in the Talmud illuminate the strictly held principle of "no digging with the crown."

Johanan ben Zakkai, a contemporary of Jesus, once lectured to his students in the shade of the temple. The learned rabbi was then criticized for having received material benefit from religious things. That is, he was accused of "digging with the crown." Later rabbinic tradition excused him because what happened inside the temple was religious but the shade outside was not. The text reads:

---

[5]There was a seat in the synagogue designated as "Moses' seat" (Mt 23:2), and in the temple those who sold pigeons had "seats" (Mk 11:15; Mt 21:12), but the word *kathedra* (chair/seat) does not occur again anywhere in the New Testament. Likewise, the word *trapeza* (table) appears as a table for money changers (Mt 21:12; Jn 2:1) and as a bank (Lk 11:23). Rich men have tables for meals (Mt 15:27; Lk 16:21), and the great banquet with the Messiah at the end of all things will be at a table (Lk 22:30). Only Luke 22:21 refers to a table in the upper room. The *krabattos* of the Gospels is a pallet that the sick man at the pool of Bethzatha could pick up (Jn 5:2-9). The other word for a bed in the Gospels, *klinē,* is also something a healed sick man could carry (Mk 9:2, 6; Lk 5:18).

[6]The occasional farm implement would also be shaped by the village carpenter/builder. The Greek words for *plow* (Lk 9:62), *winnowing fork* (Lk 3:17; parallel Mt 3:12) and *yoke* (Mt 11:29-30) each occur in only one account in the Gospels.

[7]R. A. Batey, *Jesus and the Forgotten City,* pp. 65-82.

[8]Mishnah, *Avot* 4:5, trans. Danby, p. 453.

It was related of R. Johanan b. Zakkai that he was sitting in the shadow of the Temple and teaching all day. Now here it was impossible [not to lecture], and he intended [to benefit from the shade], and is it permitted? But Raba said: The Temple was different, because it was made for its inside.[9]

The stipulation of "not digging with the crown" harmonized smoothly with the major task of the sages, which was to interpret and apply the Torah to *everyday life*. Thus, if they had one foot in the work-a-day world and the other in the world of the Torah and its law, it would be easier to make the connection between the two.[10]

Shemmai and Hillel, two of the greatest rabbis, lived one generation before Jesus. Shemmai was a stonemason, and Hillel probably earned his keep as a porter. Thus, Jesus (carpenter) and Paul (tentmaker) were not exceptions to the rule but were concrete examples of established practice. Unlike the contemporary Western world, the world of Jesus *expected* the scholar to be engaged in a trade such as carpentry. The question that naturally follows is: What sort of intellectual life would have been available to a young man growing up in an isolated village?

In Jesus' day, across the villages of Galilee and Judea, there were associations of serious-minded Jews who called themselves the *haberim* (the companions/friends).[11] The name was taken from Psalm 119:63, which reads, "I am a companion *[haber]* of all who fear thee, / of those who keep thy precepts." These associations were composed of men who were employed in secular trades but who spent their spare time debating the Law and trying to apply it to their world. A young Jew in his early teens had the option of joining such a group. If he decided to do so, he was committed to becoming a "student of the rabbis" and participating in their discussions. Those Jews who wished to spend their spare time in activities other than scholarly debates were not a part of these associations. The rabbis called such types *am ha-arets*, "the people of the land." This title was not a compliment, and considerable hostility developed between these two groups.[12] It seems natural to assume

---

[9]Babylonian Talmud, *Pesahim* 26a.

[10]Rabban Gamaliel, the son of R. Judah the Patriarch, is reported to have said, "Excellent is the study of the Law together with worldly occupation, for toil in them both puts sin out of mind" (Mishnah, *Avot* 2:2, trans. Danby, p. 447).

[11]Shemuel Safrai, "Religion in Everyday Life," *The Jewish People in the First Century*, 2:793-833. Note especially pp. 802-5, 820-81, 824.

[12]Babylonian Talmud, *Pesahim* 49b.

that Jesus joined the *haberim.* The story about him in the temple at twelve years of age emphasizes his intelligence and his scholarly bent (Lk 2:41-51). With this pattern of culture in mind, it is easy to assume that Jesus went on to spend eighteen years in sustained discussion with the brightest and best thinkers in Nazareth and the surrounding villages. When, at the age of thirty, Jesus began his public ministry, he demonstrated time and again considerable skill in the rabbinic style of debating, and, therefore, it is not surprising that the community called him "rabbi."

The title *rabbi* emerged in first-century Judaism as a title of respect for a scholar. Students used it for a teacher, and the community at large used it for the scribes and sages. Eduard Lohse states, "When Jesus is called Rabbi by His disciples and others, this shows that He conducted Himself like the Jewish scribes."[13] David Flusser, the able Israeli scholar writes, "It is easy to observe that Jesus was far from uneducated. He was perfectly at home both in holy scripture and in oral tradition, and he knew how to apply this scholarly heritage."[14] Flusser goes on to note that carpenters in particular had a reputation for learning. With this in mind Flusser then rejects "the common, sweetly idyllic notion of Jesus as a naive and amiable, simple, manual workman."[15]

In summary, Jesus was a master in the use of metaphor, parable and dramatic action. His audiences were often composed of scribes and Pharisees. The reader of the Gospels needs to be aware that when a scholarly audience is specifically mentioned, it can be assumed that a sophisticated scholarly exchange is underway.[16] When this assumption is made, new perceptions of Jesus and his message emerge. The following text provides an example.

Jesus' first sermon and the crowd reaction to it are recorded in Luke 4:16-30. In that famous scene Jesus reads from Isaiah 61:1-2. The text, however, is edited in four places. One phrase from the text before him is omitted. A line is borrowed from Isaiah 58:6 and added to the reading. One key word is changed from "say" to "proclaim," and the final verse is cut in half. Who did the editing? The Mishnah stipulates that in any public reading of the Prophets, the reader is permitted some editing. The rules for the reading of the To-

---

[13]E. Lohse, "Rabbi," in *Theological Dictionary of the New Testament,* 6:961-65.
[14]David Flusser, *Jesus,* p. 30.
[15]David Flusser, *Jesus,* p. 33.
[16]For a fuller discussion of this topic, cf. K. E. Bailey, "Jesus as Metaphorical Theologian," and "Jesus Within First Century Judaism," in *Finding,* pp. 15-28.

rah of Moses were stricter.[17] The editor of the text of Isaiah 61:1-2 that appears in Luke 4:18-19 (whoever he was) followed those rules, and thus, said editor is best understood to be a first-century Jew. Did Jesus do the editing? Or was it the apostles who remembered and later recorded, and edited, the scene and the text of Isaiah that Jesus read on that occasion? Or was it Luke who tried to summarize his understanding of what the ministry of Jesus was all about? If Jesus was no more than a simple carpenter, it is difficult to imagine that he was the editor. If he was a scholar with eighteen years of training in rabbinic thinking, then it is entirely reasonable to imagine him judiciously editing the text. The presuppositions we have about Jesus as a "simple man" or as a "serious theologian/scholar" determine the eyes with which we look at the text and how we understand it.

When the finely tuned nature of Jesus' presentations to his contemporaries is examined within the world of first-century rabbinic scholarship, it is possible to see Jesus as the first mind of the New Testament and Paul as the second. From Jesus we have indescribably profound theological perceptions of the faith available to us.

As noted, the intent of this book is to examine how Jesus the theologian has created a new story, with himself at its center, which is linked again and again to the saga of Jacob. But such an inquiry is not possible unless we are confident that the Synoptic Gospels in general, and the Gospel of Luke in particular actually present an authentic account of what Jesus said and did! Strident voices on one side insist that Jesus left Spirit-inspired mental tape recordings of exactly what he said. Some scholars from the extreme on the other side insist that the Gospel records are imaginative creations by a second, third or even fourth generation of Christians who invented stories to meet their spiritual needs and that these stories have very little to do with the mysterious figure called Jesus who all but disappeared into the mists of time early in the first century. Yet others claim that the Gospels are a record (in story form) of the religious experience of the early Christians, not a record of what Jesus said and did. Is there any assurance of the *authenticity* of the Synoptic accounts as historical records of Jesus? To this question we now briefly turn.

---

[17]Mishnah, *Mo'ed* 4:4. Around A.D. 200 the Mishnah recorded the traditions of the past. It is not possible to prove that these regulations for synagogue reading were in force at the time of Jesus. What is striking is that they are followed in the Lucan text. The Talmud expands these same regulations into a set of six rules (Minor Tractates, *Soferim* chap. 11 [39a(2)-39b(2)]).

2

THE JESUS TRADITION AND THE
QUESTION OF AUTHENTICITY

For centuries the world of Islam has claimed that the Gospels are *muharrif* (corrupted) because they do not offer readers an accurate record of what Jesus said and did. For different reasons, some modern scholars have come to the same conclusion. The debate over the authenticity of the Gospels as records of what Jesus said and did raged over most of the twentieth century and continues on into the twenty-first. The issue is of the essence for all the material in the Gospels and for the subject of this book. Are the three parables in Luke 15 the theology of Jesus, or are they stories created by the disciples long after his time? Were they composed by Luke for Gentile readers and attributed to Jesus, or can they be traced to the "theologian of Nazareth"?

Having previously discussed these matters at some length in another setting, only a brief summary is necessary here.[1] The following five important aspects of the topic need to be kept in mind.

JESUS THE RABBI
The rabbinic tradition was accustomed to orally passing on the sayings of the important figures in its tradition. After centuries of oral preservation, this material was finally recorded in writing, first in the Mishnah and then in the two Talmuds. The "movers and shakers" who fashioned Judaism, as it survived across the centuries, did not record their teaching in books. Minor scholars,

---

[1]K. E. Bailey, "Informal"; "Oral Tradition"; "The Historical Jesus: A Middle Eastern View."

such as Ben Sirach, composed documents, which were sometimes copied and preserved. But the teaching of the truly great early figures, such as Hillel, Shammai, Johanan ben Zakkai, Gamaliel, Simeon ben Gamaliel, Eleazar, Akiba and Judah the Prince were, for more than a century, remembered only through oral tradition. Although he wrote nothing, Akiba (first and second centuries) is quoted more than 270 times in the Mishnah alone. It can be assumed that over the centuries extra material was added to earlier tradition. But there *was* an earlier tradition to pass on, and that tradition was honored and preserved.

Indeed, within the rabbinic tradition the oral was the chosen method of preservation and transmission. The rabbis possessed written scriptures, but the sayings of the sages were by choice preserved in oral form for a very long time. There are two discernible reasons for this preference. If the material remained in oral form, the reciter could control who heard the sacred tradition. Unworthy ears would not be given access to it. It is far more difficult to monitor who will read a book; oral tradition demands a reciter. Furthermore, if the material is of an oral nature, the reciter can ensure that there is time for adequate explanation of that which has been recited. These two reasons are readily understandable to people the world over irrespective of their culture.

Every human being has a very personal sacred tradition that is almost always kept oral for the same two reasons. We want to control who will hear our most personal stories, and we want to make certain that there is an opportunity to explain the meaning of those stories if and when we choose to reveal them. That which all of us understand instinctively on the personal level functions on the community level in the Middle East. Like other well-known rabbis, Jesus attracted disciples. It is only natural to assume that he, like his contemporaries, deliberately passed on to them, in oral form, those insights into the mysteries of God that he considered important. In a monumental work of scholarship, Birger Gerhardsson has documented this entire process as it applies to the New Testament.[2]

The *Haflat Samar*

Middle Eastern traditional culture as I have known it engages in what is called in Arabic *haflat samar* (party for preservation; pl. *haflaat samar*). All present

---

[2]B. Gerhardsson, *Memory and Manuscript*. For a critical summary of Gerhardsson's case, cf. W. H. Kelber, *The Oral and the Written Gospel*, pp. 8-14.

at such gatherings sit in a circle and participate in a single conversation. No formal "storytellers" are designated as reciters. Anyone is free to participate. The purpose is to delight, entertain and inform the gathering. Jokes and casual stories are told at such occasions, but they are not considered important and the recitation of such material is not controlled. However, the proverbs and stories that form the identity of the community are preserved with great care, because through those wisdom sayings and stories the people in the community remember and affirm who they are. No one dares recite such stories carelessly, or change them at will. Doing so invites public correction and thereby public humiliation. The community exercises control over these, often centuries-old, stories. In the above-mentioned essays I have described how these social events function, what types of material are recited and the ways in which the material is controlled.[3] But there is more.

REMEMBERING KEY PEOPLE AND EVENTS

As an amateur yet serious student of the American Civil War, I am constantly amazed at the sheer volume of material, which was preserved orally for half a century and longer, surrounding the key figures in that conflict. These recollections are called "reminiscences." The Americans involved in the war knew they were experiencing events critical for their very existence as a nation. Abraham Lincoln, Robert E. Lee and T. J. (Stonewall) Jackson were key figures in those events. Authors of books and essays on the American Civil War have drawn on these reminiscences, which flowed from people who knew and interacted with those towering personalities. Colleagues remembered what Lincoln and Lee said and did because of their pivotal roles in the conflict and because the conflict itself was an identity-forming epoch. Reminiscences of historic personalities were also passed down through the twentieth century.

Television documentaries made in recent decades about Winston Churchill and John F. Kennedy naturally include interviews with eyewitnesses. In these documentaries people who knew these famous men are asked questions. As they reply, with recollections of fifty-year-old conversations or stories, their voices pick up, the pace quickens and their eyes begin to flash. How can they remember back that far? Why are these recollections so vivid?

---

[3]A brief summary of my analysis of the *haflat samar* and how it functions is provided by N. T. Wright in his book *Jesus and the Victory of God*, pp. 133-37. Wright notes, "Bailey's proposal has, to my mind, the smell of serious social history about it" (p. 135).

The answer is simple—the eyewitnesses know they are talking about key figures in critical events, and, as a result, their memories reproduce those sayings and stories with accuracy and ease.

Russian historian Edvard Radzinsky recently collected oral tradition about Czar Nicholas II focusing on the last six months of his life, a period for which there are almost no documents. Once the Russian public learned that Radzinsky was seeking information about the czar, individuals began to search him out and tell him their stories. The events they described had been passed from grandfather to son and then to grandsons and granddaughters for more than seventy years. They were recalling the *czar!* How could they forget?! Radzinsky was often able to confirm the material he heard by cross checking the same story as it came to him from a variety of sources. While there were sometimes differences, the similarities were striking. In the end Radzinsky produced a 430-page book, much of which came from seventy-year-old oral tradition.[4] All of this took place among the Russians—without the controls I discovered in the Middle East. Was the Russian grandfather telling the truth or trying to impress his grandchildren? There was no surrounding community to correct the recitation. In the Middle East there is.

In the 1990s Winston Churchill's granddaughter, Celia Sandys, set out to write a book about her famous grandfather. She intended to dedicate one chapter to the eight months Churchill spent in South Africa during the Boer War. Consequently, she traveled to South Africa to visit the places where Churchill was known to have been. During a national television interview she asked viewers to contact her if they had any information about her grandfather. They did. Sandys was overwhelmed and delighted by the deluge of calls, faxes and letters she received and decided to write not a chapter but an entire book about Churchill's sojourn in South Africa.[5] The book, now published, focuses entirely on the eight months he was in the country, and the information she gathered was almost all passed on orally, again, without any community controls. By the time those conversations and stories were related to her they were nearly one hundred years old. How could people remember? The simple answer is—it was *Churchill!* He was already a well-known figure when he went to South Africa. The question is: How could they forget?

The early apostolic community was composed of Jews who had accepted

[4]E. Radzinsky, *The Last Tsar.*
[5]C. Sandys, *Churchill Wanted Dead or Alive.*

Jesus as the Messiah of God. Not all their Jewish neighbors and family members endorsed that decision. Recalling and remembering the stories of what Jesus said and did was critical for their new identity as "messianic Jews." To forget would be to forget who they were. Controlling the tradition of/about Jesus (with some freedom of individual expression permitted) was essential to that identity. Free composition would have been as unthinkable as it clearly became for Lincoln, Lee, Nicholas II and Churchill. These kinds of human realities need to be factored into perceptions of how and why the "eyewitnesses and ministers of the word" (Lk 1:2) managed to authentically preserve the stories of and from Jesus of Nazareth and pass them on to Luke and the other Gospel authors. Kelber has written, "Many of the individual disciples, apostles, prophets, teachers, and ordinary followers of Jesus will forever remain anonymous, but that is not the same as saying that the Jesus traditions are rooted in the anonymous matrix of the community."[6]

LUKE AND THE "WE SECTIONS" OF THE BOOK OF ACTS

In the book of Acts, Luke occasionally uses the second-person plural pronoun *we*. Then, suddenly, the pronoun disappears. The sections where it is present have been called the "we sections" of Acts. Across the twentieth century a number of scholars put forth the idea that the use of *we* was simply a literary device that has little to do with history. In a recent essay Joseph Fitzmyer, the renowned American Catholic scholar, argues that on examination the evidence against historicity collapses. Fitzmyer concludes that Luke was an honest man who used *we* when he was with Paul and used *he* and *they* when he was apart from Paul.[7] With this view in mind, the reader can trace Luke's use of *we* on Paul's last journey to Jerusalem. In chapter twenty-one "we" (Paul and Luke) travel to Cos, Rhodes, Cyprus, Tyre and on to Caesarea (Acts 21:1-8). Finally *we* arrive in Jerusalem (Acts 21:17-18) and are received by James and the elders. Paul is then arrested, taken back to Caesarea and imprisoned for two years. During this two-year period the pronoun *we* does not appear in the text. But when Paul demands that his case be examined by Caesar and that he be sent to Rome, suddenly "we" set sail for Italy (Acts 27:1). After that, "we" pass through many ports and are shipwrecked on Malta; finally "we" (Acts 28:14) arrive in Rome. Following Fitzmyer's view of the historicity of

---

[6]W. H. Kelber, *The Oral and the Written Gospel*, p. 28.
[7]J. Fitzmyer, *Luke the Theologian: Aspects of His Teaching*, pp. 16-22.

these "we sections," it is clear that Luke was with Paul on his last journey to Jerusalem. Luke had no access to Paul when the latter was arrested and imprisoned for two years. But when the authorities decided to send Paul to Rome, Luke was able to join him for the journey. Thus Luke, by his own indirect admission, was in Jerusalem from approximately A.D. 57 to 59. [8] He was not, however, with Paul.

So what did Luke do for those two years? He was an educated man, probably a medical doctor. As well, he was deeply committed to Jesus and naturally was living as part of the messianic Jewish community (most likely) in Jerusalem. The simplest and most obvious answer to the above question is to suppose that Luke engaged in field research for his Gospel. Many people complete research some time before they are able to organize their findings into readable or printable form. I am not trying to solve the Synoptic problem (which Gospel was first and who copied from whom) here.[9] Rather, I would note that, by his own indirect admission, Luke was in Jerusalem for two years, at a time when literally thousands of eyewitnesses to the historical Jesus were available to him. Thus, the stories of and from Jesus that he gathered at that time are early and reliable. For me, the key is authenticity not "tape recordings" of what was said and done. I am convinced that the Gospel of Luke is a *primary* witness to Jesus of Nazareth and a *secondary* witness to the theology of Luke. The material Luke presents was collected from living witnesses to the events described some twenty-seven to twenty-nine years after the cross and resurrection, which causes one to reflect on what Luke himself said were his sources.

THE "EYEWITNESSES AND MINISTERS OF THE WORD"

Luke is the only Gospel author who tells his readers about his sources (Lk 1:1-4). He affirms his knowledge of documents when he writes, "Many have undertaken to compile a narrative of the things which have been accomplished among us." He then mentions "eyewitnesses and ministers of the word." The first is easily understood, but to what, precisely, does the latter phrase refer?

Initially, it can be noted that the phrase contains one definite article and two nouns. That is, Luke writes, "*the* eyewitnesses and ministers of the

---

[8] R. Jewett, *Dating Paul's Life,* pp. 100-104.

[9] My own view is that Luke did indeed compose the "first edition" of his Gospel at that time. Some years later he expanded his Gospel into the form we have now. But this discussion takes us too far afield.

word." In nearly all cases in Greek grammar when a single definite article is followed by two nouns, the two nouns refer to the same thing. This means that the eyewitnesses are the ministers of the word and the ministers of the word are the eyewitnesses. The definition of the word *eyewitness* is clear. But what does the phrase "minister of the word" actually mean?

In Greek, the word *minister* is *hypēretēs*. The question then becomes: What is the meaning of the word *hypēretēs* in a first-century Jewish context? *Hypēretēs* is well known as the Greek translation of the Hebrew word *hazzan*. The *hazzan* was the single paid employee of a synagogue. He was not the head of the synagogue but rather its "minister" *(hazzan)*.[10] Of this official's responsibilities, Shemuel Safrai writes, "The head of the Synagogue had an adjutant the *hazzan* (חזן), undoubtedly the ὑπηρέτης of Luke 4:20, who acted as executive officer in the practical details of running the synagogue. . . . Officers with similar functions had been attached to the Temple."[11]

In the New Testament the *hazzan* appears as an official both in the synagogue (Lk 4:20) and in the temple (Mk 14:54, 65). Among the various tasks the *hypēretēs/hazzan* of the synagogue carried out was responsibility for the scrolls. Again, Safrai notes, "During the era of the Second Temple and for a long time after, the chest with the books was brought in [to the synagogue] when required from an adjoining room and brought back there afterwards."[12]

As Safrai noted in his reference to Luke 4:20, this official *(hazzan)* appears in the story of Jesus reading in the synagogue in Nazareth (Lk 4:18-20), where he is clearly the person in charge of the worship. In this text, English versions often translate *hypēretēs* as "attendant," which sounds like some kind of a janitor. But clearly this official was the keeper of the scrolls and a worship leader. It is clear from Luke 4:20 that Luke knows and uses the word *hypēretēs* with its first-century Jewish meaning. How then can this same word best be understood in Luke 1:2?

In Luke 1:2 the person in question is a "*hypēretēs* of the *word,*" not a "*hypēretēs* of the *synagogue.*" Furthermore, the "minister *[hypēretēs]* of the word" in this text is also an eyewitness to Jesus of Nazareth. What conclusion can be drawn from this?

Putting all of this together, it is possible to conclude that at the very begin-

---

[10]S. Safrai, "The Synagogue," pp. 913-17, 933-37.
[11]S. Safrai, "The Synagogue," p. 935.
[12]S. Safrai, "The Synagogue," p. 915.

ning the apostles and the rest of the messianic Jewish community (the earliest church) took a title from their Jewish background and reused it. They had no buildings and were not officially organized into synagogues, so a paid official (*hypēretēs* of the synagogue), who kept the scrolls in a chest that he moved into the middle of the synagogue for worship each Saturday, was unnecessary. Besides, they had no scrolls about Jesus. But they did have disciples of Rabbi Jesus who had heard him, had learned from him and could share their memories with others. These special eyewitnesses were given a title, namely, "*hypēretēs* of the word." What word did they keep? These *hypēretēs*, who are listed by Luke as one of two major sources for his Gospel, appear to be the reciters of the tradition about Jesus, which is why they had to be eyewitnesses to qualify as *hypēretai* of the word. They were the guardians of the oral tradition from and about Jesus. When the community met for worship, they could not carry a box of scrolls about Jesus into the gathering, but the eyewitnesses among them could recite! Those who were not eyewitnesses, such as Luke, could hear what was recited, but only eyewitnesses had the title and the responsibility to pass on this sacred oral record in public. All of this is very Jewish. The students of Hillel and Shammai were contemporaries of these disciples and recited the traditions from and about their respective masters.

But twenty-seven years after the resurrection, when Luke arrived in Jerusalem, these "eyewitness and ministers of the word" were no longer young, and it was obvious that one day there would be no eyewitnesses left. What then could be done?

The messianic community could have opted to allow students of the students to continue reciting, which was common practice in the rabbinic world. But apparently the messianic Jews decided that the sayings of Rabbi Jesus were too sacred to allow non-eyewitnesses to do the reciting. There was only one other alternative: Authorize the composition of documents.

By the time Luke arrived in Jerusalem, the writing of such documents had already begun. Indeed, Luke affirms that "many have undertaken to compile a narrative" (Lk 1:1). The documents were in addition to the "the eyewitnesses and ministers [guardians?] of the word [about Jesus]." For two years he worked with these two sources (written and oral), and the Gospel of Luke is the result.

Finally, the same "ministers [guardians?] of the word" were not only important sources of information; they were also, inevitably, a board of review. When Luke finished, they almost certainly read the "orderly account" (Lk 1:3) that he compiled and edited. The community would eagerly await the review of Luke's efforts. If he had used his imagination to create stories out of thin air, or manufactured accounts to express his religious experience, their response would have been:

> We did not give Dr. Luke this material! It does not represent the Jesus we heard, knew and followed! We have not suffered and endured rejection for following someone's imagination. We are committed to Jesus of Nazareth, and we know very well what he said and did! This document is a fabrication and we want nothing to do with it!!

If this had been the judgment of the people who gave Luke his material there would *never have been a second copy of the Gospel of Luke.* Theophilus might have enjoyed it, but the church would not have preserved it. The fact that the church did preserve it means that this group of specialists, knowledgeable about Jesus of Nazareth, were pleased with Luke's efforts. It also means that authenticity for us is assured.[13] Of course the final work represents Luke's agenda. He recorded what he thought was important. He polished the language, organized the material, added his own interpretive nuances and created smooth connectives. But this editorial process does not mean that he created the material he edited.

This book's discussion of the parables in Luke 15 proceeds with the full confidence that these three parables are stories created in the mind of Jesus, preserved orally by eyewitnesses and finally recorded in some kind of written form by Luke in Jerusalem no more than twenty-seven to twenty-nine years after the resurrection. All of which brings us to a consideration of the underlying culture of the stories themselves, and to this subject we now turn.

---

[13]N. T. Wright affirms, "The stories of Jesus that circulated in the first generation are in principle to be taken as just that: stories of Jesus" (*Jesus and the Victory of God,* p. 136).

3

The Importance of
Middle Eastern Culture for
New Testament Interpretation

There are at least two basic ways to do theology. The first is by using concepts and the second is via story and metaphor. Both are influenced by culture. In working with concepts, the tool of choice is reason. But Lesslie Newbigin, theologian and bishop of the Church of South India, has argued cogently that reason is profoundly shaped by the culture and tradition of which each of us is a part. The problem begins with language. Newbigin writes:

> We cannot reason except by the use of language. Language embodies the ways in which a continuing community has learned to grasp its experience in a coherent way. It expresses the concepts which give shape to its understanding. The language is only learned as, from early childhood, we use it in the way that our parents and teachers and older contemporaries use it. In learning a language we are being inducted into a tradition, and we have no way of developing our powers of reasoning except through the use of this language.[1]

He goes on to add:

> The development of a tradition of rationality is never unrelated to the social, political, economic, military, and cultural changes which the society in question is going through. The tradition is never a merely cerebral one. The rationality which is accepted is part of and is embodied in the total life of a community. It responds to the new experiences which that community is having—whether they come from outside or from within. The tradition of thought is not a disem-

---

[1]L. Newbigin, *The Gospel in a Pluralist Society,* pp. 53-54.

bodied ghost which has a life apart from the total life and the society which carries this tradition. The rationality is embodied in *this* society, with all its elements of contingency, particularity, and sheer happenedness.[2]

And he continues:

Reason does not operate in a vacuum. The power of a human mind to think rationally is only developed in a tradition which itself depends on the experience of previous generations. . . . The definition of what is reasonable and what is not will be conditioned by the tradition within which the matter is being discussed.[3]

Newbigin observes that the "plausibility structures" we absorb through our various cultures become "like the lenses of our spectacles," namely,

It is not something we look at, but something *through* which we look in order to see the world. The lenses of our spectacles are performing exactly the function that the lenses of our own eyes are made to perform. In that sense, they are part of us. We indwell them. So with a vast amount of our culture—its language, its images, its concepts, its ways of understanding and acting. It is only when we are exposed to a totally different culture and a different language, shaped by a widely different history, that we can turn back and see that what we always took for granted as only one way of seeing things.[4]

This reality then profoundly influences the way we look at the Bible, argues Newbigin. He writes:

It is obviously true that we have no way to understanding the Bible except through the concepts and categories of thought with which our culture has equipped us through our whole intellectual formation from earliest childhood.[5]

Thus, the very reason we employ to link our concepts together is shaped by the language and culture of which we are a part. What then of theological meaning that is created through metaphor and story?

If the cultural conditioning of language, history, economics, politics and military influence the way we do our *reasoning,* how much more does culture influence what we mean when we *use metaphors and tell stories* to create meaning! In this latter case, the cultural assumptions of the storyteller and his or her audience become the worldview within which the storyteller cre-

---

[2]L. Newbigin, *The Gospel in a Pluralist Society*, p. 54.
[3]L. Newbigin, *The Gospel in a Pluralist Society*, pp. 8-9.
[4]L. Newbigin, *The Gospel in a Pluralist Society*, p. 35.
[5]L. Newbigin, *The Gospel in a Pluralist Society*, p. 192.

ates that meaning. An outsider will probably understand the primary intent of the story, but the inner nuances will be out of focus. At least some of the climaxes, dramatic turning points, deep meanings, subtle humor and inner tensions will be blurred, if not missed altogether. What is to be done if the reader of a story does *not* participate in the culture of the storyteller and his audience?

A number of options ignore this problem or solve it superficially. The most common of these is to pretend the problem simply does not exist. The reader, whatever his or her culture, can project that culture into the parable. This alternative can be found all across church history. But surely it is not good enough. In Matthew 5:14-15, quoted in chapter one, we read, "You are the light of the world. . . . Nor do *they* light a lamp." The RSV translated the latter phrase "nor do *men* light a lamp." In the world of Jesus, women lit the lamps. Jesus' listeners heard "nor do they light a lamp" and knew that Jesus was talking about women lighting lamps. Such cultural fine tuning is a vital component of the task of interpretation.

A second option is to assert that the parables of Jesus are universal in nature and apply to all cultures. On the one hand this is true. Every culture has compassionate fathers, rebellious younger sons and stick-in-the-mud older brothers. The three major figures in the story of the parable of the prodigal son can be found in any culture. Thus, potentially the story has authentic impact in every culture. But this view necessarily overlooks important treasures to be found beyond these universals.

Yes, all cultures have families with problems similar to the family Jesus describes. But, as will be shown below, in Middle Eastern traditional culture, the prodigal's request for his inheritance while his father is still alive means *he cannot wait for his father to die.* The father is expected to explode and drive his son out of the house. He doesn't. Instead, he grants his son's request. In so portraying the father, Jesus affirms that an Oriental patriarch is inadequate as a model for God. This is a crucial aspect of what the parable meant in Jesus' world. Surely it behooves us not to miss it. Thus, to assume that the universal cultural patterns in the parables are all that are necessary for interpretation is to inadvertently overlook many rich treasures in the text. But there is another fork in the road.

A third option is to plead Hellenism. In the fourth century B.C. Alexander the Great conquered the Middle East and spread Greek culture from one end of it to the other. In short, the Middle East was Hellenized. But the question remains: Is Greek culture an adequate lens through which to examine and understand the culture of the parables of Jesus the Jew?[6]

The Lebanese have spoken French for a thousand years. But they are Lebanese, not French. The Indians of the subcontinent make wide use of English. Indeed, it is the second language of the country, and even the Indian parliament is conducted in English. English has been a part of India for centuries, but the Indians are Indians, not British. British influence—yes; British identity—no. Greek was the crosscultural language of the Eastern Mediterranean at the time of Jesus. As noted previously, when Jesus was growing up, Herod Antipas was building a new capital in Sipphorus, four miles away. Greek influence was no doubt strong in that city even though in all likelihood it was still a Jewish town, which may have had a Greek theater. Yet, Nazareth was a small solidly Jewish town and remained Jewish for centuries after the time of Jesus. Jesus was a Jew, not a Greek, and the struggle to maintain Jewish identity was a profound part of his world. How then can we in the twenty-first century enter into his cultural world?

When we read the Bible in our own language, it is full of resonances that are shaped by our mother tongue, as Newbigin has observed. The question becomes: Where do I find a place to stand from which I can look at myself and my cultural assumptions from the point of view of the Bible when my very reading of the Bible is itself so fashioned by my language and culture? Newbigin uses the illustration of a bus. How can I push a bus when I am riding in it?

He concludes:

> The only way in which the gospel can challenge our culturally conditioned interpretations of it is through the witness of those who read the Bible with minds shaped by other cultures. We have to listen to others. This mutual correction is sometimes unwelcome, but it is necessary and it is fruitful.[7]

This becomes crystal clear when examining Christology. Newbigin observes how various cultures at various points in history have seen the person of Jesus. He writes:

---

[6]In a recent book, *Prodigality, Liberality and Meanness in the Parable of the Prodigal Son: A Greco-Roman Perspective on Luke 15:11-32,* David Holgate points to Greco-Roman themes in the parable. These parallels make clear how a Greco-Roman mind, trained in moral philosophy, could well have understood the parable. It does not help us understand how the audience of Pharisees and scribes would have reacted to that same parable.

[7]L. Newbigin, *The Gospel in a Pluralist Society,* pp. 196-97.

It is simply a fact of history that Jesus has been and is portrayed in an amazing variety of portraits from the Byzantine Pantocrator through the medieval crucifix and the Jesus of the scared heart, to the blue-eyed blond of American Protestantism and the Che Guevara freedom fighter of liberation theology.[8]

For Newbigin, all of this was illustrated when he discussed the scriptures with his Indian colleagues. He tells of how when listening to those colleagues he could quickly spot their syncretism and through them, his own. He says:

> When I went as a young missionary to India, I could find the elements of syncretism in Indian Christianity. I saw how, inevitably, the meaning of sentences spoken by my Christian friends was shaped by the Hindu background of the language. The words used, the only available words for God, sin, salvation, and so on, are words that have received their entire content from the Hindu religious tradition. I thought I was in a position to correct this syncretism. Only slowly did I come to see that my own Christianity was also profoundly syncretistic. Many times I sat with groups of Indian pastors and evangelists to study together a passage of Scripture. Over and over again their interpretation of the text, as it spoke to them in their language, called my interpretation into question. And it was not always clear that my interpretation was in fact more faithful to the text. Many times I had to confess that my reading of the text, which I had hitherto taken for granted, was wholly shaped by my own intellectual formation in what we call the modern scientific worldview. My Christianity was syncretistic, but so was theirs. Yet neither of us could discover that without the challenge of the other. . . . We do not see the lenses of our spectacles; we see through them, and it is another who has to say to us, "Friend, you need a new pair of spectacles."[9]

If Newbigin can discover such a corrective to his interpretations of Scripture from contemporary Indian Christians, how much more important is it for us to take seriously both the commentaries and the biblical perceptions of early (and modern) Middle Eastern Christians who live in societies closer to the cultural world of Jesus than do both the Indians and ourselves.

If we desire to break out of our own cultural imprisonment to hear the Gospel as its first listeners heard it, it is obvious that we must turn to the Hebrew Scriptures, the Dead Sea Scrolls, and many other Jewish documents from before the time of Jesus to understand the culture of his world.[10] But

---

[8]L. Newbigin, *The Gospel in a Pluralist Society,* p. 192.

[9]L. Newbigin, *A Word in Season,* pp. 68-69.

[10]Cf. the work of the distinguished Israeli New Testament specialist David Flusser. Particularly significant are *Judaism and the Origins of Christianity* and *Jesus.*

Middle Eastern sources, written in the early centuries after the time of Jesus, are also important. The rabbinic tradition created and eventually recorded a vast literature, which has been preserved. The Mishnah and the two Talmuds are great treasures that reflect traditional Jewish culture and consequently need to be considered. Naturally, the rabbis before and shortly after Jesus are the most important. But we are still "on the bus." We are still sifting this data using *our* categories. In short, we are trying to push the bus in which we are riding. What is to be done?

Beside and beyond these early Jewish documents is the literature of the Eastern Christian churches. At the Council of Chalcedon in A.D. 451, the Semitic churches of the Middle East and the churches of the Greek and Latin traditions parted company. Since that time, contact between these two great parts of the larger body of Christ has been minimal. In the Middle East, after that date, the Coptic Orthodox, Chalcedonian Orthodox, Syriac Orthodox and Armenian Orthodox churches lived their lives, developed their liturgies, translated and retranslated their New Testaments, composed their sermons, and wrote their commentaries, all in a Middle Eastern cultural context. In particular, their surviving commentaries and interpretive translations of the New Testament offer important insights into the Gospels as Eastern documents. Their witness to the Gospels must surely be considered seriously, despite of the effort required to do so. Following Newbigin's advice, noted above, we need "the witness of those who read the Bible with minds shaped by other cultures."[11]

The Greek Fathers are known to the West, and their works have been translated. But what about the Semitic Christian literature written in Syriac, Coptic and Arabic? In the twentieth century, Christian scholarship at last began to take seriously the early literature of the Jewish community. It is my fond hope that in the twenty-first century Western Christianity will have the opportunity to examine the biblical treasures of the Eastern churches. What specifically are these treasures?

Two categories of material await us. The first is the Coptic, Syriac and Arabic translations (versions) of the Gospels. The Syriac church left three translations, there are two major Coptic translations, and in Arabic perhaps as many as fifty translations of the Gospels have survived (primarily from Greek, Syriac and Coptic). What is to be reaped from these translations?

---

[11]L. Newbigin, *The Gospel in a Pluralist Society,* pp. 196-97.

To translate is to interpret. There is no possible exception to this equation. Translation is hard work because the translator must understand the original text before deciding precisely how to communicate its meaning in the new language. Jesus' first languages were Aramaic and Hebrew. Syriac is a sister language to Aramaic while Arabic is a first cousin to both. Thus, when the Greek text is translated back into Syriac, Coptic or Arabic, the stories that originated in a Semitic context are returned to a Semitic language. Nuances of the original Semitic world can be gleaned through this process. Does the prodigal waste his money in the far country in "loose living" (i.e., immoral living), or does he lose it through "expensive living"? All of the Arabic versions consulted and two of the three Syriac translations read "expensive living." Does it matter? Indeed it does as we will see below.

In the parable of Lazarus, the Greek text says that Lazarus "was laid" (passive) each day outside the rich man's gate. The RSV and NRSV translate "at his gate *lay* a poor man named Lazarus" (Lk 16:20). The passive is overlooked. The cultural point is that Lazarus was too sick to walk. Because the community respected him, it did what it could for him. Each day he was carried to the gate of the only man in town who had the wealth to help him. And each night members of the community carried him back to some hovel, where his family or friends did what they could for him. The community's presence is a critical component of the story that is missed when this passive verb is overlooked. As noted, Middle Eastern versions have almost never made this mistake. With the briefest of strokes Jesus fills in an entire section of the canvas of his parable.[12] The Eastern versions can help us see those important, yet easily overlooked parts of the larger parabolic picture. These versions were translated within a Middle Eastern "plausibility structure."

The Arabic versions in particular have been neglected. Textual critics have judged them to be "late" (which they are) and "corrupted." This latter word means that the translators often slip into a "Living Bible mode" and add bits and pieces of commentary as they translate. When this occurs, the translation in question is of little value to the textual critics who are trying to confirm the wording of the original. But if the intent is to penetrate the biblical world of Eastern Christians and see how they *understood* the story, then the more such interpretive notes appear the more important and useful the

---

[12]Seeing beggars outside of mosques, churches and rich men's homes in the traditional Middle East alerts the mind to look for the same fine tuning in the text of the parable.

translation becomes. As this happens, the Eastern versions become, in effect, minicommentaries.

Beyond the versions are the commentators. One of the most important is Hibatallah Ibn al-Assal, an Egyptian Christian New Testament scholar who lived and worked in the thirteenth century. In the Middle Ages, when the lights of learning were burning dimly in Europe, classical Arabic scholarship was flourishing. A high standard of academic endeavor was maintained in all fields from the ninth through the fourteenth centuries. While Muslim scholarship of that period is known, Arabic Christian scholarship of those same centuries is almost unknown. Hibatallah was one of those Christian scholars. After collecting Arabic Gospels translated from Greek, Syriac and Coptic, he began to compare them. Discovering that they did not agree, he devised a series of symbols that made it possible for him to start with his own new translation into Arabic and then list all the other translation options (and their origins) in the margins of his work. Hibatallah's four Gospels were completed in 1252 and contain more than ten thousand marginal notes. His opus is the world's first critical edition of the four Gospels and is an amazing compendium of how the Eastern churches understood the text of the Gospels during that period and for centuries prior to his day.[13]

As authors of formal commentaries, three names from the distant past and one in the twentieth century are of particular note. The earliest is the extant work of the Syrian Orthodox scholar and bishop, Musa bar Kepha, who was born in A.D. 813 in what is now Iraq and lived until A.D. 903. His commentaries on Luke and Matthew have survived. His work on Luke has at long last been translated from Syriac into Arabic and English by Dr. 'Abd al-Masih Saadi, who has graciously allowed me access to his manuscript.[14] The commentary on the four Gospels by Abdallah Ibn al-Tayyib of the eleventh century, from Takrit in Iraq, is complete, and his influence has been felt all across the Eastern churches.[15] Following him two centuries later in the Syrian Orthodox exegetical tradition was Diyunisiyus Ibn al-Salibi. In the mid-twentieth century, Ebrahim Said, a Protestant scholar in Cairo, Egypt, published a thoughtful Ar-

---

[13]The present writer is part of a team endeavoring to publish this overlooked work. As the world's first critical edition of the Gospels, it is centuries earlier than similar efforts in Europe.

[14]The only complete Syriac text of the commentary on Luke by Musa bar Kepha is a microfilm held in the Syriac Institute for Manuscript Studies at the Lutheran School of Theology, Chicago, Illinois. Its shelf number is Mardin 102. Dr. 'Abd al-Masih Saadi is the director of that institute.

[15]This work was translated from Syriac into Arabic in the eighteenth century. The Arabic was first published in Cairo in 1908 by Yousif Manqariyus.

abic-language commentary on Luke's Gospel. Said did his own thinking within his own Middle Eastern heritage and did not imitate commentaries from the West. His work is a garden of delights and is significant for our topic. Yet, the question remains: Are these sources too recent to help in studying a first-century text?

The centuries of separation between Eastern and Western Christianity have been a great tragedy, and the great divide remains. The sayings of Jesus can be compared to a spring at the top of a mountain that flows down opposite sides of that mountain. The Western side is known to us. But what of the Eastern side? The Gospels originated in that Eastern world from which we have been isolated since A.D. 451. Surely Western Christianity is the poorer if it fails to do its best to recover the ways in which the Eastern Semitic Christian tradition has understood the text of the New Testament. Naturally, we are eager for the earliest available sources. But, anything of quality from the other side of the mountain can be of assistance. Such Christians are "outside of our bus." If Newbigin can discover the flaws in his culturally conditioned perceptions of Scripture by talking to twentieth-century Indians, how much more valuable is the ancient Middle Eastern Christian biblical tradition?

Finally, there is the possibility of obtaining insights from surviving conservative traditional Middle Eastern culture. Archimedes affirmed that if given a fulcrum and a place to stand he would move the world. He was right, but no one could give him a place to stand or a place to position his fulcrum away from the surface of the earth. Traditional Middle Eastern culture provides a place for all non-Middle Eastern Christians to stand as they look at the Gospels. Definitive answers to cultural questions cannot be gleaned from contemporary Middle Eastern traditional culture. Rather, that culture poses new and important questions that we avoid at our loss. They too are outside our bus. It will not do to blithely say, "Middle Eastern traditional culture has changed over the years and thus is of little value as a grid for understanding the culture of Jesus." Superficially, this is true. But, should we fall back on our own culture? Following Newbigin, none of us can pretend to be a disembodied eye looking down on the world from 100,000 miles out in space.

In summary, the goal of this study is to examine all the available relevant Middle Eastern literature on our subject that is as close to the New Testament as possible. The cultural place to stand for this quest will be traditional Middle Eastern life rather than our own.

4

THE PARABLE OF THE PRODIGAL SON
AND THE "TRAVEL NARRATIVE" IN LUKE

Luke 9:51 reads, "Jesus resolutely set out for Jerusalem" (NIV). By the end of Luke 19 Jesus has arrived. It has long been noted that this central section of Luke's Gospel is a special collection, which is usually referred to as the "Travel Narrative." Most of it is missing in Mark's Gospel, whereas Matthew includes about half of it.

There is no discernible geographical arrangement to this travel narrative. In Luke 9 Jesus starts for Jerusalem, but by Luke 10 he is already at the home of Mary and Martha on the Mount of Olives. Three chapters later, in Luke 13:22, he is "on his way . . . journeying toward Jerusalem." Shortly thereafter, in Luke 13:34-35, there is a lament over Jerusalem. In Luke 17:11 Jesus is back "passing along between Samaria and Galilee," and in Luke 18:35-19:10 he is in Jericho. In Luke 19:28 he arrives for a second (or third?) time in Jerusalem, and there is another lament over Jerusalem.

The literature surrounding this so-called travel narrative is enormous and must not detain us. It behooves us, however, to pause and note a few of the characteristics particular to this section of Luke and to observe the placement of Luke 15 within the larger collection.

My own study of this special section of Luke's Gospel has identified a topical rather than sequential order. Ten subjects are presented followed by the same list repeated backwards.[1] This arrangement of material is usu-

---

[1]K. E. Bailey, *Poet,* pp. 79-85.

ally referred to as chiasm, but I prefer to call it inverted parallelism. Both secular Greek literature and the Hebrew Scriptures exhibit this form of rhetoric. Thus, both Greek and Jewish readers of Luke's Gospel would have been able to follow its outline. The suggested topical arrangement is seen in figure 1.

Approximately 5 percent of the verses in these chapters do not fit the above outline. Apparently, first a collection was assembled and at a later stage several other sayings were added.

Rather than calling it "The Travel Narrative" a more appropriate name might be "The Jerusalem Document." The document's noticeable features include the following points:

(*a*) The city of Jerusalem is prominent and appears at the beginning, the middle and the end (a feature common to this rhetorical style).[2]

(*b*) A lament over Jerusalem occurs in the middle of the Jerusalem Document, and a second lament takes place at the end.

(*c*) The Hebrew parallelisms in the material are intact. When the same material appears in Matthew, it is almost always expanded, indicating that the Lucan version is earlier.

(*d*) The words for weights and measures are often Hebrew words written with Greek letters (transliterated rather than translated).

(*e*) At times the spelling of *Jerusalem* is the Hebrew word written with Greek letters instead of the Greek spelling for the name of the city.

(*f*) Extensive use of Hebrew stylistics, seen in the classical writing prophets, particularly Isaiah, appear.

These features support the conclusion that the document is both Jewish and early, and could have been assembled by the "eyewitnesses and ministers of the word" (Lk 1:2) discussed in chapter two. Because of the prominence of Jerusalem in the document, their center was probably Jerusalem. As a collection, the document may have been given to Luke, and consequently it is a product of one or more of the "many" who have "undertaken to write" whom he mentions in his introduction to the Gospel. Luke polishes the language and adds a few shorter pieces out of the tradition but basically leaves the document as it is. The material includes the trilogy of parables on finding the lost.

---

[2]Cf. K. E. Bailey, *Poet,* pp. 44-74; cf. also K. E. Bailey, "Recovering," pp. 265-96. In the 1 Corinthians passage discussed in these articles (1 Cor 1:17—2:2), the theme of the cross appears at the beginning, the middle and the end of a hymn on the cross.

1. Jerusalem (saving events) (9:51-56)

   2. Follow me (9:57—10:12)

      3. What shall I do to inherit eternal life? (10:25-41)

         4. Prayer (11:1-13)

            5. Signs and the present kingdom (11:14-32)

               6. Conflict with the Pharisees: Money (11:37—12:34)

                  7. The kingdom is not yet and is now (12:35-59)

                     8. The call of the kingdom to Israel (13:1-9)

                        9. The nature of the kingdom (13:10-20)

                           10. Jerusalem (saving events) (13:22-35)

                      9'. The nature of the kingdom (14:1-11)

                     8'. The call of the kingdom to the outcasts and to Israel (14:12—15:32)

                  7'. The kingdom is now (16:1-8)

               6'. Conflict with the Pharisees: Money (16:9-31)

            5'. Signs and the coming kingdom (17:11-37)

         4'. Prayer (18:1-14)

      3'. What shall I do to inherit eternal life? (18:18-30)

   2'. Follow me (18:35—19:9)

1'. Jerusalem (saving events) (19:10-48)

Figure 1. Topical arrangement of the "Travel Narrative"

What can be gained by noting that this is a possible pre-Lucan collection with the above suggested outline?

The first half of the proposed overall outline reduced to its bare bones is

- Jerusalem—salvation.
- Follow me.
- What do I have to do?
- Prayer is important.
- The signs are fulfilled.
- There will be conflict with some.
- The kingdom has come and is coming.
- Israel is called.
- The nature of the kingdom
- Jerusalem—salvation.

As mentioned, this list of topics then repeats backward. The list summarizes the types of ideas that naturally were prominent in the teachings of Jesus as he approached the cross, as well as being important for the church that proclaimed his person and message. After the resurrection, the apostolic community wanted to present Jesus, the Messiah of Israel, to the Jewish community. A collection of sayings and events from the life of Jesus, focusing on the above topics, would have been useful for such an endeavor. Thus, this collection, highlighting the critical teachings of Jesus as he approached the cross, may have been assembled to present his person and message to the Jewish community. When the church was asked, "Who is this Jesus and what is his message?" the "Jerusalem Document" would have provided answers, and this is a possible reason for the compilation of the material.

Luke 15 appears in the second half of the document. Frequently in the Bible when topics are presented sequentially and then repeated backward, the second presentation of those same topics fills out or completes the first. It is, therefore, important to check carefully what is said in the appropriate place in the first list before looking to see what is added in the inverted repetition. Very often the two are two sides of a single coin. When applying this principle to the material under study, two parts of a single topic can be observed.

In the first list of major topics there is a clear *call to Israel to repent.* Turning to the second half, both *Israel* and *the outcasts are called.* The structure of calls to Israel and the outcasts can be seen in figure 2.

First half	Second half
2. Follow me	*2′. Follow me*
The people come to Jesus	The blind man (an outcast)
The mission of the Seventy	Zacchaeus (an outcast)
8. The call to Israel	*8′. The call to Israel* and *to the outcasts*
Repent or perish	Outcasts at the banquet
The fig tree	Lost sheep, lost coin and lost son

Figure 2. Jesus' call in two parts

Clearly, the theme of the Gospel *for Israel and for the outcasts* is introduced in the second half of the outline as noted above. The reader discovers first that Jesus has come *for Israel* and then discovers that both Israel and *the outcasts within Israel* (blind man, Zacchaeus, second set of guests at the banquet, the prodigal son and even those brought in from the highways and byways) are welcome. In this manner the great trilogy in Luke 15 has a prominent place in defining, in story form, the nature of the salvation that is achieved in Jerusalem.

In summary, Luke 15 presents parables that are central to the theology of Jesus and to the presentation of the Gospel by the apostolic community to its fellow Jews. Luke could have received this finely crafted document and added a small amount of new material to it before including the edited result in his Gospel. He no doubt polished the Greek, and he endorses the material by including it in his Gospel.

It will never be possible to detect definitively the exact words of Jesus and isolate them from those added by the oral reciters, the recorders of the tradition and the editorial polishing of Luke. Nor need we try. The text contains stories of and about Jesus that are enriched by authoritative insider interpretation. To quote Hultgren's apt comment, "Our purpose is to interpret the parable in its canonical setting."[3]

Having looked briefly at a possible setting for Luke 15 in the Gospel of Luke as a whole, we now turn to the question of "the one and the many" in the interpretation of parables.

---

[3]A. J. Hultgren, *The Parables of Jesus,* p. 85.

5

THE ONE AND THE MANY
IN PARABOLIC INTERPRETATION

A story is first created and then told by a particular person in a particular place and time. If it is a good story well told, and if those listening are perceptive, the storyteller's intention will be clear. We learn in 2 Samuel 11:1—12:14 that King David stole his neighbor's wife and then arranged to have her husband killed in battle. Subsequently Nathan the prophet created a story and told it to David. The story is about a rich man who had many sheep and a poor man at his gate who had but one lamb. A guest dropped in to see the rich man, who then stole the poor man's lamb, which he proceeded to kill, cook and offer to his guest. What, asked Nathan, did the great King David think about this rich man? David declared that the man should die. Nathan thundered in reply, "You are the man!" (2 Sam 12:7). David got the message and repented. Psalm 51 is a record of his remorse.

But there is a problem. I am not King David. I am living three thousand years later and have neither stolen my neighbor's wife nor arranged for her husband's death. So what does this particular story have to say to me? Or is it simply a quaint tale from a very distant past?

This is not an easy nut to crack. One solution is to moralize. That is, to take a look at the morals of the people in the story and decide if they are worthy of praise or blame and by so doing gain something for our day. Such a method asserts that the point of the story is: "Don't engage in lust" and "Don't steal your neighbor's wife." Granted, David's acts are unacceptable by any moral standard. But is that all?

For centuries, the Eastern and Western church allegorized the parables of the Bible. That is, it attached symbolic meanings to various people, things and actions in a story without reference to the original setting and in this manner extracted meaning applicable to any age.[1] The difficulty with this method is that it created an interpretive style in which "anything goes." For hundreds of years people found all manner of meaning in the parables that Nathan, Jesus or Paul could never have imagined.

Granted, the stories do contain symbols, i.e., allegorical signposts. In Nathan's parable the rich man represents David while the poor man is Uriah the Hittite and the lamb is Bathsheba. The story makes no sense at all unless the reader is able to see these symbolic identifications. If David had not made these connections instinctively he would not have been moved to repentance. But to go further and say, "The lamb is killed and thus it represents Christ," is to introduce an idea totally foreign to Nathan's intention, and impossible for David to have concluded. The history of the interpretation of biblical parables is full of farfetched interpretations of this sort. For readers, what other options are there?

In the late nineteenth century a German scholar by the name of Adolf Jülicher wrote two volumes documenting the total confusion that the allegorical method produced.[2] He managed to discredit that method once and for all for serious interpreters of the parables. Julicher offered an alternative, namely, that "Each parable has one point." Although he influenced many across the twentieth century, there are two difficulties with his perceptions.

First, biblical stories are not akin to the skin of an orange. The skin of an orange is only useful to hold the fruit until it ripens. The skin is discarded after the orange is peeled or squeezed. The inside of the orange is what matters. The same is true with an egg and an eggshell. But biblical parables are not like this. A biblical story is not simply a "delivery system" for an idea. Rather, the story first creates a world and then invites the listener to live in that world, to take it on as part of who he or she is. Biblical stories invite the reader to accept them as *his or her* story. In reading and studying the Bible, ancient tales are not examined merely in order to extract a theological principle or ethical model. Instead, the Bible is read to rediscover who we are and what we must

---

[1]The well-known English language classic *Pilgrim's Progress* by John Bunyan is an example of this style of writing. Allegories are presented on almost every page.
[2]A. Jülicher, *Die Gleichnisreden Jesu*.

yet become, because the biblical story of sin and salvation, law and grace, is *our* story.

When Paul writes to the Corinthians, he is clearly addressing the "Jews and Greeks," a fact that he mentions again and again. Yet he also says, "our fathers were all under the cloud, and all passed through the sea" (1 Cor 10:1). Later in the same letter, writing to a mixed crowd of Christian Jews and Greeks he states, "Back when you were Gentiles you were led astray by dumb idols" (1 Cor 12:2; author's translation), and in Romans 11:13-24 he talks about the Gentile believers being grafted into the olive tree. The olive tree about which he is talking is Israel. In short, the new Gentile believers, theologically speaking, *joined Israel,* and thus Israel's story became their story. In like manner, the parables invite us to "inhabit them." Their entire worldview is meant to become ours. As readers, we are a family of older and younger brothers with a compassionate father who is willing to pay an enormous price to come to us and reconcile us to himself. The parable is a perception of reality that we are asked to inhabit. So, does the story contain "ideas" at all?

Indeed it does, which is Jülicher's second weakness. Operating on the assumption that the parables were simply illustrations for an idea, Jülicher insisted that each parable had only a single idea. His goal was to break the back of the allegorical method, and his weapon of choice was to insist on one idea per parable. Some interpreters accepted this principle. Others, who may have never read or even heard of Jülicher are still influenced by him and follow the notion that "every parable has one point." Yet, since Jülicher, many interpreters have found his view inadequate. If, as readers, we are invited to inhabit a parable, then the parable can be likened to a house with a number of rooms. If someone lives in such a house, there are usually windows, doors, a kitchen and a living room. The house has various sections, and life within that building would be disorganized without them. Or, it may be a simple house with only one room and one door. Granting readily that a parable contains ideas, it is clearly too dogmatic and restrictive to insist that each parable has but one. Jülicher (and those who followed him) thought that admitting to more than one idea was to start down the slippery slope to a renewal of allegory with its irresponsible conclusions. But is this truly the case?

As a verse in Scripture, John 3:16 has a unity that is composed of parts. The verse speaks of the love of God, the person of Christ, the needy world, faith, self-giving, perishing and eternal life. What would happen if the interpreter insisted that John 3:16 contained only one theological idea? Trying to apply such a principle to John 3:16, it would be necessary to select one of the above meanings and pretend that the others were not there. In like manner, attempting to select a single meaning from the parable of the prodigal son would force the interpreter to ignore a great deal of the story's theological content. The parable speaks of arrogance, being lost, broken relationships, false repentance, costly love, joy, rejection, sonship, the fatherhood of God and acceptance of being found. Should all the items on the above list be scratched off save one? How then would we chose the winners? Some have suggested that "there are three major characters in the parable and thereby three theological themes for the story." But the list cited above contains more than three. Which are to be ignored and why? Clearly, with many parables such a method is inadequate. So what is to be done?

Yes, a parable invites the reader/listener to dwell in its worldview. But that worldview can encompass a number of components. A story often has symbols, but only those that the original storyteller intended should be admitted. The very joy of living in the world of the parable is related to the various parts of the house the reader is asked to make his or her own. It is these parts that I have called "the theological cluster." There is no need to worry about a parable having one idea (which sometimes occurs) or a major idea with a series of secondary ideas (which sometimes happens) or a series of ideas, all of which appear to be important. The only theological content that should be considered valid in a parable is that which the original storyteller could have intended and was available to the original audience. We must do our best to enter the world of the storyteller. By so doing, we will hear Jesus addressing first-century Jews who were sinners in need of grace. Jesus is speaking to the human predicament. The reader must stand at the back of Jesus' original audience; only after focusing on what Jesus was saying to that audience is it possible to discover what his words mean for people in any other time and place.

With this in mind we have a twofold task. First, the three parables of Luke 15 need to be examined briefly as a single unit. This level of the text was available to all of Jesus' listeners. Second, with that understanding as a foundation, it will then be possible to listen for what the scholarly scribes and Pharisees heard vis-à-vis the interaction between the saga of Jacob and the parable of the prodigal son.

II

The Parable of the Prodigal Son in Luke 15 Compared with the Saga of Jacob in Genesis 27—35

The Setting in Luke 15

6

THREE STORIES, ONE PARABLE
Seeing the Three Stories of Luke 15 as a Unity

The fifteenth chapter of Luke comprises three parallel stories whose heroes are the good shepherd, the good woman and the good father. The selection of these three metaphorical symbols can only be deliberate. I will argue that all three are symbols for God, and that all three evolve into symbols for Jesus. The first question that needs to be addressed regarding this trilogy is: Why these three particular metaphors?

The first of the three characters to appear on stage is the good shepherd. As will be seen below, the parable of the good shepherd (as it appears in Luke 15) would naturally invoke Psalm 23 for almost any first-century scholarly Jew. That psalm begins with the familiar affirmation, "The LORD is my shepherd."[1] With Psalm 23 at the back of Jesus' mind (as well as in the minds of his original audience) it must then be asked: What are the primary metaphors for God in the Psalter from which Jesus may have made this selection?

The metaphors for God in the psalms fall easily into two types. The first is inanimate objects. From this category come: The Lord is my/our rock, fortress, tower, refuge and shield. All these have to do with security in the face of danger. A second category personalizes God by invoking human images. The most common is: "The Lord is King." Naturally, the king is a powerful figure who, like the images of rock, fortress and tower, also provides security. But a thin stream of metaphors for God is composed of people who are not

---

[1]For a full discussion of the relationship between Psalm 23 and Luke 15, cf. K. E. Bailey, *Finding.*

(like the Lord in Isaiah 6:1) high and lifted up, seated on a throne at a great distance from the worshiper. Three and only three metaphors compose this stream, and each deserves scrutiny.

Personal Metaphors for God

The three personal, compassionate metaphors for God in the Psalter are: Shepherd, Mother and Father. These metaphors are rare and relevant to our topic.

1. God the Good Shepherd. Psalm 23 is the obvious high point of the Psalter's reflection on God the Good Shepherd and will be examined below. In addition, the following lines appear:

> Give ear, O Shepherd of Israel,
>> thou who leadest Joseph like a flock! . . .
> Restore us, O God;
>> let thy face shine, that we may be saved! (Ps 80:1, 3)

Unlike a king who is necessarily distant from common folk, the shepherd personally leads his flock to pasture in nearly every kind of weather and provides for each sheep. Psalm 23 particularly mentions food, drink and security. Here in Psalm 80 salvation is added to the list. Given the prominence of Psalm 23, in both Jewish and Christian piety, it is surprising to find the symbol of God, the Good Shepherd, so seldom used in the Psalter. But such is the case.

2. God as Father. Two texts employ this metaphor. The first reads,

> Father of the fatherless and protector of widows
>> is God in his holy habitation.
> God gives the desolate a home to dwell in;
>> he leads out the prisoners to prosperity. (Ps 68:5-6)

The second affirms,

> As a father pities his children,
>> so the LORD pities those who fear him.
> For he knows our frame;
>> he remembers that we are dust. (Ps 103:13-14)

As is true throughout the Hebrew Scriptures, so here in the Psalms; the image of father invokes recollections of compassion for the weak. In this text, children, widows, the desolate and prisoners are specifically mentioned. The father, who is personal and near, acts with compassion.

3. The Mother. Only Psalm 131:1-2 is in this category. The original Hebrew allows for numerous shades of meaning. With the weight of the pre-Christian Syriac translation for support, I have chosen the NIV, which reads,

My heart is not proud O LORD,
   my eyes are not haughty;
I do not concern myself with great matters
   or things too wonderful for me.
But I have stilled and quieted my soul;
   like a weaned child with its mother,
   like a weaned child is my soul within me.
O Israel, put your hope in the LORD
   both now and forevermore.

A number of Hebrew Scripture texts specifically refer to God as mother. Isaiah 42:14 is prominent among them.[2] In Psalm 131 the psalmist addresses God and then likens himself to a weaned child with its mother, the strong inference being that the mother is a symbol for God. In the aforementioned list of three personal, accessible and compassionate metaphors for God, the first two are obvious. The psalmist refers to God both as a shepherd and as a father. There is the strong possibility that the image of mother in Psalm 131 can be added to the list. What then of Jesus?

It is hardly coincidental that these same three metaphors are the foundation stones upon which Jesus builds the three parables of Luke 15. It appears that when Jesus wants to talk about a compassionate, incarnate, personal God he turns to almost the same three images. The one difference is that the psalmist includes "mother" while Jesus confines himself to "woman." Has Jesus borrowed this trilogy from the psalms? Quite likely. In any case, such a possibility helps clarify both the selection of these three metaphors and the importance of seeing them as three parts of a whole. With these ideas in mind, the setting of this trilogy in Luke's Gospel deserves attention.

THREE PARABLES AS ONE

Luke 15 opens with this scenario, "Now the tax collectors and sinners were all drawing near to hear him. And the Pharisees and the scribes murmured, saying, 'This man receives sinners and eats with them.' So he told them *this parable*" (italics added).

---

[2]Others will be noted when we examine the parables of the good woman and the lost coin (Lk 15:8-10).

The word *parable* in Luke 15:3 is a singular. The collection of three stories follows. Luke (or his source) clearly understood the three as a single unit. Weighty internal reasons support Luke's use of the singular. Among them are the following:

1. The three parables are addressed not to "the crowd" but rather to a group of scholars (the scribes and Pharisees). Consequently, the reader is expected to see the stories as part of a scholars' debate rather than as a simple discussion with fisherfolk. The academic guild of the day was angry. Jesus was known to be an intellectual and was called rabbi. Interlocking three stories into an extended, carefully orchestrated presentation is consistent with the work of a scholar presenting his case to other scholars.[3]

2. The setting of meals and eating links the three stories. Each of the three parables ends with a party, which necessarily means that people and food are involved. Each host invites a circle of "friends and neighbors" to "rejoice with me" or to "make merry and be glad."

The rabbis were expected to gather followers from among those who were doing their best to keep the Law in a precise fashion. And at meals, only those insiders who attempted to do so were allowed to join. This was important to the Pharisees because of the Essenes, who composed the famous Dead Sea Scrolls.

The Essenes had decided to withdraw from the cities and towns into a monastic community. They believed that the law of Moses could not be kept properly by anyone who lived among the *am ha-arets* (people of the land) discussed in chapter one. The Pharisees, on the other hand, opted to remain in the populated towns. But when they sat down to eat, they were very careful to maintain ceremonial purity and, therefore, did not eat with the population at large. But Jesus ate with sinners.

The Middle East is famous for its lavish hospitality. This well-deserved reputation is on display in the story of Abraham and his three visitors (Gen 18:1-8) and continues to this day. As with Abraham, the entertaining of guests always involves serving something to drink, or eat, or both. In the three parables in Luke 15, only the third (Lk 15:23, italics added) specifically states, "Let us *eat* and make merry," but any Middle Eastern reader of the text (ancient or

---

[3]A similar scene occurs with Paul when he is invited to defend himself before scholars on Mars Hill (cf. Acts 17:22-34). Paul's speech is a carefully constructed unit addressed to scholars. The passage in Acts may be a brief summary of his lecture.

modern) knows full well that when the shepherd and the woman invite their friends into their respective houses, there will be eating and drinking. There has to be. The culture demands it. There is, therefore, not one story concluding with a party (which involves eating and drinking) but rather three, a fact that unites this trilogy.

3. Each story has a special "finder," and the three story lines are parallel. Thus, the good shepherd, the good woman and the good father need to be seen together. Strangely, the church's traditional understanding of the three stories fails to make this connection. The average reader easily identifies Jesus as the good shepherd but fails to see the good woman as a second symbol for him. The two are clearly linked. I would submit that it is impossible to see Jesus symbolized in the first story without noting him in the second. If he is "the good shepherd," he is necessarily also "the good woman." If Jesus is not the good woman, it follows that he cannot be seen as the good shepherd. These traditional interpretive blind spots must be overcome if the text is to be taken seriously. Jesus is clearly talking about himself in both parables.[4] But what of the father? Is it possible that the symbol of the father in the third story is also a symbol for Jesus? And if so, how?

Naturally, the father in the story of the prodigal son is a symbol for God[5] (as are the good shepherd and the good women; cf. Ps 23; 131). But is he *only* a symbol for God? This theme will be examined more closely in a later chapter. The good shepherd finds the lost sheep and has a party while the good woman discovers her coin and also holds a party. Finally, the good father finds his son and hosts a party. As we have seen, the shepherd and the women evolve into symbols for Jesus. What about the father? The text necessitates an examination of if, when and how the symbol of the father evolves into a symbol for Jesus. The same question is pressed upon the listener/reader in another way.

The Pharisees went to Jesus complaining "*This man receives sinners and eats with them*" (Lk 15:2). When the Pharisees say, "*This man* receives sinners," they mean Jesus, who replies and says, as it were,

---

[4]Jesus also refers to himself as a mother hen (cf. Lk 13:34).

[5]Some commentators have taken the phrase "I have sinned against heaven and before you" (Lk 15:21) to mean that the father is not a symbol for God. But this phrase is a quotation from Pharaoh talking to Moses (Ex 10:16). It is my conviction that it is the *quotation* that determines the selection of words, not Jesus' ideas about who the father represents. Cf. the discussion of father on pages 138-46.

You accuse me of eating with sinners. You are absolutely right. That is precisely what I do. But as a matter of fact I not only sit down and eat with sinners, I rush down the road, shower them with kisses and drag them in that I might eat with them. It is much worse than you imagined! Let me tell you a story to explain how this happens.

In telling the story of the father who orders a banquet so that he can sit down and eat with a sinner (the prodigal), Jesus is clearly talking about himself. Of course, the symbol for father begins as a symbol for God as does the good shepherd and the good woman. But all three evolve into symbols for Jesus. Finally, at the end of the parable the little boy tells the older son that the father has received a sinner (the prodigal) and will eat with him. This scene will also be examined later in greater detail. Here, it is sufficient to note that the shepherd, the woman and the father all evolve into symbols for Jesus, a fact that unites the three stories in a powerful manner.

4. In each of the three stories something is lost. But there is an important progression. In the first story, one in a hundred is lost, in the second, one in ten, and in the third, one in two.

5. The arena within which the missing animal/coin/son must be found narrows. In the first story, the sheep is lost in *the wide wilderness.* In the second, a coin is lost in *the house.* In the third, the son (sons?) is lost from within *the inner circle of a father's love.*

6. There is movement from animals and coins to people. This occurs in Psalm 23, in which David begins with a discussion of sheep and concludes with people at a banquet.[6] Jesus makes this same progression in the central section of Luke's Gospel, where he first talks about untying an ox or an ass on the sabbath (Lk 13:15), then defends his action in "untying" a woman from her bond (Lk 13:16). In Luke 14:1-6 the same two items (animals and people) are linked in a single story, but the order is reversed. Jesus heals a man from dropsy (a human problem with water) on the sabbath and defends himself by pointing out that his audience would certainly pull an ass or an ox out of a well (an animal problem with water) on the sabbath. In summary, the connecting of animals to people in a single discussion can be seen in Psalm 23 and appears twice in miracle stories told by Jesus. This connection supports the idea that the three stories in Luke 15 were composed together and preserved together.

---

[6]For a full discussion of the connections between Luke 15 and Psalm 23, see K. E. Bailey, *Finding.*

7. In each story there is a price to be paid. The shepherd must expend a great deal of energy not only to find but also to restore the lost sheep to the village. Of necessity he carries the fifty- to seventy-pound animal on his shoulders over rough terrain. The woman, we are told, searches "diligently" for her coin, and the father runs out of his house and down the road in self-emptying humiliation to reconcile and restore his lost son. As we will see, the son returns home imagining that the best he can hope for is to become a servant. And the father, at great cost, reconciles him as a son.

These seven points of connection lead us to view the three stories as a single parable with three scenes in which Jesus begins with animals and coins before turning to people. This raises the question of why such a movement was delibserately selected by both David and Jesus.

PROGRESSION IN THE PARABLES OF LUKE 15

I have a good friend who is a monsignor in the Roman Catholic Church. For nearly ten years he was my colleague in Jerusalem. The good Father is both a Jesuit priest and a skilled therapist with a doctorate in psychology who has explained to me how deeply the topic of money is buried in the human psyche. In the past, patients often went to him with a series of layered problems that had almost destroyed them. At times, one of those layers was a pattern of self-destructive behavior relating to sexuality. After a number of sessions, the doctor-patient relationship reached a deep level of mutual trust, and the patient was willing to discuss his or her sexual life and problems regarding it. Occasionally, in a later session, my friend asked how much money his patient had and how it was spent. At that point, the patient would withdraw in shock with the expressed or unexpressed question, "Why are you invading my privacy?" The conclusion that my friend and other therapists have come to is that an individual's money and how he or she spends it is embedded more deeply in the psyche of a person than is sexuality. Personal sexuality, it seems, can be discussed more easily than personal finance.

This understanding of how human beings are "wired" was obviously known to David as well as to Jesus. David began with sheep (money) and then talked about people. Jesus is challenged about why he "receives sinners." He replies, "If a sheep (money) was lost and it was *yours*, what would you do?" He knows, and they know, that the answer is, "I would go after it!" Jesus then reinforces his point by talking *directly* about money. "What if a woman lost a day's wages? Would she go after it?" he asks. She would and does. Only then do lost people appear on the stage in the form of two lost sons. This connection between financial loss and human loss makes it even more certain that these three stories were composed and coordinated into a single whole by Jesus and not by a later editor. Which leaves a final question: the question of memory.

To imagine that the community remembered individual stories is easier to accept than the idea that it recalled a longer presentation composed of three parts. Is the latter really possible?

Jesus, as we know, went from village to village preaching the good news of the coming of the kingdom of God. The most natural assumption is that, like a candidate for political office, at every stop he was obliged to answer many of the same key questions. Naturally, over time, he would develop polished answers that he delivered again and again. In the modern world, the press reporters who follow politicians can, at the end of the campaign trail, repeat almost verbatim the candidate's answers to major questions. Jesus' disciples hailed from among the common people, the "people of the land" discussed above. Jesus would have been challenged repeatedly regarding his association with such folk. These three parables may have been his "stump speech" answer. Having heard this trilogy on numerous occasions, the early disciples would have had no difficulty in remembering and recording it as a unit.

Keeping in mind the seven connectives between the three stories that were identified in this chapter, it behooves us to turn to the parable of the lost sheep, in which is embedded many of the major ideas that reappear in the parable of the prodigal son. These theological trajectories are among those ideas that tie the parable of the prodigal with the saga of Jacob.

7

THE PARABLE OF THE LOST SHEEP

The First Warm-up Story (Lk 15:3-7)

Jesus begins his "parable of finding the lost (in three scenes)" with the story of the good shepherd and the lost sheep.[1] The parable exhibits a rhetorical structure, illustrated in figure 3.

1. *What man* of *you*, having a hundred sheep,	YOU
2. and having lost *one* of them,	ONE
3. does not leave the *ninety-nine* in the wilderness,	NINETY-NINE
A. and go after the *lost* one LOST	
B. until he *finds* it? And having *found* it,	FIND
C. he places it upon his shoulders, *rejoicing*.	REJOICE
D. And coming *to the home*, he calls *to the*	
friends and neighbors,	RESTORE
C'. saying to them, "*Rejoice* with me,	REJOICE
B'. because I have *found* my sheep	FIND
A'. which was *lost*." LOST	
4. Even so, I say to *you*, that thus there will be more *joy* in heaven	YOU
5. over *one* sinner who repents	ONE
6. than over *ninety-nine* righteous persons who need no repentance.	NINETY-NINE

Figure 3. The lost sheep (Luke 15:4-7)

---

[1]This chapter is revised and expanded from K. E. Bailey, *Finding*, pp. 54-92.

A number of rhetorical features are significant for interpretation. The three themes (#1-3) at the beginning (you, one, ninety-nine) are repeated in the same order at the end (#4-6).[2] The center has seven phrases. Four ideas are presented (lost, find, rejoice, restore) and then repeated in reverse sequence. As noted earlier, I prefer to call this type of rhetoric "inverted parallelism." The theme of "restore" is in the center and is the climax of the story part of the parable. These rhetorical styles are highly developed in the Old Testament writing prophets. Thus Jesus is steeped in this literary tradition and uses it with great skill. Because the explanation of the meaning of the parable (#4-6) is thematically tied to the beginning, it is best understood as part of the original composition.[3] With these carefully crafted Hebrew stylistics in mind, the parable needs to be examined with some care.

CONNECTIONS TO PSALM 23

Here Jesus is retelling a classical story already well known to his listeners. His scholarly Pharisaic audience will first think of Psalm 23 and then ponder Jeremiah 23:1-6 and Ezekiel 34:1-31. Why?

The traditional translation of Psalm 23:3 is "He restoreth my soul" (KJV). In the English translation tradition, this verse has come to mean "He lifted my depression" or "He helped me recover a sense of joy" or some sense of a restoration of faith and worth. But buried under these time-honored meanings is the original Hebrew text, which reads *nafshi yeshobeb. Nafshi* means "myself/soul/person/life." The verb *shub* is the great Hebrew word for "repent/return."[4] Thus Psalm 23:3 can be translated "He brings me back" or "He causes me to repent." For centuries, Arabic versions in the Middle East have read *yarudd nafsi* (he brings me back). The other option, "he causes me to repent," is an important component of what David is saying in the psalm. He is reflecting on his personal journey of faith that includes repentance *(shub),*described as God coming after him and bringing him back. The Hebrew original of the psalm is built on the concrete picture of a good shepherd who goes after a lost sheep, picks it up and carries it home. The sheep cannot find its way home by itself. Once lost, it crawls under a rock or bush and begins to bleat. It must be

---

[2]I have called this "step parallelism"; cf. K. E. Bailey, *Finding,* pp. 45-47.

[3]In the rabbinic tradition, a parable is called a *mashal,* and the extra interpretive information attached to it is called *nimshal.* Cf. C. Thoma, "Literary and Theological Aspects of the Rabbinic Parables," pp. 26-41.

[4]*Yeshobeb* is an intensive form of the verb *shub.*

rescued quickly before a wild animal hears it, finds it, kills it and eats it. When found by the shepherd, it is so terrified that its legs will have turned to rubber and it is unable to stand. The only way the shepherd can restore it to the flock and finally to the village is to carry it home over his shoulders.[5]

The phrase that immediately follows in Psalm 23 expands this picture of restoration. It reads, "He leads me in the paths of righteousness." The assumption of the text is that the psalmist was wandering in the paths of unrighteousness. The good shepherd (God) went after him, picked him up and carried him back to the paths of righteousness. The shepherd caused him to repent/return *(shub)*. The psalm continues with assurances of security from death and evil, whereupon the imagery suddenly changes.

In Psalm 23:5 the story shifts from animals to people. God, the good shepherd, suddenly becomes God, the generous host, who prepares a meal, anoints my head and fills my cup. The story concludes in the house (Ps 23:6), where the psalmist intends to dwell "to the end of the days" (author's translation).[6] This unforgettable combination of dramatic images is not easily forgotten. Indeed, a few hundred years later, Jeremiah repeats the same story with several important changes.

CONNECTIONS TO JEREMIAH 23:1-8

Jeremiah 23:1-8 opens with sharp criticism of the bad shepherds of Israel (its leaders) who have lost their flock. This is a new element not found in the original psalm. The individual lost sheep of Psalm 23 becomes an entire flock, and after the shepherd's failure God promises to appear in person and "bring them back." The verb *shub* (repent/restore) reappears in the phrase "I will bring them back" (Jer 23:3 NRSV). The anticipated return is no longer a return to God; it has become a return to the land. The similarities and contrasts between these two texts can be seen in figure 4 (p. 68).

David's psalm contains no bad shepherd, no flock and no return to the land. The only return is to God, and the only house is the house of God. Jeremiah focuses on the flock. He turns David's personal story of how God

---

[5]These details have been explained to me by shepherds in Lebanon and the West Bank in Israel/Palestine.

[6]My translation here is a literal rendering of the Hebrew text. Does it mean "God's days"? Such an understanding is behind the use of the word *forever* in the King James Version. But perhaps it means "our days"; the NRSV chooses this option and translates the verse as "my whole life long." Could it be both?

brought him back to the paths of righteousness into a tale of the good shepherd (God) and the lost flock (Israel), which God himself will one day lead back to "their fold" (i.e., the land of Israel). After their return to the land (not to God), "David a righteous Branch," will reign as king with justice and righteousness (Jer 23:6-8). No celebration takes place, and the only dwelling that is mentioned is the "house of Israel." Jeremiah builds on and revises David's psalm. The revisions showcase some of Jeremiah's main concerns as he reflects on the fall of the nation of Israel and the hope for a future return. But the biblical history of this particular set of dramatic images is not over.

David (Psalm 23)	Jeremiah (Jeremiah 23:1-8)
1. ——	Bad shepherds
2. Lost sheep	Lost flock
3. The problem: a sheep is lost	The problem: shepherds destroy/scatter the flock
4. Good shepherd: God	Good shepherd: God plus David
5. Incarnation implied	Incarnation promised
6. Price paid: bring back	Price paid: gather, bring back
7. Repentance *(shub)*: return to God	Restoration *(shub)*: return to the land
8. Celebration	——
9. Story ends in the house of God	Story ends in the land

Figure 4. Two renditions of the same story

CONNECTIONS TO EZEKIEL 34

Ezekiel, the prophet of the exile, tells the same story for the third time (Ezek 34). Clearly, he has access to Jeremiah's retelling in that he follows and dramatically expands Jeremiah's outline. Indeed, the story lengthens with each telling. David relates his tale with six verses. Jeremiah expands to eight, while Ezekiel needs thirty-one verses to present his version of the same parable. Ezekiel opens with a blistering attack on the "shepherds of Israel" (Ezek 34:2). It takes him a full ten verses to tell his readers how angry God is with Israel's leaders. Not only have they scattered and neglected the flock, but they are also *devouring it!* The flock needs rescuing from the shepherds themselves! Obviously, a radical solution is necessary.

At the end of verse 10 God promises to rescue the flock *himself,* and verse

11 repeats the promise of incarnation first voiced clearly in Jeremiah's account. God says, "Behold, I, I myself will search for my sheep, and will seek them out" (Ezek 34:11). He continues with "I myself will be the shepherd of my sheep, and I will make them lie down, says the Lord GOD. I will seek the lost, and I will bring back *[shub]* the strayed. . . . I will feed them in justice" (Ezek 34:15-16).

After this a new element appears, namely, *bad sheep.* Some sheep feed on good pasture and tread down that which remains. They drink clean water and foul the rest with their feet (Ezek 34: 17-19). The strong attack the weak (Ezek 34:21-22). It is clear that God is going to go after them not because they are good sheep but because he is the good shepherd. He has no illusions regarding the quality of the flock he intends *in person* to rescue!

As in Jeremiah, David is again waiting in the wings to take control of the flock once God the good shepherd has them rounded up and brought back to the land. As this rescue unfolds, they will "know that I, the LORD their God, am with them, and that they . . . are my people, says the Lord GOD" (Ezek 34:30). God's intervention in returning them to the land will prove (to them) that they belong to God.

Jesus is accused by the Pharisees and the scribes: "This man receives sinners and eats with them" (Lk 15:2). His first response is to recount this classical story already familiar to his audience in these three versions.[7] No doubt the listening audience is amazed that he presumes to align himself with David, Jeremiah and Ezekiel. But it is worse than they imagined! For in Jesus' version he has clearly written himself into the play as the lead character. He is the good shepherd. Jesus is saying:

> You wonder why I receive sinners and eat with them? I do so because in my person God is fulfilling his great promise hinted at in David's shepherd psalm and spelled out clearly in Jeremiah and Ezekiel. Through those prophets he pledged himself to come in person and round up the lost sheep. He also pledged himself to rescue the flock from the shepherds who destroy them. This is who I am, and this is why I do what I do.

These four accounts of the same story must now be brought together.

---

[7]The book of Zechariah (9:16; 10:2-3, 11:3-17; 13:7-9) has many of the same shepherd images. The bad shepherds, the flock of God and the incarnation of God as the good shepherd who brings them back *(shub)* all appear in the text. Yet, these themes are random images scattered through a number of prophetic oracles rather than a structured story with a biblical lineage. For this reason these texts have been left out of this discussion.

Thematic Similarities to Three Old Testament Passages

Jesus' parable (Lk 15:4-7) begs to be compared thematically to the three previous renditions of the same story. Figure 5 illustrates the similarities.

David (Psalm 23)	Jeremiah (Jeremiah 23:1-8)	Ezekiel (Ezekiel 34:1-31)	Jesus (Luke 15:4-7)
1. ——	1. Bad shepherds	1. Bad shepherds	1. Bad shepherd
2. Lost *sheep*	2. Lost flock	2. Lost flock	2. Lost *sheep* (Flock in wilderness)
3. The problem: A sheep is lost	3. The problem: Shepherds destroy/scatter the sheep	3. The problem: Shepherds scatter/eat the flock	3. The problem: The shepherd loses a sheep
4. Good shepherd: God	4. Good shepherd: God plus David	4. Good shepherd: God plus David	4. Good shepherd: Jesus
5. Incarnation implied	5. Incarnation promised	5. Incarnation promised	5. Incarnation realized
6. Price paid: Bring back	6. Price paid: Gather, bring back	6. Price paid: Search for, save, deliver, bring back	6. Price paid: Search for, find, carry back
7. *Repentance: Return to God*	7. Restoration: Return to land	7. Restoration: Return to land	7. *Repentance: Return to God*
8. ——	8. ——	8. Bad sheep	8. Bad sheep (?)
9. *Celebration*	9. ——	9. ——	9. *Celebration*
10. The story ends in *the house*	10. The story ends in the land	10. The story ends in the land	10. The story ends in *the house*

Figure 5. Three Old Testament passages and Jesus' parable

The italicized words in the figure highlight the points in the story where, in his version, Jesus has returned to the original account of the good shepherd in Psalm 23. That is, in four cases out of ten Jesus sets aside Jeremiah and Ezekiel as he *returns* to the content of Psalm 23.[8] In four additional

---

[8]Cf. numbers 2, 7, 9 and 10.

points the idea *originates* with the psalm.[9] Only in numbers 1 and 8 do new ideas begin with Jeremiah or Ezekiel. A brief comment on each of the above points seems appropriate.

1. The nature of the shepherd. Briefly stated, David presents a single good shepherd. Jeremiah and Ezekiel offer two kinds of shepherds, the bad (Israel's leaders) and the good (God present among them). Jesus' parable opens with a bad shepherd who becomes a good shepherd. This transition from bad to good shepherd requires some reflection.

In Psalm 23, David describes the many good qualities of God the shepherd. God leads the sheep to green pastures and to still waters. He rescues the lost sheep, leads it in the paths of righteousness and protects it from all dangers. By contrast, Jeremiah and Ezekiel open with stinging criticism of the bad shepherds of Israel, shepherds who destroy, scatter and finally devour their own sheep. After describing the bad shepherds, both prophets record the promise of God (the good shepherd) who will compensate for the errors of the bad shepherds and come *himself* to rescue the sheep. Thus Jeremiah and Ezekiel describe the bad shepherds as the shepherds of Israel and the good shepherd as God.

As noted, like Jeremiah and Ezekiel, Jesus opens with a bad shepherd. He begins with the phrase "if he has lost one of them [the sheep]." Clearly, the shepherd is blamed. This is a "Bo Peep" story. But that same bad shepherd accepts responsibility for the error of his ways and pays the necessary price to find the animal and carry it home (the question of the price paid will be examined below). Jesus has evidently taken the bad shepherd and good shepherd images from the two prophets and combined them into a single person. The bad shepherd becomes the good shepherd. Jesus seems to be saying to his audience of scribes and Pharisees:

> You are the shepherds of Israel. You have lost your sheep. You should go after them, but you have failed to do so. To compensate for your mistakes *I* am going after them. You should *rejoice* with me. Instead you come *complaining!* Can't you see that I am making up for your mistakes?!

This combination in a single person of *(a)* the bad shepherd who loses his sheep with *(b)* the good shepherd who goes after it is a daring, risky use of metaphorical language. The opening description of the bad shep-

---

[9]Cf. numbers 3, 4, 5 and 6.

herd represents the audience, while the second part, which deals with the good shepherd, is clearly Jesus himself. By going after the lost sheep, Jesus is doing what they should be doing. But in this parable, Jesus includes another striking, albeit subtle, example of the joining of two figures in a single person.

In Jeremiah and Ezekiel, the good shepherd is God, but David is waiting in the wings to take over the flock. After God comes in person and finds/restores the lost flock, he intends to turn responsibility over to David. Jesus' version has no God + David. He presents only himself as the good shepherd who finds and restores the lost sheep. Whatever happened to David? The answer is obvious to Luke's readers. In the first chapter of Luke, the angel promises Mary that the child to be born will be given "the throne of his father David, and he will reign over the house of Jacob forever; and of his kingdom there will be no end" (Lk 1:32-33).[10]

Throughout the Synoptic Gospels, Jesus is known as the son of David. As indicated, Jesus is shaping his version of this classical tale in the light of the three previous accounts of the same story. His scholarly audience could hardly have missed what he was doing. Jeremiah and Ezekiel promised God + David, and thus Jesus is indirectly saying,

> In me you have both promises in one person! I represent the divine presence in the community, and the mantle of the house of David has been placed on my shoulders.

2. The lost sheep (and a lost flock). David tells the story of his personal walk of faith when he says "The LORD is my shepherd." In David's account there is no reference to any flock. Jeremiah and Ezekiel, as noted, turn the story into a tale of Israel's exile and hoped-for return to the land. In the process, the lost sheep becomes a lost flock. Jesus combines the two with a lost sheep *who is part of a flock.* But, amazingly, at the end of Jesus' parable that flock *remains in the wilderness!*[11] The shepherd *"leave[s] the ninety-nine in the wilderness, and go[es]"* (Lk 15:4). What happens to those ninety-nine? We are not told. Yes, they represent the ninety-nine "righteous persons who need no

---

[10]The same information is also given to the reader of Matthew, where the genealogy of Jesus includes Jesus (Mt 1:1-17) and Joseph is addressed by the angel as "Joseph, son of David" (Mt 1:20; cf. also 12:23; 15:22; 21:9). In Mark 10:47 the blind beggar addresses Jesus with "Jesus, Son of David."

[11]In the story line the parable makes sense. The assumption is that the shepherd has an assistant who takes responsibility for the rest of the flock in the temporary absence of the shepherd.

repentance" (Lk 15:7). But as Arland Hultgren notes, as addressed to the Pharisees this "must be taken as sarcastic."[12] There can be no rejoicing over the ninety-nine back in the village when no one knows where they are!! The point is subtle, but it is nonetheless there. Are the ninety-nine (the scribes and Pharisees) still in the wilderness? Are they still lost? Do they continue to be in exile? This powerful theme reappears in the third story, as will be seen. It is important to note its introduction in this first story.

At times it is helpful in Scripture to think cinemagraphically and follow the camera. What precisely is the camera focused on? Jesus opens his parable with the camera centered on the flock. A quick shot reveals that the ninety-nine are being left in the wilderness. The camera then moves to the lost sheep and the search for it by the shepherd. Then comes the return to the village. The last scene is one of rejoicing with friends in the village at the success of the shepherd's efforts. But—what about the rest of the flock? The camera never swings back to tell us of its return. The parable is silent. In this sense the parable has a missing ending like the parable of the prodigal son. All we have is the *nimshal* (the interpretive conclusion) that follows the action and reflects on it. So is the parable only dealing with a lost individual (such as David), or is there a flock unaccounted for out in the wilderness (as with Jeremiah and Ezekiel)? Or is Jesus concerned for both? These questions remain mysteries until the third story unfolds.

3. The problem. When David writes, "He brings me back/causes me to repent," he is affirming that he was lost and that God, the good shepherd, brought him back. The text does not reveal how he became lost. It could have read, "When I wander off the path, he brings me back/causes me to repent." The first phrase is assumed rather than stated. Surely David means that he (not God) is responsible for his lost condition. But in Jeremiah, Ezekiel and Luke 15, as noted, the shepherds are faulted.

4 and 5. The good shepherd: the incarnation of God/Jesus. (These two ideas are two sides of a single coin and therefore need to be discussed together.) For all three previous authors, the good shepherd is God. Jesus retells this classical story with himself at its center. He is clearly affirming that, in his ministry, the great promises of God, written in Jeremiah and Ezekiel, are being fulfilled.

In the New Testament, the Christology of this passage needs to be placed

---

[12]A. J. Hultgren, *The Parables of Jesus,* p. 60.

alongside the great christological hymns in Philippians 2:5-11 and Colossians 1:15-20. The good shepherd as presented by Jesus can be called "hermeneutical Christology." By this I mean that in this parable it is possible to see who Jesus is by tracing how he takes an Old Testament symbol for God, reshapes it and applies it to himself.

Across the centuries, the church has studied the titles for Jesus as a means of understanding who he is. The titles Son of God, Son of Man, Savior of the world, Messiah, Son of David and so forth have rightly been rigorously examined. A second method of trying to understand Jesus has been called "functional Christology." This endeavor says, Let us look to see what Jesus *does,* and through a study of his actions we can discover who he is. He forgives sin. He heals the sick and raises the dead. These actions will unlock the secrets of who he is.

Both of these methods are important. But in this, and other Gospel passages, a third method is employed. By taking Old Testament language for God and applying it to himself, Jesus is perhaps offering the most profound insights of all into the mystery of his person.[13]

Another way to approach the above endeavor is to ask, "What if Alexander the Great had marched West rather than East?" If that had happened in the fourth century B.C., there would have been no Greek conquest of the Middle East and no Middle Eastern Hellenism. The New Testament would have been written in Hebrew or Aramaic, and the dominant intellectual forces in the early church would have been Aramaic rather than Greek. Obviously, that did not transpire. Yet, it is fruitful to engage in what I like to call the re-Semitization of our Christology.

By means of the Nicene Creed (A.D. 325) the Greek world gave the church a brilliant definition of who Jesus is. The creed's language is both familial and philosophical. It states:

> We believe in one Lord, Jesus Christ, the only Son of God, eternally begotten of the Father, God from God, Light from Light, true God from true God, begotten, not made, of one Being with the Father.[14]

---

[13]The eminent Israeli scholar David Flusser authored a thought-provoking essay in which he discusses the fact that the great Rabbi Hillel (one generation before Jesus) did exactly the same thing; cf. "Hillel's Self-Awareness and Jesus," in D. Flusser, *Judaism,* pp. 509-14.

[14]*The Book of Common Prayer According to the Use of the Episcopal Church* (New York: Oxford University Press, 1990), p. 326.

But in this parable, the *foundation* for this theology is presented in Jewish/biblical word pictures rather than in Greek philosophical language. Thus the parable of the lost sheep presents a Jewish metaphor for God which is set in a classical Jewish story reshaped by Jesus. This makes clear that a lofty understanding of who Jesus is can be traced to Jesus himself. His disciples did not turn the proclaimer into the proclamation a generation or more after his earthly life. Rather, some of the most profound affirmations of who Jesus is come from Jesus himself. As seen here, those affirmations stem from the parables he created to declare who he was and what his gospel was all about. The disciples discovered gold; they did not create gold. Incarnation is at the heart of Jesus' self-understanding.

Briefly tracing the movement of incarnation from David, through Jeremiah, Ezekiel and Isaiah, to Jesus is the next task.[15]

Psalm 23 uses language for God that invokes incarnation. God is not only seated in the heavens looking down on the world. He is also "my shepherd" who leads me to pasture and water. I see his rod and staff and feel safe as a result. Granted, in the Hebrew Scriptures, God is primarily present among his people in the temple.[16] And in a general sense the presence of God is everywhere.[17] But in this psalm, David uses metaphorical language that describes God as being present with him in a specific, localized sense, guiding him along the paths of righteousness. Here David speaks of God as present for him in the concrete person of a shepherd.

Jeremiah and Ezekiel move the reflection on incarnation a giant step forward. As noted above, each of these prophets specifically affirms the promise of God, that one day in the future "I, I myself will search for my sheep, and will seek them out" (Ezek 34:11). Incarnation becomes even more real as the prophet spells out all that God the good shepherd will do for his lost and scattered flock. In addition to these three Old Testament texts, incarnation also appears in a brief important passage in Isaiah to which we now turn.

The prophetic promise of incarnation is powerfully affirmed in the well-known text of Isaiah 55:6-11 which breaks into three interlocking stanzas.

---

[15]A similar movement will be observed below in studying the father in the Old Testament (as a model for God) and the figure of the father in the parable of the prodigal son.

[16]Habakkuk 2:20 reads, "The LORD is in his holy temple; / let all the earth keep silence before him."

[17]Cf. Psalm 139:7-12: "Whither shall I flee from thy presence?" (v. 7).

The passage begins with three double lines:

Stanza 1
Seek the Lord while he may be found,
call upon him while he is near

let the wicked forsake his *way*
and the unrighteous man his *thoughts*;

let him return *(shub)* to the Lord, that he may have *mercy* on him
and to our God, for he will abundantly *pardon*

These three double lines are called "Hebrew parallelisms" because each of the three ideas is repeated twice. The believer is called on to (1) seek the Lord *while he may be found* and *while he is near*. He must then (2) forsake his *ways* and *thoughts*. Only then can he (3) return/repent *(shub)* to the Lord and receive *mercy* and *pardon*. Obviously, God is not always near and cannot always be found. Thus the question that arises is: When is he *near*, and where *can* he be found? The plot thickens in stanza two:

Stanza 2
For *my thoughts* are not *your thoughts*
    neither are your *ways* my *ways*, says the Lord
        For as the *heavens* are higher than the *earth*,
    so are *my ways* higher than *your ways*,
and *my thoughts* than *your thoughts*.

The center of the first stanza talks about "ways and thoughts," while in this second stanza "ways and thoughts" open and close the five lines. Thus, the *center* of the first stanza becomes the *outside* of the second. In this second stanza the *ways* and *thoughts* of God are affirmed to be as far from our *ways* and *thoughts* as the *heavens* are higher than the *earth*. We as readers are pushed to despair. In stanza one, we are to seek God "while he is near," but in stanza two we discover that he is *not near*. Instead, God, with his ways and thoughts, is in the heavens, and we are very much upon the earth. God's mercy and pardon are unavailable because he cannot be found. What can possibly be done? The resolution of this critical problem appears in stanza three:

Stanza 3
For as the rain and the snow come down from *heaven*
    and return not thither but water the *earth*,

> making it bring forth and sprout
> > giving seed to the sower and bread to the eater

So shall *my word* be that goes forth from my mouth;
> it shall not return to me empty,
> > but it shall accomplish that which I purpose,
> > and prosper in the thing for which I sent it.

This stanza begins with a "parable" about the *heavens* and the *earth.* That is, once again Isaiah has taken the center of the previous stanza (the heavens and the earth) and used it to formulate the following stanza (stanza three). The third stanza opens with the rain/snow that is in the *heavens* (far away where God dwells) and notes that it comes down upon the *earth* where people live. As it comes down, it achieves God's purposes. This parable *(mashal)* is followed by its interpretation *(nimshal).* God's word is like the rain and snow. That word also comes down and achieves God's purposes. What purposes we ask? The simple answer is "mercy and pardon." When God is near, the believer can receive those great benefits. In the heavens, they are neither near nor available. But the word comes down like rain and snow falling from the sky, and as this happens, God draws near and his mercy and pardon are consequently available.

Remembering that the Word of God is not merely the *speech* of God but includes the *actions* of God, it is clear that: The Word of God equals the ways and thoughts of God. So the outside of the second stanza (ways and thoughts) is directly related to the climactic conclusion of stanza three. The problem has a solution, which is the incarnation of God's word. Rain comes down to us from the heavens and so does the Word of God. Each accomplishes God's purposes for us. A summary of the movement in the three stanzas is illustrated in figure 6.

Stanza One: My *need*
Seek God while he is near and receive pardon.　　　(But when is he near?)

Stanza Two: My *problem*
God is in the heavens—I am on the earth.　　　(God is far away, so what can I do?)

Stanza Three: *God's solution* to my problem
The rain and snow come down. Even so God's word　　　(*Incarnation* solves my problem).
comes down (and thereby comes near to me) and
achieves God's purposes, which are mercy and
pardon for me.

Figure 6. Movement in the three stanzas of Isaiah 55:6-11

This affirmation of the incarnation of the Word of God that brings mercy and pardon to the believer is in harmony with the image of the good shepherd who "brings me back" (David), who "restores/saves the flock" (Jeremiah/Ezekiel) and finally who "finds and rescues the lost" (Jesus). In Jesus' telling of this classical tale, incarnation is fully realized. The good shepherd (God), who promised to come himself and gather the flock, is present in the person of Jesus, son of David. Along with Isaiah 55, all four good shepherd texts present *incarnation* as a critical component of *salvation.*

6. The price paid. This theme is closely related to the following topic of "repentance." "Repentance" includes the *sheep's response* to the shepherd's saving acts. Here the focus is on what the *shepherd does,* but again they are two sides of a single coin.

As with other topics in this list, there is progression through the four texts. David simply affirms that "He brings me back." The reader is given no further details. Jeremiah expands the role of the shepherd in the rescue operation by describing (God) the shepherd as "gathering" and "bringing back" *(shub)* the fold. God will also "set shepherds over them" and promises to "raise up . . . David" (Ezek 23:4-5). But Ezekiel has more.

Ezekiel eloquently expands the description of the saving acts of God the good shepherd. In his version God searches, seeks, rescues, gathers, feeds, herds, brings back, binds up, strengthens and saves. All this is the catalog of what God will do *before* they arrive home. After he returns them to the land, there is an additional list of promises.

Jesus' telling of this story summarizes the actions of the good shepherd in Jeremiah and Ezekiel, particularly Ezekiel. Search, find and bring back are the sharp focus of Jesus' version. But with this emphasis he adds a striking new element not found in the previous three stories. In Luke 15 the shepherd *picks up* the lost sheep and *carries* it back on his shoulders (i.e., around the back of his neck on both shoulders). He does so *rejoicing* rather than *complaining.* The average sheep weighs fifty to seventy pounds. Struggling across hilly pastures with a sheep over one's shoulders is dangerous and exhausting. As mentioned earlier, the animal is too terrified to walk. Carrying it is the only way the shepherd can rescue it from certain death. The price paid to rescue the sheep is enormous. This unique emphasis is freighted with atoning power and can be seen to elucidate the theme of redemptive suffering.

The future personal entry of God into human history to save is already clearly affirmed by each of the two prophets, but this picture of the price paid goes beyond the stories they tell.

7. *Repentance/return.* The key word *shub* (repentance/return/restoration) occurs in each of the four Hebrew texts and reappears in Greek dress *(metanoeō)* in the parable under consideration in Luke 15. In his concluding comments, Jesus declares, "There will be more joy in heaven over one sinner who *repents* than over ninety-nine righteous persons who need no *repentance*" (Lk 15:7).[18]

This application of the parable comes as a big surprise. If asked what the parable was all about one might conclude:

- It is about a bad shepherd who loses his sheep.
- It is about a good shepherd who goes after it.
- It is about the price paid to find the sheep and carry it home.
- It is about rejoicing in community when the shepherd carrying the lost sheep arrives home.

All of these ideas are present in the parable. But Jesus affirms that the main point is: *repentance!* Clearly, the lost sheep is a symbol of repentance! How can this be? All the lost sheep does is become lost. This startling new definition of repentance deserves examination. Indeed, it is critical for all three parables in Luke 15 and for comparisons with the saga of Jacob. Thus, it is necessary to look briefly at what the three previous texts have to say on this subject.

David's psalm is a personal testimony. He was lost, and the good shepherd (God) went after him, and *yashubib nefshi.* As noted, in the psalm the weight of the meaning of this phrase is "He causes me to repent." Is this an act of David or an act of God? In some undefined sense, it is surely both. It is clear that David is not stuck in Egypt or Babylon needing to return to Jerusalem. Instead, he is estranged from God and needs to be brought back to the paths of righteousness and life with God. God acts to bring him back, and, by implication, David accepts God's action. But details of the rescue effort are not provided.

As noted, Jeremiah and Ezekiel turn the parable into a story of political exile. There is no hint of any return to God in their version. God comes as the good shepherd and restores them to their land. In this act they recognize that God is in charge but no more.

---

[18]The Greek word for "repentance" in this text is *metanoeō*. This word is a New Testament Greek equivalent to the Hebrew word *shub.*

Jesus' account restores the narrative to a personal testimony and focuses on the costly efforts of the shepherd in searching for, finding and returning sinners to himself. In the process he expands the tacit definition of repentance in the psalm. With Jesus, repentance equals acceptance of being found. To understand what he is doing, it is necessary to briefly place what Jesus is saying into the context of the evolving rabbinic theology of his time.

The topic of repentance was important in both the Hebrew Scriptures and in the rabbis' reflection on them. George Foot Moore, in his monumental work on the theology of the early rabbis, dedicates two chapters to the topic of repentance in rabbinic thought.[19] He provides a summary of this topic:

> To the Jewish definition of repentance belong the reparation of injuries done to a fellow man in his person, property, or good name, the confession of sin, prayer for forgiveness and the genuine resolve and endeavor not to fall into the sin again.[20]

Thus, to be made right with God, a sinner must:

- make compensation for the sin to the person wronged
- confess the sin and seek forgiveness
- resolve and endeavor not to sin again

These actions, in rabbinic thought, gradually became a means of atoning for sin. This idea is as early as the wisdom of Ben Sirach, who some two hundred years before the time of Jesus wrote, "and in the time of [committing] sins, show forth repentance . . . and wait not till death to be justified."[21] Clearly, for Ben Sirach, repentance accomplishes justification/righteousness before God. This theme is often repeated in rabbinic literature. A summary of ideas from a variety of rabbis appears in *Tractate Yoma* of the Babylonian Talmud, which reads:

> Great is repentance, for it reaches up to the Throne of glory, . . .
>
> Great is repentance, because it brings about redemption, . . .
>
> Great is repentance, for because of it premeditated sins are accounted as errors, . . .
>
> Great is repentance, because it prolongs the [days and] years of man, . . .

---

[19]G. F. Moore, *Judaism,* 1:507-34. For a second highly respected study of the rabbis, cf. E. E. Urbach, *The Sages.* Urbach discusses repentance in a variety of places as evidenced in the following discussion.

[20]G. F. Moore, *Judaism,* 1:117.

[21]Sirach 18:21-22 (as translated by E. E. Urbach, *The Sages,* 1:467). The key word is *dikaiothenai,* which Urbach rightly translates "to be justified."

As to the character of one of flesh and blood, if one angers his fellow, it is doubtful whether he [the latter] will be pacified . . . by mere words. But with the Holy One, blessed be He, if a man commits a sin in secret, He is pacified by mere words, as it is said: *Take with you words, and return unto the Lord.*

Great is repentance, for on account of an individual who repents, the sins of all the world are forgiven.[22]

A second summary reads:

Men asked Wisdom, What is the doom of the sinner? It answered, "Evil pursues sinners" (Prov. 13,21); they asked Prophecy the same question, and it answered, "The soul (the individual) that sins shall die" (Ezek. 18,4); they asked the Law, and it answered, "Let him bring a trespass offering *(asham)* and it shall be forgiven him, as it is said, 'And it shall be accepted for him to make atonement for him' " (Lev. 1,4). They asked the Holy One, blessed is He, and he answered, "Let him repent, and it shall be forgiven him."[23]

This summary is attributed to Rabbi Phinehas, a fourth-century Palestinian rabbi.[24] At the same time, Judah b. Simon (a first-century Palestinian rabbi) said, "Return, O Israel, unto the Lord thy God (Hosea xiv 2)—even if you have denied the primary principle of the faith." Urbach quotes this passage and then comments, "Thereby he [Judah b. Simon] wished to say that there is no sin for which repentance does not atone."[25]

For an insight into what Jesus is saying, it should be observed that in all of these references there is no incarnation. God, the good shepherd, does not need to come to us. Instead, through repentance, we go to God. Moore quotes the rabbinic saying, "An arrow carries the width of a field; but repentance carries to the very throne of God."[26] And again,

Great is the power of repentance, for as soon as a man meditates in his heart to repent, instantly it (his repentance) rises, not ten miles, nor twenty, nor a hundred, but a journey of five hundred years; and not to the first firmament but to the seventh; and not to the seventh firmament only—it stands before the glorious throne (Hos. 14:2).[27]

---

[22] Babylonian Talmud, *Yoma* 86b.

[23] *Pesikta,* f. 158b, edited by Martin Buber (quoted by G. F. Moore, *Judaism,* 1:533).

[24] E. E. Urbach, *The Sages,* 1:463-64.

[25] E. E. Urbach, *The Sages,* 1:469. His quote is from the Tosefta, *Sotah* 13:5.

[26] The passage is taken from *Pesiqta Rabbati,* f. 163b; cf. G. F. Moore, *Judaism,* 1:530.

[27] The passage is taken from *Pesiqta Rabbati,* f. 185a; cf. G. F. Moore, *Judaism,* 1:530-31.

Urbach notes that early Israel was not called on to repent. It was the prophets who made such demands.[28] Furthermore, the prophets and the early sages did not have "a single style for calling to repentance."[29] In summary, repentance was important; it was a work required of the believer. The power of repentance was related to atonement and, for many, a substitution for it. But, incarnation was not necessary. The saving prayer of repentance pierced the clouds and reached the very throne of God.

As this theological world was developing, Jesus tells the story of the shepherd who rescues his lost sheep. Supported by the theology of Isaiah 55:6-11, David, Jeremiah and Ezekiel, Jesus emphasizes *the need for God to come to us*. His word must come down and bring God near so that we might receive mercy and pardon (Isaiah). The Lord is like a shepherd who remains near us (David). God, the good shepherd, pledges himself, to come, gather and save the flock (Jeremiah, Ezekiel). In the process, the good shepherd pays a high price. He must find the sheep, pick it up and carry it back to safety in order to save its life (Jesus).

In the context of the Hebrew Scriptures and the developing rabbinic tradition, what does Jesus contribute to this discussion? And what would his audience, on reflection, hear him saying? Clearly there are five points:

(a) Incarnation. As Jesus defined it, there can be no repentance without incarnation. The shepherd leaves the flock and enters the wilderness to find the lost sheep. He dare not wait hoping that it may come home. He knows that it cannot do so.

(b) The price paid. Repentance/restoration is not possible if the shepherd is unwilling to pay the high price required to carry the lost sheep back to the village. Finding it is not enough; it must be carried home.

(c) A redefinition of repentance. Repentance is no longer something the sheep does to assure its acceptance by the shepherd. The sheep becomes lost and "accepts being found."

(d) Repentance calls for a celebration in the community. For the psalmist, God "prepares a table." There is a celebration. But it is a table for one. In Jesus' retelling of this tale, the shepherd calls in "his friends and his neighbors" (Lk 15:6) for a party. This element is missing from all three previous accounts.

(e) Joy. The emotion attached to repentance is that of joy. The joy of the

---

[28]E. E. Urbach, *The Sages,* 1:462-71.
[29]E. E. Urbach, *The Sages,* 1:463.

shepherd (and the community) is affirmed. The story assumes that the sheep participates in that joy. Once lost, the sheep is afraid a wild animal will kill it. Suddenly, the shepherd appears and carries it back to the village. One of the theological implications of this new definition of repentance is that joy at being found overcomes remorse over having become lost. In this parable Jesus describes a lost animal. The second story is centered on a lifeless coin. In the third story, people walk on stage whose words and actions, in light of the sheep and the coins, will need to be examined with care. So much for Jesus' affirmation of the meaning of repentance.

8. Good and bad sheep. The first two stories contain no criticism of the sheep. Ezekiel's critique of them is a new element. He describes strong sheep who eat from good pasture, drink clear water and leave crushed feed and befouled water for the others. These same strong sheep are told "you push with side and shoulder, and thrust at all the weak with your horns, till you have scattered them abroad" (Ezek 34:21).

In spite of these glaring faults, Ezekiel does not call on the sheep to repent. He affirms only that God will become the shepherd anyway, and will round them up, return them to their land and provide for all of their needs. There is recognition that God will bring them back to the land, but in these texts no restored relationship with God is discussed by Ezekiel or Jeremiah. The best that God, the good shepherd, seems to hope for is that after these mighty acts to save the people will indeed recognize him as their God.

In his reference to "the ninety-nine righteous who need no repentance" (Lk 15:7), Jesus picks up on the theme of "good and bad sheep" in Ezekiel 34:17-19. As noted, Jesus is talking tongue in cheek. Isaiah the prophet wrote, "All we like sheep have gone astray" (Is 53:6). Ecclesiastes observes, "Surely there is not a righteous man on earth who does good and never sins" (Eccles 7:20).

9. Celebration in the community. A celebration concludes Psalm 23. It is indeed a table for one, but it is still a party with a cup that is running over. The celebration disappears in Jeremiah and Ezekiel only to be reintroduced in Jesus' parable as a community affair. The shepherd is part of a community that celebrates with him. But the language Jesus chooses contains a layer of meaning that has gone unnoticed.

We have already discussed the rabbinic societies consisting of the *haberim*, which translates "the friends." Thus when Jesus tells his listeners that the shepherd calls in "his friends," the language has a special ring for a Pharisaic audience. Jesus is saying, "You are the *haberim,* the 'friends.' This shepherd finds his lost sheep, carries it home and has a party. *His* friends rejoice with him. Why can't you, the 'friends,' rejoice with me?"[30] This theme of celebration will resurface when we look at the saga of Jacob.

   10. The location of the ending. David's story concludes "in the house of the LORD" (Ps 23:6), where the psalmist intends to dwell "to the end of the days." This can mean the end of God's days, that is, "for ever" (KJV), or "my whole life long" (NRSV). Perhaps it means both. In any case, the story concludes in the house of God.

   Jeremiah and Ezekiel make a substitution. Rather than ending up in the house of God, the flock is taken back to the land. The only house mentioned in either account is "the house of Israel" (Jer 23:8), where the word *house* refers to people not to a place. Jesus' story, like Psalm 23, concludes in "the house."

THE THEOLOGICAL CLUSTER OF THE PARABLE OF THE LOST SHEEP (LK 15:1-7)

To summarize, I would suggest that this great parable reflects the following cluster of theological ideas, many of which will reappear in the discussion of the saga of Jacob and the parable of the prodigal son.[31]

   1. Failed leadership. The parable contains criticism of leaders who lose their sheep and do nothing but complain about others who go after them.

   2. Freely offered grace. The lost sheep offers no special service to the shepherd and thereby fails to earn the right of rescue. It comes as a gift.

   3. The atonement. The shepherd pays a high price both to *find* the sheep and to *restore* it to his home. Thus, the heart of the atonement is affirmed in this parable.

   4. Sin. Humankind is depicted as lost and unable to find its own way home.

   5. Joy. The parable rings with the joy of the shepherd and the community (and presumably the sheep) at the success of the saving event.

   6. Repentance. Repentance is defined as acceptance of being found. The sheep is lost and helpless and yet is a symbol of repentance. Repentance becomes the act of the shepherd as he carries the sheep back to his home in the village (and includes the sheep's acceptance of that rescue).

---

[30]The Hebrew word *haburah* survives in this verse in a medieval Arabic version of the Gospel of Luke. Cf. Vatican Arabic #18.

[31]This section is revised from K. E. Bailey, *Finding,* p. 92.

7. *The individual and the community.* As told by Jeremiah and Ezekiel, the story of the lost sheep (Ps 23) becomes a story of a lost flock (Israel), which God in person will one day restore to the land. Jesus combined these two elements in his new telling of the old story. He recovers David's tale of a lost sheep that is carried home by the self-giving act of a good shepherd, but Jesus also includes the flock that is left dangling "in the wilderness." Do they arrive home? We are not told. This foreshadows the parable of the prodigal.

8. *Christology.* Jesus is clearly talking about himself. As the good shepherd, he is God's unique agent who restores the lost sinner to God. (The joy *in the home* of the shepherd is equated in the parable to joy *in heaven*.) The shepherd must personally make the costly demonstration of love in order to restore the helpless sheep. Three Old Testament texts stand behind the parable: Psalm 23, Jeremiah 23:1-4 and Ezekiel 34:11-16. This Old Testament background makes clear that the shepherd is more than merely an agent. He is the one who fulfills the promises of David, Jeremiah and Ezekiel, namely, that God himself will come to his people and seek his lost sheep.

Jesus, it appears, looks at Psalm 23 and says to himself:

> There is good material here, but the story needs an "update." Beginning with a good shepherd who goes after a lost sheep is fine. The table-for-one special meal is also good. But David did not integrate these two elements in his psalm. I will rewrite the story, put these two elements together, add the presence of the community and place myself at the center of it all.

But Jesus is not finished. After this amazing discussion of the good shepherd and the lost sheep, he dramatically introduces the good woman and the lost coin. To that second parable we now turn.

8

The Lost Coin

And Also Some Women (Lk 15:8-10)

This parable contains at least three points of special interest. First, why does Jesus tell a story about a woman? Second, what is the meaning of the story, and what does it say that is not already conveyed in the first story? And finally, what is the importance of this parable for the theme of the relationship between Jacob and the prodigal?

Before turning to reflect on these three questions, the parable's distinctive rhetorical style requires examination (figure 7). A few notes on the cultural setting of the parable will follow.

1. Or what *woman*, having *ten silver coins*,   INTRODUCTION

    2. if she *loses* one coin,   LOST

        3. does not light a lamp and sweep the house
           and *seek diligently* until she *finds* it?   FOUND

           4. And finding, she calls together
             her friends and neighbors,
             saying, *'Rejoice with me*,   REJOICE

        5. for I have *found* the coin   FOUND

      6. which I had *lost.'*   LOST

7. Even so, I tell you, there is *joy*
   before the angels of God
   over one *sinner* who *repents*."   CONCLUSION

Figure 7. The good woman and *the lost coin* (Luke 15:8-31)

As seen in figure 7, the parable falls into seven brief stanzas/units.[1] By noting the key words on the right of the text, the inverted form of the parable is evident. Four ideas are presented. The climax in the middle describes a party at home with female friends. The ideas then begin to repeat backwards, and the parable concludes with an interpretation of its meaning. This seven-scene structure is important for understanding the parable as a whole. What then can be said of the cultural and indeed geographical setting?

Jesus established a headquarters for his public ministry in Capernaum on the northern shore of the Sea of Galilee. In that district the native building material for houses was, and is, a beautiful and very black basalt. Simple one-room village homes were about the size of an American one-car garage. Windows were really only ventilation slits in the walls, approximately three inches high and located some seven feet off the ground.[2] The poor used flat stones of basalt for flooring while large slabs of basalt stretched from arch to arch to form the ceilings.[3] Faced with walls, floor, and a ceiling constructed of black stone, and with almost no light from three-inch ventilation slits, it is little wonder the woman had to light a lamp and search diligently for her coin.

The coin mentioned is a *drachma,* which was taken out of circulation in the days of Nero[4] and replaced by the *denarius.*[5] In Jesus' day the drachma was a day's wages for a working man. The woman's ten coins represented a third of a month's wages. In all likelihood married, she is clearly trusted by her husband and thus reflects a woman of worth, somewhat like the good wife described in Proverbs 31:10-31[6] This good woman, like the shepherd, hosts a party. On that occasion she is more open and honest than the shepherd, who told his friends about the sheep "that *was lost.*" In contrast she tells her friends about the "coin that *I lost,*" admitting publicly that the loss was her fault.

---

[1]The material in this chapter is revised from K. E. Bailey, *Finding,* pp. 93-108.

[2]Reconstructions of such homes in Chorazin (overlooking the Sea of Galilee) have windows that look like gun slits. Significantly the word *thura* (door) appears twenty times in the Gospels, but the word *thuris* (window) is completely absent from all four Gospels. Doors were an important functional part of life. Windows were not.

[3]Cf. V. C. Corbo, *The House of St. Peter at Capharnaum,* p. 39.

[4]Nero ruled Rome A.D. 54-68.

[5]Cf. Fitzmyer, *Luke,* 2:1081. The word *drachma* occurs only here in the entire New Testament. Its presence in the text is another piece of evidence for the authenticity of the parable as a creation of Jesus. Luke leaves this reference to the archaic *drachma* in the text rather than "contemporizing" the account by changing it into a denarius.

[6]Ben Sirach (Ecclesiasticus) specifically warns the husband with an evil wife to lock things up, to issue supplies by number and weight, and to keep careful written records (Sirach 42:6-7). Cf. K. E. Bailey, "Women in Ben Sirach and in the New Testament," pp. 56-73.

WHY A WOMAN?

With the preceding brief background in mind, the question naturally arises, why a story about a woman? The question is important. Jesus could have created a parable about a *man* who lost his coin. Such a story was told by Rabbi Philian, a second-century sage. It is as follows:

> If a man loses a *sela'* or an *obol* in his house, he lights lamp after lamp, wick after wick, till he finds it. Now does it not stand to reason: if for these things which are only ephemeral and of this world a man will light so many lamps and lights till he finds where they are hidden, for the words of the Torah which are the life both of this world and the next world, ought you not to search as for hidden treasures?[7]

Having read Rabbi Philian's story, one must ask: If an Eastern Jewish man could search for a lost coin without losing his dignity, why did Jesus tell this type of story about a *woman?* The answer is simple: Women were as important to him as men. Indeed the entire New Testament restores women to a place of equality with men.[8] This restoration effort begins with the actions and teachings of Jesus. It is confirmed by the inclusion of women among Jesus' disciples.

The popular mind in the church thinks of the band of disciples as composed entirely of men, but that was most certainly not the case.[9] A number of texts make this clear. Among these are

1. The word *mathētria* (disciple) in its feminine form appears in Acts 9:36 applied to Tabitha (Dorcas).

2. In Matthew 12:46-50 Jesus is approached by his family, who wants to speak with him. He replies:

> "Who is my mother, and who are my brothers?" And stretching out his hand *toward his disciples,* he said, "Here are my mother and my brothers! For whoever does the will of my Father in heaven is my brother, and sister, and mother."

In Middle Eastern culture it is impossible to gesture to a room full of men and make such a comment. One can say, "Here are my brother, my cousin

---

[7]*Midrash Rabbah, Song of Songs* 1.1.9, ed. Freedman and Simon, 9:11.

[8]For a full discussion of this topic, cf. K. E. Bailey, "Women in the New Testament: A Middle Eastern Cultural View," *Anvil* 11 (1994): 7-24.

[9]The original twelve apostles were all men. The woman Junia is called an apostle in Romans 16:7; cf. J. D. G. Dunn, *Romans,* 2:894.

and my uncle," but not "Here are my brother and sister and mother."[10] The latter remark can only be made to an audience of *men and women.* Jesus makes such a speech, gesturing to those in front of him, while calling them "disciples." There is no doubt that women were among them.

3. The most telling text of all is Luke 8:1-3, which reports that men and women in the apostolic band traveled together from village to village. Moreover, the women were paying for the movement, and a man (Luke) admits this astonishing fact in public by including it in his Gospel. The church provided Luke with this "scandalous" information, which he in turn faithfully recorded.

4. Mary, the sister of Martha, "sat at the Lord's feet and listened to his teaching" (Lk 10:39). To "sit at the feet" of a rabbi means to become a disciple of that rabbi. The same phrase is used for Paul in reference to his discipleship under Gamaliel (Acts 22:3). Having noted the presence of women among the disciples, it is easy to understand Jesus' teaching that reflects their presence. This emphasis includes parables from the life experiences of women. Examples are readily available.

Jesus often tells his parables in doublets: one story from the daily life of men and a second out of the world of women. As noted earlier, Jesus says, "You are the light of the world." He then clarifies what he means with two metaphors: the city set on the hill and the lamp lit and placed on a lamp stand in a home (Mt 5:14-15). Everyone knows that men build buildings and that women light the lamps in Jewish homes. On another occasion Jesus teaches, "The kingdom of God . . . is like a grain of mustard seed which a man took and sowed in his garden" (Lk 13:18-19). He goes on to compare the kingdom to "leaven which a woman took and hid in three measures of meal" (Lk 13:20-21). The first of these grew out of a task common to men, while the second reflected the experience of women. The double parable of the good shepherd and the good woman is another example of this commitment to communicate with both women and men.

To this can be added the further evidence that Luke's Gospel contains a striking series of parallel accounts that match men with women.[11] In the central section of Luke alone the following are observable:

• Martha (Lk 10:41-42) and the ruler (Lk 18:22) each lack one thing.

---

[10]This is not a uniquely Middle Eastern attitude. Is there any culture, East or West, where a speaker can gesture to a group of men and say, "Here are my sister and mother"?

[11]My own study has unearthed twenty-seven such parallel passages in Luke alone; cf. K. E. Bailey, *Finding,* pp. 97-99.

- There are two parables on assurance of answers to prayer (Lk 11:5-8; 18:1-8).
- The men of Nineveh and the queen of the South are paired (Lk 11:29-32).
- Justice is for female and male servants (Lk 12:45-46).
- Divisions in one house include men and women (Lk 12:51-53).
- A woman and a man are each healed on the sabbath (Lk 13:10-16; 14:1-6).
- A "daughter of Abraham" (Lk 13:16) and a "son of Abraham" are healed (Lk 19:9).
- The mustard seed and the leaven in the meal illustrate the kingdom (Lk 13:18-21).
- Disciples are expected to honor Jesus above family (men and women mentioned, Lk 14:26-27).
- The lost coin parallels the lost sheep (Lk 15:4-10).
- Description of the days of the Son of Man contains examples of women and men (Lk 17:34-35).

As noted, some of these male and female doublets are attributed to Jesus. Others may be selections made by Luke's apostolic sources. He himself may be responsible for yet others. In any case, the message is clear: Beginning with Jesus and extending on into the early church there is a concerted effort to include men and women together on all levels of the new fellowship formed around Jesus, the Messiah of God.[12] But for Jesus there is more.

We have seen that the Hebrew Scriptures affirm God as a person, not as an impersonal force. To communicate such an idea to people, personal metaphors must be used. The prophetic answer was to employ both male and female imagery. The metaphors of the psalms have been mentioned. To the above can be added the case of the two images appearing together in Isaiah:

---

[12]So far I have discovered no cases of a rabbi presenting two parallel metaphors or parables, one from the world of men and a second from the life experience of women. But the rabbis did on occasion make men parallel with women in their accounting of the tradition of the past. One such example occurs in the *Midrash Rabbah, Song of Songs* (2.7.1, 2.9.4), where the patriarchs and matriarchs are mentioned together in parallel; cf. Freedman and Simon, 9:113, 121. (This Midrash is generally known to be compiled in Palestine. Its date of composition is unknown, but much of the material is from early sources, some of them pre-Christian. For our purposes it should be noted that it reflects community attitudes that were available to Jesus. He participated in a tradition that he could expand upon.)

The LORD goes forth *like a mighty man*,
like a man of war he stirs up his fury;
he cries out, he shouts aloud,
he shows himself mighty against his foes.

For a long time I have held my peace,
I have kept still and restrained myself;
now *I will cry out like a woman* in travail,
I will gasp and pant. (Is 42:13-14)

Psalm 131, with its female image applied to God, has already been cited. A further obvious case appears in Isaiah 66:7-9, where the prophet likens Jerusalem to a mother. The returning pilgrims are compared to her young children, who drink from her breasts and are dandled on her (Jerusalem's) knees (Is 66:10-12). Suddenly, the imagery shifts:

As one whom his mother comforts,
    so I will comfort you;
    you shall be comforted in Jerusalem. (Is 66:13)

Clearly, Jerusalem has become the *place* where comforting occurs. God is now the comforter who comforts like a mother.

In conclusion, Jesus builds on Hebrew Scripture traditions concerning the equality of men and women, traditions that are rooted in the psalms and in the prophetic witness to the nature of God. With women disciples, and with an eagerness to speak to them on as deep a level as he speaks to the men, he adds the parable of the good woman to the story of the good shepherd. But what is Jesus saying in the parable?

THE THEOLOGICAL CLUSTER OF THE PARABLE OF THE LOST COIN: PARALLEL THEMES

There are seven theological themes in this parable that are similar to those in the previous parable but yet have their own distinctive nuances.

1. Faulty leadership. A careless woman loses her coin.

2. Costly grace. A good woman lights a lamp and searches diligently to find her coin.

3. Atonement. Thanks to great diligence, the women succeeds. The coin cannot find itself. The theme of restoration through costly effort is unmistakably present. This restoration is a part of atonement.

4. Sin. Humankind is here likened to a coin rendered useless by being lost in the dirt between the cracks of a stone floor in a dark room.

5. Joy. The friends and *haberoth* (companions) rejoice with the woman. The possibility that they might sit in judgment over her for her saving efforts is absurd. Heaven itself rejoices over a restored sinner. How could the *haberim* (Pharisees) fail to do so?

6. Repentance. The lost coin is completely inanimate and yet is a symbol of repentance. The sheep's bleating provides *some* help for the shepherd who seeks his lost charge. Here, the total unqualified weight of the rescue operation rests on the woman. Thus, once again "repentance is *being found.*" (The third story will set forth the importance of the prodigal's *acceptance* of being found. Here, the emphasis is on the woman's *actions in searching* and *finding.*)

7. Christology. The first story presents "Jesus the good shepherd." This text reflects "Jesus the good woman."

THE THEOLOGICAL CLUSTER OF THE PARABLE OF THE LOST COIN: NEW MEANINGS

At the same time, the reader cannot skip over the parable by saying, "Oh yes, we have already covered this subject in the first story." This parallel parable creates new meanings that go beyond the first story. The following can be noted:

1. The unchanged value of the coin. The undiminished worth of the coin has a unique (implied) emphasis in this parable. The sheep may be sick, and its wool may be damaged. The prodigal may be "messed up" as a person by his experiences in the far country. If so, they will leave scars. But the coin loses nothing of its previous value for having been lost.

2. The worth of women. The reader of Luke's Gospel has just seen where Jesus likens himself to a mother hen (Lk 13:34). Here he is a good woman. In the first parable Jesus says to his pharisaic audience, "You should be like this 'unclean' shepherd." In this parable he affirms, "I am like this woman! I search for the lost. You should do likewise." By his choice of imagery Jesus elevates the worth of all women.

3. Hope of success in finding the lost. This theme is clearly intensified. The outcome of the shepherd's hunt, in spite of his determination, is uncertain. He must search a vast, empty wilderness. Not so the woman who has no servant and does the sweeping herself. She does not look outside because she knows that the coin is in the house. The details of the story assist the reader in realizing that a one-room peasant home is the parable's setting. Such homes were about the size of a one-car garage and contained very little furniture. The house is dark even during the day; it has no windows—only ventilation slits high on the wall. In such a home there are not many places where a coin can lie undetected. The woman's diligence is assured success. The coin is definitely *in* the house, and it *can* be found.

IMPORTANCE OF THIS PARABLE TO JACOB AND THE PRODIGAL

Finally, the third question: Why is this parable important for the overall subject of Jacob and the prodigal? This topic will be covered in detail in the discussion of the mother in the Jacob saga. Here, a brief note seems appropriate.

If, as proposed, Jesus is rewriting the Jacob story, that story contains a father (Isaac) and a mother (Rebekah). Jesus' parable of the prodigal son has no mother. Why? The simple answer is that Jesus has elevated the father in his new story from an Oriental patriarch (Isaac) and refashioned him into a metaphor for God. Jesus cannot use a double metaphor in one parable without compromising his understanding of the unity of God. If the new story has a mother and a father, then there are two gods, one male and one female. Jesus tells three stories, but each of them has a single central figure. There is one shepherd (not a shepherd and his wife). In like manner there is one woman (not the woman and her husband). Finally, the father has no wife. The unity of God is preserved, and God who is spirit and is neither male nor female is portrayed as having the characteristics of each.

This is in harmony with the story of creation where humankind is made in the image of God. The text reads:

So God created humankind[13]
in his own image . . .
male and female created he them. (Gen 1:27 NRSV)

This text makes clear that both the male and the female are created in the image of God, and if this is true then the nature of God necessarily encompasses the natures of males and females. The trilogy of stories under consideration is a continuation of this same theology, and the tale of the good woman is a critical part of that larger whole.

In addition, as will be seen in discussion of the Jacob saga, Rebekah is a deeply flawed character who shamelessly deceives her husband and older son. After that scene she is not heard of again until her death. Jesus drops her

---

[13]The Hebrew word *adam* is rightly translated "humankind." In this text it is not a title.

from his new story (based on the old). But in her place he creates a strong, positive female image as he formulates the parable of the good women. As a result, his female (and male) listeners can be instructed and moved by the good shepherd, the good woman and the good father. All three are images for God, and in this threefold parable they all become images for Jesus.[14] The inclusion of this story of the good woman thus becomes an important part of Jesus' strategy as he creates a new story about exile and return modeled on the saga of Jacob.

The third parable in the trilogy is the climax of the three. To that story we now turn.

---

[14]In the Epistles all three become images for early Christian leadership. Paul sees himself as a "father" to the Corinthians (1 Cor 4:15). He tells the Galatians that he is "*in travail* until Christ be formed in you!" (Gal 4:19). Peter tells his readers to "be *shepherds* of God's flock" (1 Pet 5:2 NIV).

9

TO FIND THE LOST

The Parable of the Two Lost Sons (Lk 15:11-32)

Before turning to reflect on comparisons between Jacob and the prodigal, the famous parable itself must be examined.[1] My goal is to compare Jacob's story with the parable of the prodigal as Jesus intended it to be understood. To do this it is necessary to observe the carefully constructed rhetorical style of the parable and then turn to a series of interpretive barnacles that have attached themselves to the story in the mind of the church. First, the rhetoric.

The parable is a drama in two acts. Act one is the exile and return of the prodigal. This act focuses on three themes set in three scenes, which are followed by the prodigal's speech in the far country. That speech falls into two parts. The three themes are then reversed (and presented in inverse order) in the three scenes that follow the speech.

The second act is the drama of the older son and his father. In this case, the identical outline appears; only the final scene is missing. These two rhetorical masterpieces can be depicted as in figure 8 (pp. 96-97).

NOTES ON ACT ONE (THE PRODIGAL)

As will be seen below, act one opens (1) with the prodigal wishing his father *dead*. At the conclusion of the first half of the parable, after achieving reconciliation with the prodigal, the father announces (7) that he has brought the

---

[1]For a fuller exposition of my interpretation of the parable of the prodigal son, see K. E. Bailey, *Poet*, pp. 158-206; *Finding*, pp. 109-93. In this chapter I present only a brief summary.

Act One: The Younger Son

1. There was a man who had two sons;   DEATH
    and the younger of them said to his father,
    "Father, *give me* the share of *property*
    that falls to me."
    And he divided his living between them.

2.   *Not many days* later, the younger son *sold all* he had   ALL IS LOST
        journeyed into a far country,
        and *wasted* his property in *extravagant living*.
        And when he had *spent everything*,
        a great famine arose in that country,
        and *he* began to be in *want*.

3.   So he went and joined himself   UNQUALIFIED
            to one of the *citizens* of that country,   REJECTION
            who *sent him* into his fields to *feed pigs*.
            And he would gladly have eaten the pods
            that the pigs ate;
            and *no one gave him anything*.

4a.   But when he *came to himself* he said,   THE PROBLEM
                "How many of my father's *craftsmen*   (?)
                have *bread enough and to spare*,
                but *I perish* here with *hunger!*

4b.   "I will *arise* and go to my *father*, and say to him,   THE SOLUTION
                'Father, I have sinned against heaven and before you;   (?)
                I am no longer worthy to be called your son;
                fashion out of me a *craftsman*.'"
                And he arose and came to his father.

5.   And while he was at a *great distance*,   UNQUALIFIED
            his *father saw* him   ACCEPTANCE
            and had *compassion*, and *ran*
            and *embraced* him and *kissed* him.

6. And the son said to him,   ALL IS RESTORED
    "Father, I have sinned against heaven and before you;
    and am *no more worthy to be called your son*."
    But the father said to the servants,
    "Bring quickly the *best robe* and put it on him;
    and put a *ring* on his hand and *shoes* on his feet;

7. "and bring the *fatted calf* and kill it,   RESURRECTION
    and let us eat and make merry;
    for this my son was *dead, and is alive*;
    he was *lost, and is found*."
    And they began to make merry.

Figure 8. A drama in two acts.

Act Two: The Older Son

8. Now his **elder son** was **in the field**,   HE STANDS ALOOF
    and as he came and drew near to the house
    he heard **music and dancing.**
    And he called one of the **boys**
    and asked **what this meant**.

9. And he said to him,   YOUR BROTHER—
    "**Your brother** has come,   PEACE (a feast)
    and your **father** has **killed the fatted calf**   ANGER!!
    because he received him **with peace**,"
    But he was angry and refused to go in.

10. So his **father came out**   COSTLY LOVE
    and was **entreating him**,

11a. but he answered his father,   MY ACTIONS
    "Lo, these many years **I have served you,**   MY PAY
    and I **never disobeyed** your command;
    yet you never gave me a **kid,**
    to make merry with **my friends**.

11b. "But when **this son of yours** came,   HIS ACTIONS
    who has devoured your living   HIS PAY
    with **harlots**,
    you killed **for him** the fatted calf!"

12. And he said to him, "My dear son,   COSTLY LOVE
    you are always with me,
    and **all that is mine is yours**.

13. "It was fitting to make merry and be glad,   YOUR BROTHER—
    for this **your brother was dead and is alive**,   ALIVE (a feast)
    he **was lost and is found**."   JOY

THE FATHER EARNESTLY LONGS FOR THE STORY TO END

(14?) And the older son entered the house,
    and joined in the festive banquet,
    and was reconciled to his brother and father.
    And the father rejoiced with the two sons he had found
    and brought to life.

prodigal from *death to life*. The prodigal, who initially wishes his father *dead*, is himself discovered to be *dead* and in need of *resurrection*.

In the second scene (2) the prodigal loses everything and fails in his attempt to regain his losses. But the father, in the matching scene (6), welcomes him and then restores the him to the family and community by dressing him in the father's best robe and giving him the signet ring of the house. *Unqualified rejection* (by the son) in scene (3) is matched by *unqualified acceptance* (by the father) in scene (5). In the very center the prodigal delivers a speech in two parts (4a-b) skillfully crafted (as will be seen) with a view to gaining yet further benefits from his father.

NOTES ON ACT TWO (THE OLDER SON)

The older son's journey also starts in the field (8) and moves toward the house, where he stands aloof. The first scene of this act (8) has no final matching stanza due to the missing ending. (My imaginative addition to the text tries to express the kind of a conclusion the father fervently longs to accomplish). The older brother then demands an explanation for the festivities (9). On discovering a celebration of reconciliation he becomes angry and insults his father in public. In the matching scene (13) the father responds to that anger with an appeal for joy. The third part of the drama with the older son (10) shows the father's self-emptying love, a love offered at greater cost than that extended to the prodigal. The father's love in action (10) is sealed with love expressed in words (12). At the center of this second act is a speech by the older son, which falls into two parts (11a-b). Like the prepared speech of the prodigal, the older son is also trying to "work" his father for greater benefits. At the very least he hopes to be given a goat, if not much more.

As seen above, each half of the parable exhibits inverted parallelism (chiasm), and the parallels between the two speeches uniquely tie the two halves together. A wide spectrum of meanings to be discussed below is here reinforced by the rhetorical style of the parable. Sophisticated first century listeners/readers would identify the matching stanzas and clearly sense the dramatic tensions of the missing ending that the Pharasaic audience alone could resolve by accepting to be found by Jesus. The prodigal moves from estrangement through acceptance of being found to reconciliation. Will the older son be willing to play his part in that same journey?

To the interpretive barnacles so often attached to this great parable, we now turn.

SCRAPING OFF THE BARNACLES OF CENTURIES

One of the realities of the history of the interpretation of Scripture is that the more familiar a passage becomes, and the more central it is to the life and faith of the church, the more interpretive "barnacles" it acquires. A clear case of this development is the birth stories of Jesus.

Everyone knows (?) that *three* wise men visited the holy family. Actually, we are not told how many there were. We only know that they took three different kinds of gifts: gold, frankincense and myrrh. Three could have taken gold. Perhaps four appeared with frankincense and three with myrrh, making a total of ten wise men. Luke does not say how many there were. The average Christian thinks Jesus was born the night the holy family arrived in Bethlehem, but the text says, "And *while they were there,* the *days* [plural] were accomplished that she should be delivered" (Lk 2:6 KJV). That is, they were in town some days before the baby was born. The point is that this story is very, very familiar. Over time, special ways of seeing the story have developed that, in the minds of many readers, become fused with the text itself.

This process has perhaps proceeded further with the great parable of the prodigal son than with any other New Testament story. My intention here is limited to a brief review of a series of fifteen points in the story that need to be clarified in the light of the cultural world of Jesus. Many of these will be discussed in greater detail when comparisons with Jacob are considered.[2] These points are as follows:

1. The request. The younger son requests his inheritance while his father is still alive and in good health. In traditional Middle Eastern culture, this means that the prodigal cannot wait for his father to die. As noted above, if the father is a traditional Middle Eastern parent, he will strike the boy across the face and drive him out of the house. Is such a response unique to the Middle East? Surely not. What happens to a young farm boy in any culture who presses his father to give him his share of the family farm while the father, in good health, is still operating it? This kind of request is surely outrageous anywhere in the world. The prodigal is not simply a young lad who wants to make his way in the world. Rather, he asks for something unthinkable in the Middle East and beyond. The father is expected to refuse, but he does not.

---

[2] The following summary is revised from K.E. Bailey, "Pursuing," pp. 34-40.

2. The community. Too often this parable is seen as a story about three people and no more. The family home is imagined as a great house on the top of a hill standing in grand isolation. Such is not the case. Agricultural land is scarce in the Holy Land. In both Old and New Testament times the average village was about six acres. Farmers rarely lived on their farmland, residing instead in tightly compacted villages. This was and is because of the need to reserve every bit of land for farming, but people also gathered in small villages for reasons of security. The parables of Jesus are stories about people living in communities that are nearly always mentioned or assumed.

In each of the first two parables in this trilogy the community is called to gather for a celebration. In this particular story an inheritance is sold to the community. At the end of the tale, a father runs down the village street in full view of the community. After embracing his wayward younger son at the edge of the village, the father turns to address his servants (who have run after him). Like the shepherd and the woman, the father invites the community to a festive banquet. Anticipating a crowd, he orders the butchering of a calf rather than a sheep or a duck. Community-based professional musicians are hired for the occasion. The older son has a circle of friends who live nearby and could attend a party for him. In short, this is a parable about three people *living in a community,* a community that is just offstage throughout the parable. Each twist and turn of the story expects the reader/listener to be aware of that offstage presence.

3. The significance of the father's initial gift. The father grants the prodigal the freedom to inherit and to sell his portion of the estate. At five points in the parable the father does not behave in the manner of a traditional Oriental patriarch. The first instance occurs here when he grants the prodigal's request. The inheritance is substantial. This wealthy family has a herd of fatted calves and a herd of goats. House servants/slaves are in evidence. The house itself includes a banquet hall large enough to host a crowd capable of devouring a fatted calf in one evening. The father can afford professional musicians for the party. Transferring such an inheritance is a delicate matter that should only be dealt with by the father as he approaches death (as in the case of Isaac, examined below). So what is the significance of the father's response to this request?

Ebrahim Sa'id, an Egyptian Protestant scholar commenting on Luke 15 in Arabic, in 1935 wrote:

The shepherd in his search for the sheep, and the woman in her search for the coin, do not do anything out of the ordinary beyond what anyone in their place would do. But the actions the father takes in the third story are unique, marvelous, divine actions which have not been done by any father in the past.[3]

Sa'id was an able Middle Eastern Christian scholar. He looked at this text and at his own culture and affirmed that Jesus does not use an Oriental patriarch as a model for God. In the contemporary West, Jesus is often accused of having done just that. But such was not the case. Rather, Jesus, in creating this image of a father, has broken all the bounds of Middle Eastern patriarchy. No human father (or mother) is adequate as a model for God. Knowing this, Jesus elevates the figure of father beyond its human limitations as he reshapes it into his primary metaphor for God.

4. The hurried sale. The text implies that the father (in violation of long-established custom) grants both the inheritance *and the right to sell,* knowing full well that the exercise of this unprecedented privilege will expose the family to public shame.

The sale is referred to in the phrase traditionally translated "he gathered all together" (Lk 15:13 KJV) or "he gathered all he had" (RSV). The Greek verb used here is a financial term that means "turned into cash."[4] As that happens, this horrendous break of relationships within the family becomes public knowledge, and the family is shamed before the entire community. First-century Jewish law provided for the division of an inheritance (when the father was ready to make such a division) but did not grant the children the right to sell until after the father's death.[5]

The prodigal sells *"not many days* later" (Lk 15:13). He is obliged to move quickly because village anger against him is rising as a result of his having shamed his father. It is this community anger that presses him to conclude the process as expeditiously as possible and quit the village.[6] The prodigal appears totally indifferent to the pain he is causing the family. All he cares about is liquidating his assets and getting out of town.

---

[3]E. Sa'id, *Luqa,* p. 395 (author's translation).

[4]Cf. I. H. Marshall, *Luke,* pp. 607-8; J. Fitzmyer, *Luke,* 2:1087. The New English Bible uses the phrase "turned into cash." For the Greek word in the text of Luke *(synagō),* cf. W. Bauer, *Greek-English Lexicon,* p. 782.

[5]Mishnah, *Bava Batra* 8.7, trans. Danby, p. 377.

[6]Selling his inheritance would not have been easy. Someone on the fringes of the community would buy, but the prodigal would probably sustain a loss. No family in good relations with the prodigal's father would have dealt with him.

5. The kezazah ceremony. In the Jerusalem Talmud and elsewhere in the writings of the sages, we are told that at the time of Jesus the Jews had a method of punishing any Jewish boy who lost his family inheritance to Gentiles. Such a loss was considered particularly shameful, and the horror of that shame is reflected in the Dead Sea Scrolls. *The Testament of Kohath* reads:

> And now, my sons, be watchful of your inheritance that has been bequeathed to you, which your fathers gave you. Do not give your inheritance to gentiles, . . . lest you be regarded as humiliated in their eyes, and foolish, and they trample upon you for they will come to dwell among you and become your masters. [7]

To discourage any thought of committing this heinous offense, the community developed what was called the *kezazah* ceremony (the cutting-off ceremony). [8] Any Jewish boy who lost his inheritance among Gentiles faced the ceremony if he dared return to his home village. The ceremony itself was simple. Fellow villagers would fill a large earthenware pot with burned nuts and burned corn and break it in front of the guilty individual. While doing this, they would shout, "So-and-so is cut off from his people." From that point on, the village would have nothing to do with the hapless lad. As he leaves town, the prodigal knows he *must not* lose his money among the Gentiles. He does. In the far country he lives among people who own and thereby eat pigs. They are obviously Gentiles. Fear of the shame of this ceremony and the need to earn enough to recoup his losses are important aspects of the parable.

6. Expensive living. The prodigal spent his money in "expensive living" rather than "loose living" or "riotous living." The Greek text says that the prodigal "wasted" *(diaskorpizō)* his resources in "expensive" *(asōtōs,* Lk 15:13) living. Does this word necessarily imply immorality? Hultgren writes, "The young man's life is described as 'dissipated' or 'wild and disorderly' *(asōtōs)*—whether immoral as well . . . is not clear from the Greek term used."[9] For eighteen centuries, Syriac and Arabic translations in the Middle East (with

---

[7] 4Q542, fragment 1 column 1 (lines 4-7). Cf. R. H. Eisenmann and M. Wise, *The Dead Sea Scrolls Uncovered,* pp. 149-50.

[8] *Midrash Rabbah, Ruth* 7.11, ed. Freedman and Simon, 8:87; Jerusalem Talmud, *Ketubbot* 2:10; *Qiddushin* 1:5. Cf. K. E. Bailey, *Poet,* pp. 167-68.

[9] A. J. Hultgren, *The Parables of Jesus,* p. 75; K. E. Bailey, *Poet,* p. 170.

one exception) have avoided any reference to immorality.[10] The words used in these translations are "expensive," "indolent," "luxurious" and "wasteful."[11] Jesus gives no hint of how the prodigal lost his money. The listener/reader is only told that the prodigal was a spendthrift. At the end of the story the older son publicly accuses his brother of wasting the money with harlots. But he makes this claim after arriving "from the field" without even knowing that his brother is back in the village. Clearly he wants to exaggerate his brother's failures. The unjust nature of this attack on the prodigal by his older brother almost disappears when the prodigal's life in the far country is described with translations that imply immorality.

7. *The search for employment.* When his money is spent, the prodigal's obvious option is to go home. But he has broken the rules. He has lost his money among the Gentiles and knows all too well that the *kezazah* ceremony awaits him if he returns to the village empty-handed. Thus, he is desperate to somehow recoup his losses. To do so he needs a paying job and on two occasions tries to find one. The first attempt is in the far country. The second is the game plan he vocalizes on the eve of his return home. Both attempts deserve reflection.

The first plan is initiated when the prodigal becomes a pig herder. But it does not pan out. The text deliberately affirms, "No one gave him anything" (Lk 15:16). Like Lincoln's Gettysburg Address, this parable contains no extra verbiage. Each phrase is carefully crafted to convey precise meaning. This phrase tells the reader that the owners of the pigs fed the prodigal but did not pay him. The first-century Jewish listener/reader *knows* the prodigal must earn back the money he wasted if he is to avoid the *kezazah* ceremony. Having failed at his first attempt, he opts for one last desperate roll of the dice. He will go home, get job training, find employment, earn his way and acquire the necessary capital to pay back what he has lost! His father owns slaves. The prodigal does *not* offer to join them! He *must have a paying job,* and he knows that no skilled craftsman will accept him as an apprentice without his father's endorsement. But how can he convince his father to trust him *one more time?*

8. *The self-serving plan.* Perhaps the most theologically damaging traditional misunderstanding of this parable is found in the popular perception of

---

[10]The point here is that Eastern Christians from the second century onward have understood that there is no hint of immorality in the description of how the prodigal spent his money. (The Old Syriac is the only exception.)

[11]The word *musrif* (wasteful) is the most common.

the phrase, "he came to himself" (Lk 15:17). As will be seen, this can be read "he returned to himself." The phrase "he came to himself" is often interpreted as meaning "he repented." When understood in this fashion, the text loses its cutting edge, and the theological unity of the chapter is broken. As noted, the good shepherd must traverse the wilderness to find his sheep. The good woman lights a lamp and searches diligently to find the lost coin. Both the sheep and the coin must be *rescued.* But if the prodigal manages to make his way home, in the fullest sense of that word, by his own efforts, then the third story is the *exact opposite* of the first two. In the first story the lost sheep is a symbol of repentance, which we determined is defined as "acceptance of being found." The second story confirms this definition. But if the prodigal truly repents in the far country and struggles home on his own, theological confusion reigns. Either repentance is an elastic concept open to two directly opposite interpretations, or Jesus himself is confused.

Theological debates in church history reflect the tension between "God must come after us" and "Unaided we can return to God." In the early fifth century, a British monk by the name of Pelagius argued that humans are able to do God's will and return to him unaided. Augustine, of North Africa, opposed Pelagius by insisting that God, in Christ, must come to save humankind because without assistance humans cannot return to God or fulfill his will. Does Jesus set forth the view later championed by Augustine in the first two stories and in the third parable offer a foundation for Pelagius? Or is he just confused? I find both options unacceptable. Is there an alternative?

We have already seen that in telling the parable of the good shepherd Jesus invoked Psalm 23. In that psalm God brings me back to himself ("he brings me back" [Ps 23:3, author's translation]). When the phrase "he came to himself" is read in the light of Psalm 23, a new meaning emerges. God brought the psalmist back (to God) and caused him to repent. But the prodigal is going to solve his own problems: *he* came to *himself.* See figure 9 for a comparison.

Psalm 23:3	Luke 15:17
The text:	The text:
He (God) brings my *nefesh* (self) back to God.	The prodigal acts to return to his own *nefesh* (self).
The actor: God	The actor: The prodigal
The goal of the return: God	The goal of the return: Himself

Figure 9. Repentance in Psalm 23 and Luke 15

Who does *what* with the *nefesh* (self)? For the psalmist, God brings my *nefesh* (self) back to God, while for the prodigal, he returns to his own *nefesh* (self).[12]

The rich twelve-hundred-year-old history of New Testament Arabic versions contains a number of illuminating translations of the phrase "he came to himself." Some read "he got smart." Others translate "he took an interest in himself." Also to be found are "he thought to himself" and "it then occurred to him." None of these translators saw the prodigal in the far country as repenting. Other Christian translators of the text into Arabic use the phrase, "he *returned* to himself." This translation has lasted for more than a thousand years in Eastern Christian Gospel texts, and for the last two hundred years has often appeared. What does it imply?

As seen in the previous two stories, *repentance* also means "return." David affirmed that he cannot "return" *(shub)* on his own: God, the Good Shepherd, must come after him, and his return is *to God*. As noted, the same theology is set forth in the parable of the woman with her coin. But here, we are told that the prodigal returned to *himself,* not to his *father*. Thus the cluster of texts examined offers three kinds of return. These are:

- For David (Ps 23) and Jesus (Lk 15:2-10): The return is *to God*
- For Jeremiah (Jer 23:1-8) and Ezekiel (Ezek 34:1-31): The return is *to the land*
- For the prodigal (in the far country): The return is *to himself*

The prodigal is returning neither to God nor to the land. Instead, he returns only *to himself!* In such a game plan the father is simply an instrument to be used by the prodigal to get what he wants, which is *something to eat!* The obvious question arising from this thoughtful Arabic translation is: On the basis of the Greek text is this a legitimate translation?

Literally Luke's text reads, "He came *[erchomai]* to himself." The verb *erchomai* is used by Luke a number of times to mean "return." One of these is in Acts 1:11: "Men of Galilee, why do you stand looking into heaven? This Jesus, who was taken up from you into heaven, will come *[erchomai]* in the same way as you saw him go into heaven."

Clearly, in this text *erchomai* carries the meaning of "return." Furthermore, there is a case in the Greek translation of the Hebrew Scriptures where the

---

[12]In the Syriac and Arabic translations all across the centuries the same word, *nefesh* (Syriac) and *nefs* (Arabic), appears in both texts in each language tradition.

Hebrew verb *shub* (return/repent) appears in the Greek text as *erchomai.*[13] In this connection the little boy's speech to the older son in Luke 15:27 becomes important. The older son asks the youngster what is going on. The boy answers, "Your brother *has appeared [hēkei]*." The word *erchomai* (come/return) is not used.[14] A more literal translation of the Greek in Luke 15:27 is "Your brother is here." The Arabic New Testaments mentioned above say the prodigal *"returned* to himself." By contrast, these same versions tell us that the little boy in Luke 15:27 says, "Your brother is present *(hadara)*." This Middle Eastern scriptural tradition clearly views the prodigal in the far country as returning to *himself,* while what he really needs is a heartfelt return to *his father's love and fellowship.* Upon the prodigal's arrival the little boy says that "he is here," not that "he has returned." In all these Arabic versions the prodigal in the far country is never seen as repenting. What then of the prodigal's prepared confession?

On arrival, the prodigal plans to say, "I have sinned against heaven and before you" (Lk 15:18), which is often (understandably) seen as indicative of heartfelt repentance. Jesus' audience, however, comprises scribes and Pharisees who know the Scriptures *very well.* They are particularly familiar with the account of the Exodus. This sentence from Luke 15:18 is a quotation from Pharaoh when he tried to manipulate Moses into lifting the plagues. After the ninth plague, Pharaoh *finally* agreed to meet Moses. When Moses appeared, Pharaoh's opening remark to him was "I have sinned against the LORD your God, and against you" (Ex 10:16). Everyone knows that Pharaoh was *not repenting.* He was simply trying to manipulate Moses into doing what he (Pharaoh) wanted. The prodigal's actions are best understood as attempting the same thing. Hoping to soften his father's heart, the prodigal plans to offer *his* solution to the problem of their estrangement: job training. He will acquire a skill, work as a paid craftsman and be able to save money.[15] For the present the prodigal will not live at home. Only after the lost money is recovered will he presume to suggest reconciliation. Having failed to find a paying job in the far country, he will try to obtain his father's backing to become gainfully employed in his home community. *He will yet save himself by keeping the law.*

---

[13]Cf. 2 Chronicles 10:5 in the Greek Septuagint.

[14]*Hēkei* is a form of *hēkō,* "to be present."

[15]The phrase "bread enough and to spare" (Lk 15:17) means that the craftsmen who work on his father's estate are indeed able to save. They have "enough" and "to spare." The prodigal plans to join them.

Grace is unnecessary. He can manage alone—so he thinks!

The clincher in this discussion is the prodigal's soliloquy in the far country, where he confesses to the listener/reader why he is returning. Put simply, he wants to eat. He says, "My father's [craftsmen] have bread enough and to spare, and I perish here with hunger" (Lk 15:17). Aside from the manipulative quote from Pharaoh, there is no hint of remorse. He does not say to himself "I made a big mistake" or "I am ashamed of what I have done" or "I broke my father's heart." He considers neither the agony of rejected love his father has endured nor the financial loss the entire family has sustained.

The prodigal's self-confessed motive and goal are finding a way to eat. If he were a servant standing before a master, his plan would be disappointing and deeply flawed, yet somehow acceptable. But as a son dealing with a compassionate and loving father, his projected solution is grossly inadequate. The prodigal thinks the problem is the lost money. His anticipated solution trivializes the problem, which is not merely a matter of a broken law but is about a broken relationship.

9. The turning point. The prodigal starts home and on his way steels his nerves for a humiliating entrance into the village. He remembers the *kazazah* ceremony and braces himself to endure its shame. The painful interview with his father will not be any easier. His one hope is that his humble speech will touch his father's heart and that through it he will win his father's backing for the training he needs to become a wage earner. Time-honored custom expects him to appear, like the returning Jacob, with generous gifts for the family.[16] Not only does the prodigal struggle home empty-handed, he returns in failure after having insulted his family and the village by the manner of his departure. In his present frame of mind, he is willing to endure the painful road back home for one simple reason: he is hungry. The bottom line is "I perish here with hunger!" (Lk 115:17). But what of his father?

The father knows his son will fail. He waits day after day, staring down the crowded village street to the road in the distance along which his son disappeared with arrogance and high hopes. The father also remembers the *kezazah* ceremony. He knows only too well how the village will treat his son when he returns in rags. Thus, the father also prepares a plan for their meeting. His plan is to reach the boy before the boy reaches the village and thereby protect him from the wrath of the community.

---

[16]Jacob returns with wave after wave of expensive animals for his brother; cf. Genesis 32:13-21.

The father realizes that if he is able to achieve reconciliation with his son, *in public,* no one in the village will treat the prodigal badly. If the community witnesses the reconciliation, there will be no suggestion from any quarter that the *kezazah* ceremony should be enacted. But to achieve that goal, self-emptying humiliation will be required of the father.

The father sees the prodigal "while he was yet at a distance" (Lk 15:20). That distance is more spiritual than it is physical. The prodigal thinks that a sum of money will heal a broken heart. He is indeed a long way away!

The language of "while yet at a distance" is borrowed from Isaiah 57:19, where God affirms and creates peace for those who are "far" and peace for those who are "near." This is precisely what the father sets out to do. He intends to create peace by means of a costly dramatic action with the one who is far off (the prodigal) and then concentrate on creating peace with the one who is near (the older brother).

Once more, the pictures in our minds need revision. As noted above, the reality of the ever-present community is critical. At harvest time a farmer would build a booth and live on his field to protect his crop. Otherwise, dwellings were always crowded together in densely constructed villages. Wealthier families lived closer to the center of town. Village streets were lined with houses whose walls touched each other. Those streets were just wide enough to permit the passing of a loaded camel. Such narrow streets are assumed time and again in the Talmud where, on the sabbath, a homeowner was allowed to pass bread to a neighbor, across the road, from one second-story balcony to another. By doing this the owner was not carrying food out of the house and thereby not breaking sabbath-observance laws. A neighbor could also place a plank across the balconies and use it to cross to the house on the opposite side of the road with food in hand.[17] Obviously, such streets could hardly have been more than twelve feet wide and the balconies not more than six feet apart. In this parable the listener/reader is expected to imagine the father day after day waiting on such a balcony viewing the narrow street, teeming with life, that led out of the village.[18]

For the third time, the father breaks the mold of Middle Eastern patriarchy. Spotting the boy "while he was at a distance" (i.e., before he reaches the vil-

---

[17]Mishnah, *Mo'ed* 11:2, trans. Danby, p. 110; Mishnah, *Eruvin* 7:4, trans. Danby, p. 131.

[18]Thrown out of the window, Jezebel fell to her death in the street. Thus even the palace was built on the very edge of the street (2 Kings 9:30-37).

lage [Lk 15:20]), the father takes his long robes in his hand and runs down the crowded street to welcome his pig herder son. As he does so, he humiliates himself before the village. Out of compassion he empties himself, assumes the form of a servant and *runs* to reconcile his estranged son.

Traditional Middle Easterners, wearing long robes, do not run in public. They never have. To do so would be deeply humiliating.[19] The father runs, knowing that in so doing he will deflect the attention of the community away from his ragged son to himself. People will focus on the extraordinary sight of a distinguished, self-respecting landowner humiliating himself in public by running down the road revealing his legs. They will not even notice the ragged young man until after the reconciliation takes place at the edge of the village.

As the father reaches the prodigal, he falls on his son's neck and kisses him *before* hearing his prepared speech! The father does *not* demonstrate costly love in *response* to his son's confession! Rather, his offer of grace is a prelude to the prodigal's remarks. The boy is totally surprised. He sees his father running the gauntlet for him. Overcome by emotion, he can only offer the first part of his prepared speech, which now assumes new meaning. He declares that he has sinned and that he is unworthy to be called a son. By omitting the request for job training and servitude, he makes clear that he has no bright ideas for mending their relationship. In short, he is no longer "working" his father for additional advantages. *The father does not interrupt his younger son.* Instead, the prodigal changes his mind and in a moment of genuine repentance surrenders his plan to save himself and lets his father find him. He comes finally to *acceptance of being found.* This understanding of the text has been available for almost a thousand years in the Eastern church.

Two of the four great Middle Eastern commentators on the Gospels mentioned in chapter three comment on why the prodigal did not finish his speech. Ibn al-Tayyib wrote:

> He [the prodigal] did not complete what he was planning to say, which was "make out of me one of your paid craftsmen" . . . because he saw from the running of his father to him and the grace-filled way his father met him and embraced him that there was no longer any place for this request to be made into a craftsman. For if after such acts he had made such a request, it would have appeared that he doubted the genuineness of his father's offered forgiveness.[20]

---

[19]For a longer discussion of this critical aspect of the story, cf. K. E. Bailey, *Finding*, pp. 143-46.
[20]Ibn al-Tayyib, *Tafsir*, 2:272-75 (author's translation).

Ibn al-Salibi observes:

> Why did he [the prodigal] not say to his father, "Fashion out of me one of your
> paid craftsmen" when he had planned to say it? The answer is that his father's
> love outstripped him and forgiveness was everflowing toward him.[21]

These two influential Middle Eastern commentators make clear that the
prodigal neither forgot to finish his speech nor was he interrupted; rather, his
world was transformed by his father's costly demonstration of love. The shepherd goes forth to find his sheep. The woman searches for her coin. In like
manner, the father must go out to find his son. The new factor is that his going out is a dramatic giving of himself in public humiliation—all to find and
restore his son. The son surrenders all plans to solve his problem. He "accepts
being found."

Jesus has thus written two definitions of repentance into the story. The
first is repentance *as understood by the audience.* That is, the sinner must
confess, make compensation and demonstrate sincerity. The purpose of this
work of repentance is to restore the sinner to God's favor. The second is *the
new definition of repentance that Jesus presents here* with all its unforgettable drama and life-changing power.

The prodigal still has a critical choice to make. He can refuse the grace offered to him and insist that he will work and pay as a solution to his problem.
Or he can surrender to grace and repent, i.e., accept being found. The father's next speech indicates that he chooses the latter.

10. The father behaves like a mother. God is spirit, personal and one.
To describe God using only adjectives is to depersonalize him, while describing him as both mother and father sacrifices the unity of God. The thousand-
year-old, finely tuned sacred tradition on this topic that was available to Jesus
will be examined below. In this parable, a traditional Oriental patriarch
would be expected to sit in grand isolation in the house waiting to hear what
the wayward boy might have to say for himself. The boy's *mother* could run
down the road and shower her son with kisses. God gives birth in the New
Testament (1 Jn 3:9) even as he does in the Old (Deut 32:18). In like manner,
in this text the father appears on the road demonstrating the tender compassion of a motherly father.

11. Christology. As the father goes down and out, to reconcile his son,

---

[21]Ibn al-Salibi, *Durr*, 2:157 (author's translation).

he becomes a symbol of God in Christ. The father, as a symbol for God, ever so quietly evolves into a symbol for Jesus. By the end of the story, Jesus is clearly talking about himself because, as the conclusion draws near, the father in the parable does exactly what Jesus is accused of doing: he receives a sinner and plans to eat with him.

Abdallah Ibn al-Tayyib identified the father in his self-giving love on the road as a symbol for Jesus.[22] Joachim Jeremias of Germany made the same identification in the twentieth century.[23] This is another case of hermeneutical Christology. That is, Jesus takes a known symbol for God and quietly transforms it into a symbol for himself.

12. The meaning of the banquet. The father observes that the prodigal has accepted being found and offers no plan for how he (the prodigal) is going to solve the problem between them. Only then does the father order a celebratory banquet. In the parable the meaning of the banquet is affirmed three times by three different people. The first is offered by the father, the second by a little boy in the courtyard of the house and the third by the older son. The first two are in harmony with each other, but the third is in sharp contrast to the other two. The contemporary popular mind only recalls the third and strangely overlooks the other two. All three demand attention.

(a) The father's interpretation. Once reconciliation is assured, the father orders a banquet. He says, "Let us eat and make merry; *for* [now comes his explanation of the meaning of the banquet] this my son was dead, and is alive again; he was lost and is found!" (Lk 15:23-24).

The father does not say, "He was lost *and has come home.*" Instead, the text reads, "He was lost and *is found.*" Someone had to find him, and it was the father who gave of himself to do so. Thus, in the father's perception, the prodigal was still *lost* and *dead* at the edge of the village. Just as the shepherd was obliged to go forth and pay a high price to locate his sheep, and the good woman sought diligently to discover her coin, even so the father went down and out in a *costly demonstration of unexpected love* to find and resurrect his son. The banquet is a celebration of the success of those costly efforts.

(b) The little boy's interpretation. The older son comes in from the field, and on hearing the music and dancing calls to a *pais* (Lk 15:26). This Greek word can mean three things. The first is "son," which does not fit this text.

---

[22]Ibn al-Tayyib, *Tafsir,* 2:272.
[23] Jeremias, *Parables,* p. 132.

The second alternative is "servant," which also fails to make sense because all the servants are busy in the house serving the huge banquet.[24] And the third option is "young boy." Middle Eastern Syriac and Arabic versions have almost always chosen this third alternative.

As he approaches his family home in the center of the village, the older son naturally meets a crowd of young boys who are not old enough to recline with the elders at the banquet but are outside the house dancing to the music's beat and enjoying the occasion in their own boisterous way. The young lad assumes the role of the chorus in a Greek drama.[25] He tells the listener/reader the truth about what is really transpiring in the story. When the older son quizzes him about the party, the boy does not offer his personal point of view. Rather, he repeats the community's understanding of what is happening.

> Your brother has come, and your father has killed the fatted calf, *because* [now comes the second interpretation the banquet] he [the father] has received him [the prodigal] with peace! (Lk 15:27, author's translation)

The word translated here as "peace" is the Greek word *hygiainō*. In ordinary Greek usage this word has to do with "good health." This word is the root of the English word *hygiene*. But in the Greek Old Testament (the Septuagint), *hygiainō* appears eleven times. Ten times it translates the Hebrew word *shalom* (peace), and once it translates a cognate Hebrew word *shalam* (fulfilled), which has the same root. When first-century Jews used the word *hygiainō*, they were mentally translating the Hebrew word *shalom*, which includes "good health" but means so very much more. In essence it denotes peace and reconciliation. This evidence from the Greek Old Testament makes it almost certain that Jesus used the word *shalom* when he crafted this story—the point being that the banquet is in celebration of the father's successful efforts at creating reconciliation *(shalom)* and the community has gathered to participate in that celebration. Rather than a *kezazah* ceremony of rejection, the village is participating in the joy of a restoration achieved by the father at great cost. Thus, the young boy confirms the father's interpretation of the banquet's raison d'être. For both, the banquet is a celebration of

---

[24] A "servant/slave" *(doulos)* would have spoken of "my master" rather than "your father."

[25] Sepphoris, Herod Antipas's capital four miles from Nazareth, had a large Greek-style theater. On the basis of archeological evidence, the excavator James Strange identifies Herod Antipas as its builder (cf. James Strange, "Sepphoris," in *The Anchor Bible Dictionary*, 5:1090-93). It was an important city before Jesus was born, and Greek culture was pervasive throughout the "Galilee of the Gentiles" (Is 9:1; Mt 4:15).

the father's successful efforts at reconciling his son. The language of the young boy, "*He* has received *him*" (and plans to eat with him), reminds the listener/reader of the Pharisee's complaint, "This man [Jesus] receives sinners and eats with them" (Lk 15:2). The young boy's speech confirms that the father has clearly evolved into a symbol for Jesus. Jesus receives sinners and eats with them. In this parable the father does the same.

(c) The older son's interpretation. After the father leaves the banquet and in great public humiliation goes out to reconcile his older son, the elder son offers a third interpretation of the celebratory gathering. He says, "You killed *for him* the fatted calf!" (Lk 15:30). This claim is the exact opposite of what the little boy has just told the older son. It is also the opposite of the father's own declared purpose for the banquet. Noting that the older son contradicts the two previous interpretations of the feast, the listener/reader must choose between them. Is the banquet in honor of the *prodigal,* or in honor of the *father?* Is it a celebration of the prodigal's successful efforts at reaching home (on his own), or is it a celebration of the success of the father's costly efforts at creating *shalom* (peace)? Will the guests first congratulate the prodigal or the father? Will the father receive kudos while his son, embarrassed and nervous, stands behind him? Or will the guests congratulate the son with the father smiling in the background?

Too often the reader of the parable does not even discern the three interpretations of the banquet described above. When the older brother affirms "You killed *for him* the fatted calf," many accept this as a true interpretation of the banquet without noting that the text offers two opposing explanations of the same celebration. When the three alternatives are clear, surely the father's interpretation, reinforced by the young boy, needs to be affirmed. What then are the overtones of the banquet itself?

Meals hold a prominent place in the Gospel of Luke.[26] From the great feast in the house of Levi (Lk 5:29) and the dinner with Simon the Pharisee (Lk 7:36-50) to the master returning from the wedding banquet (Lk 12:35-38) and the parable of the great banquet (Lk 14:15-24) through to the meal with the men on the way to Emmaus (Lk 24:28-35), meals with Jesus feature prominently in his life and in his teaching. In the chapter under consideration there are three parties. The most important banquet in the Gospels is of course the

---

[26]In parable and in narrative account there are more than twenty references to meals in Luke's Gospel.

Last Supper. That sacred feast denotes different things in various Christian traditions. A part of its meaning is that it offers continuation of table fellowship with Jesus. It is also a celebration of the success of Jesus' costly sacrifice as he reconciles us to himself. Thus it is not hard to see the banquet with the prodigal, to which the older son is also invited, as foreshadowing the Holy Communion. Surely we know that Jesus is the hero of that sacred banquet and that sinners are not the center of attention. The older son thinks his brother is the hero of the celebration. But such is not the case. All glory is reserved for the father.

The older brother's self-righteousness becomes a pair of colored glasses through which he sees the world. All the brother can understand is that the prodigal lost the money and that he has been reconciled to their father without having paid back what he lost. In short, grace has been offered and accepted rather than the requirements of the law being demanded and met by the sinner. The older son's interpretation represents the point of view of many, both then and now. But the father's view of the banquet (supported by the young boy's speech) reflects the mind of Jesus. For many, grace is not only amazing—it is also unbelievable! How can it be true? After all, you get what you pay for—don't you?!

13. The older son's anger. If the banquet is a celebration of the prodigal's safe return (in good health), the older son will enter the hall immediately. Such a scenario would mean that the prodigal's position in the family was not yet determined. The older son would be *very* anxious that his point of view be represented when the family discusses the matter. Of course they are *all publicly* glad (?) that the prodigal is home and in good health! It would be churlish indeed, and very bad public relations, not to rejoice at his safe arrival.

But the young boy communicates to the older brother that it's all over! The prodigal is reconciled! Their father has already accepted him—and has done so without the prodigal paying for his sins! This is why the older son is angry. Indeed, he is *so* angry he takes the radical step of breaking his relationship with his father. For a son to be present and refuse participation in such a banquet is an unspeakable public insult to the father. A cultural equivalent might be the theoretical case of a son in the West who has a heated public shouting match with his father in the middle of a banquet after a large family wedding. Shouting match—all right—but not in public at such a celebration! The older son's rejection of his father's reconciliation with the prodigal leads the older son to sever his own relationship with the father who achieved it.

14. The father's response. For a fourth time the father breaks the accepted code of behavior for an Oriental patriarch, and for the second time in the same day he is willing to offer a *costly demonstration of unexpected love.* Only now it is offered to a law-keeper rather than a law-breaker. Amazing grace holds true for both sons. Culturally, the father is expected to proceed with the banquet and ignore the public insult. He can deal with the older son later. But no! In painful public humiliation the father goes down and out to find yet one more lost sheep/coin/son.

15. The older son's response to grace. The younger son accepts being found. He is overwhelmed by the costly love freely offered to him. By contrast, the older son is unimpressed. Instead, he mercilessly attacks both his father and his brother in public.[27] The father is expected to explode and order a thrashing for the public insults. For a fifth time, patriarchy is transcended. This is far more than a picture of a remarkable father. It is a symbol for God.

If the older son accepts the love offered him, he will be obliged to treat the prodigal with the same loving acceptance with which the father welcomed the pig herder. The older son will need to be "conformed to the image" (Rom 8:29) of his compassionate father, who reaches out in the form of a suffering servant to both kinds of sinners, offering each of them undeserved costly love. Is the older son willing to enter the banquet hall and start the process of learning to behave like his father? By this point in the story the audience is on stage in the person of the older son. Jesus is on that same stage as the father. How will the story end?

The parable has no ending. We do not know what the older son decides to do. Jesus is pointedly saying, "Your brother awaits you at the banquet. What are you going to do with him—and with me?" The listener/reader is pressed to provide the missing ending to the play.

THE PARABLE OF THE TWO LOST SONS—
THE THEOLOGICAL CLUSTER

As I have already observed, a parable is not a delivery system for an idea. Rather, it is a house in which the reader/listener is invited to dwell. That house has a number of doors, windows and rooms. Like John 3:16 (see chapter

---

[27]For a full description of the details of this attack, cf. K. E. Bailey, *Poet,* pp. 195-200; *Finding,* pp. 75-82.

five), this parable has a rich, interlocking cluster of theological themes. All of them, I am convinced, were in Jesus' mind. Most were available to his Pharisaic audience, and the entire theological cluster was perceivable to his disciples and to Luke's first-century Christian readers.[28]

1. Sin. The parable exhibits two types of sin. One is the sin of the law-breaker and the other the sin of the law-keeper. Each centers on a broken relationship. One breaks that relationship while failing to fulfill the expectations of the family and society. The second breaks his relationship while fulfilling those same expectations.

2. Freedom. God grants ultimate freedom to humankind, which is the freedom to reject his love. Humankind is free to choose its own way even if that path causes infinite pain to the loving heart of God.

3. Repentance. Two types of repentance are dramatically illustrated. The first is: Earn your acceptance as a servant/craftsman. The second says: Accept the costly gift of being found as a son.

4. Grace. The parable illustrated this freely offered love that seeks and suffers in order to save.

5. Joy. Two kinds of joy appear in the story: for the father, joy in finding; for the son, joy in being found and restored to community.

6. Fatherhood. The image of God as a compassionate father is given its finest definition in all of Scripture. That definition includes the offer of costly love to law-breakers and to law-keepers.

7. Sonship. Each son returns to the father either defining (the older son) or intending to define (the prodigal) his relationship to the father as that of a servant before a master. The father *will not* accept. He offers costly love to each, out of his determination to have sons who respond to love rather than servants merely obeying commands.

8. Christology. The father twice takes upon himself the form of a suffering servant who in each case offers a costly demonstration of unexpected love. The woman and the shepherd do some of the same on a lesser scale. In each scene there is a dramatic self-emptying. The third parable embodies a one-to-one relationship between the actions of Jesus and the actions of the father in that each welcomes sinners into table fellowship. This unity of action clearly implies a unity of person.

9. Family/community. The father offers costly love to his sons in order

---

[28]This section has been revised from K. E. Bailey, *Finding,* pp. 190-92.

to restore them to fellowship in the context of family/community. The family is Jesus' metaphor for the church.

10. Atonement. The father's two acts of redeeming love are made at great cost. Because of who he is, and because of the costly nature of the love offered, they generate incalculable atoning power. Some of the deepest levels of the meaning of the atoning power of costly love are exposed.

11. Eucharist. The son(s?) who partake of this banquet in the parable are sitting and eating with the one who offered costly love to win them into fellowship with himself. This parable foreshadows the final climactic meal with Jesus' disciples. The mood of the banquet is celebratory. The price paid by the shepherd, the woman and the father is not forgotten at the party that concludes each parable. But the atmosphere at the banquet is one of joy at the success of the costly efforts of finding the lost.

12. Eschatology. For Luke's readers, the messianic banquet has begun. All who accept the father's costly love are welcome as his guests. Table fellowship with Jesus is a proleptic celebration of the messianic banquet of the end times. The parable of the great banquet in Luke 14:15-24 precedes this parable. Luke (or his source) presents the reader with the former parable where "to eat bread in the kingdom of God" (Lk 14:15) finally means to accept table fellowship with Jesus. The same theme appears in this parable as well.

The preceding fifteen points of cultural clarification along with these twelve theological themes establish a foundation for our discussion of Jacob and the prodigal.

One final topic must engage us before proceeding. Jesus is a part of a theological and literary history. He needs to be placed within that history. Thus the question arises: How were the Jews around his time dealing with the Jacob saga? Was Jesus following set precedents, revising the methodologies available to him or charting new paths? To answer these questions, we can consult four early Jewish discussions of the saga of Jacob: *Jubilees,* Philo, Josephus and the early rabbis. To a brief survey of these texts we now turn.

III

THE PARABLE OF
THE PRODIGAL SON
IN LUKE 15
COMPARED WITH
THE SAGA OF JACOB
IN GENESIS 27—35

*The Saga and the Parable:
Comparisons and Contrasts*

10

JACOB REVISITED

*The Jacob Story in Early Jewish Tradition
and in the Mind of Jesus*

By Jesus' day the text of the Hebrew Scriptures was firmly established, as evidenced from the Dead Sea Scrolls. Yet during that period Jewish authors exercised the freedom to radically rewrite some of the key stories in those scriptures. Here my intent is to examine how four of those authors reshaped the story of Jacob.

Our interest in Jacob is limited to the story of his exile and return as recorded in Genesis 27:1—36:8. We take up his story (Gen 27:1) when his father Isaac, sensing his old age, decides that he should settle his affairs and unintentionally gives Jacob his primary blessing. Jacob flees to "a far country" (Lk 15:13) and eventually returns to the land but initially not to his father Isaac. Closure occurs when, after some time, Jacob arrives to see his father Isaac. The father dies, and Jacob's older brother Esau goes "away from his brother Jacob" (Gen 36:6) and returns to "the hill country of Seir" (36:8).

These parameters are set for us by the flow of the story of the prodigal son. Thus we need to be concerned only with this formative part of Jacob's life. Jesus revisits this story as he composes the new story of the parable of the prodigal son. But it must be asked: Is Jesus alone? Is he the only Jew in the centuries shortly before and after his time who in one way or another revisited the saga of Jacob? The answer is clear: Jesus is not alone. To understand what Jesus does with Jacob's story, we need to examine the work of others on the same story.

Four other texts deal with the story of Jacob.[1] Sometime around 140-161 B.C. the author of *Jubilees* devoted an extended section of his book to the saga of Jacob. As will be seen, within conservative Judaism he offered a fairly radical "rewrite." Contemporary with Jesus, Philo of Alexandria also dealt with Jacob, but in his own particular philosophical allegorical manner. During the last half of the first century, Josephus, a Palestinian Jew comfortably pensioned in Rome by Caesar, penned his highly colored version of Jacob's story. Finally, the exegetical reflections of a long series of rabbis on the saga of Jacob were committed to writing in the fourth century A.D. This work is entitled *Genesis Rabbah*. Each of these four sources takes liberties with the biblical account, but in different ways. To these texts we now turn.

Categorizing these four efforts is not easy. The rabbis reflected on the saga, and their interpretations were recorded. The result was a "commentary." That is, the *Genesis Rabbah* gives the text of Genesis and then offers various views as to what that text means. Philo does not move systematically through the saga; rather he philosophizes on various parts of it in many places in his voluminous writings. With allegory as his methodology, the sky is the limit to what he finds in the story. Josephus gives a continuous account of the story of Jacob and presents his readers with what reads like a first draft of a Hollywood scriptwriter's text for a movie on the story of Jacob contemporized to attract a first-century Greco-Roman audience. With little apparent concern for much of the theological content of the original, Josephus tells a good tale. He also takes many liberties. Two of these (Philo and Josephus) are writing in Greek from a position on the cultural borders between Judaism and paganism. Josephus is writing for Gentiles. Philo writes for Gentiles and Greek-speaking Jews. The other two (*Jubilees* and *Genesis Rabbah*) are composed in Hebrew for the Jewish community alone. *Jubilees* is pre-Christian, while Philo was contemporary to Jesus. Josephus followed a few years later, and *Genesis Rabbah*'s authors stretch from the first to the fourth centuries A.D. I will look briefly at each of these, starting with the two authors who worked "on the borders."

---

[1]The variants between the Greek Old Testament (Septuagint) and the Hebrew text of the Jacob saga are minor when compared with the variants in the four accounts listed. Thus the Septuagint will be omitted from the discussion.

PHILO OF ALEXANDRIA

Philo[2] was born about 15-20 B.C. into a prominent Jewish family in Alexandria, Egypt, and received a broad education in the Greek disciplines of that learned city. As an older man, in A.D. 39/40, he led a Jewish delegation to Ceasar in Rome. On the one hand, he was a philosopher and ethicist. On the other, he was a deeply committed Jew. Socially and intellectually he lived in both worlds. Peder Borgen writes of Philo, "He lived all his life in the double context of the Jewish community and the Alexandrian Greek community. Philosophy was Philo's life interest."[3]

His extensive writings received wide attention by early Christians and only centuries later by Jews. He developed the allegorical method for his particular form of biblical interpretation and was convinced that all ideas of value could be traced to Moses and that moral good had its source in Scripture, "and thus belonged to the Jewish nation and its heritage."[4] Holding this view, he naturally felt that it was important to attach all learning to the Hebrew Scriptures. His treatment of the Jacob saga illustrates his methodology. Philo's reflections on that account of exile and return are scattered through many essays. In one of them he contemplates Rebekah's advice to Jacob to flee and go to Haran. Philo writes:

> I very much admire Rebecca, who is patience, because she, at that time, recommends the man who is perfect in his soul [Jacob], and who has destroyed the roughness of the passions and vices, to flee and return to Charran. . . . And it is with great beauty that she here calls going by the road, which leads to the outward senses, a fleeing away; for, in truth, the mind is then a fugitive, when, having left its own appropriate objects which are comprehensible to the understanding, it turns to the opposite rank of those which are perceptible by the outward senses.[5]

He continues to reflect on Jacob's and Abraham's journey to Haran and writes:

> Do thou then, O my soul, travel through the land, and through man, bringing if you think fit, each individual man to a judgment of things which concern him;

[2]The information for this paragraph is taken from P. Borgen, "Philo of Alexandria," in *The Anchor Bible Dictionary*, 5:333-342, and from H. A. Wolfson, *Philo*.

[3]P. Borgen, "Philo of Alexandria," in *The Anchor Bible Dictionary*, 5:335.

[4]P. Borgen, "Philo of Alexandria," in *The Anchor Bible Dictionary*, 5:341.

[5]Philo, *On the Migration of Abraham* 38.208, in *The Works of Philo*, p. 273.

as, for instance, what the body is, and under what influences, whether active or passive, it co-operates with the mind; what the external sense is, and in what manner that assists the dominant mind; what speech is, and of what it becomes the interpreter so as to contribute to virtue; what are pleasure and desire; what are pain and fear.[6]

In like manner, page after page, using allegory and word association along with flights of imagination, Philo attaches his philosophical and ethical views to various parts of the Jacob saga and the rest of the Hebrew Scriptures. It is significant to note the remarkable freedom that is granted to him by his readership, to use the Scriptures in this way.[7]

JOSEPHUS

Josephus was born in A.D. 37 in the Holy Land to a Hasmonean family. With the benefits of a good education, he quickly became prominent in first-century Jewish affairs. He initially joined the revolt and fought Rome before deciding that the Zealots could not succeed. Switching sides, he then joined the Romans. After the war of A.D. 66-70, he was made a Roman citizen and granted a pension. Living in Rome for some thirty years, he gave himself to writing. Among other things, he retold the story of the history of the Jews from creation up to the year A.D. 66.[8] It is generally agreed that his primary readership was Gentile. He wanted to commend Jewish history and culture to a society that thought badly of the Jews because of the Jewish revolt against Rome. He also wanted to justify his actions to his fellow Jews. Our interest is in what he had to say about Jacob.

Josephus's biblical material appears in his work entitled *The Antiquities of the Jews*. In the preface of this volume he writes, "I shall accurately describe what is contained in our records, . . . and this without adding anything to what is therein contained, or taking away anything therefrom."[9] It is not clear what he means by this because of the freedom with which he retells the biblical stories. But in some sense it appears that he thinks he is offering an au-

---

[6]Philo, *On the Migration of Abraham* 39.219, in *The Works of Philo*, p. 274.

[7]In passing it should be noted that Philo's works were not preserved in the Jewish community. Thus, outside of the philosophically oriented, sophisticated Jewish community in Alexandria, he was apparently not popular.

[8]This information was gleaned from Louis H. Feldman, "Josephus," in *The Anchor Bible Dictionary*, 3:981-98.

[9]Josephus, *The Antiquities of the Jews*, Preface, 3 (17).

thentic account of his people's history. Although he does not dwell on Jacob, he does give a fairly full account of the saga of exile and return. A few of his interesting omissions and emendations to the text of Genesis 27:1—36:8 are as follows.

We are told that Isaac calls Esau in because he, Isaac, is prevented by his great age from worshiping God; that is, he is unable to worship by sacrificing. He also wants to pray for Esau (1.18.5 [267]).[10] When his mother suggests her game plan to Jacob for deceiving Isaac, Jacob is nervous about getting involved in this "evil practice" (1.18.6 [270]). (There is no attempt at damage control over the deception. It is openly admitted as an evil act. By admitting this, Jacob appears noble.) Isaac prays over Jacob (masquerading as Esau) and asks God to "make him terrible to his enemies, and honorable and beloved among his friends" (1.18.6 [273], an interesting crosscultural translation of Gen 27:29). Esau returns from the hunt, finds that he has been tricked and asks for a blessing. Isaac prays that he might excel "in arms" and "obtain glory forever on those accounts" (1.18.7 [275]). (This is an upgrade for Esau that improves on Gen 27:40. In the post-biblical tradition, Esau is usually downgraded as a villain.) Jacob leaves Canaan because he "hated the people of that country" (1.19.1 [278]).

During Jacob's ladder vision God tells him that he, God, brought Abraham out of Mesopotamia "when he was driven away by his kinsmen" (1.19.2 [281]). (No covenant is mentioned, and Abraham's great decision of faith disappears.) Jacob is promised that his posterity will "fill the entire earth and sea" (1.19.2 [282]). The romantic details about the love at first sight between Jacob and Rachel are expanded. On meeting Jacob, Laban presses Jacob about how he could leave his aged mother and father when they need his care (1.19.6 [294]).

After Jacob wins the two sisters as his wives and prepares to leave, Rachel steals the household gods in order to have some bargaining chips in case Laban comes after them and captures them (1.19. 9 [311], a nice dramatic addition). When Laban catches up with the fleeing Jacob and his family, the missing idols become "sacred paternal images which were worshiped by my forefathers" (1.19.10 [316], more Greco-Roman contextualization of the story). When questioned about why he was running away, Jacob tells Laban

---

[10]I will list the traditional numbers of the book, chapter and paragraph. At the end of each notation the paragraph numbers of the Loeb Classical Library series will be added.

that he was impelled by "the love of his native country" that God "implants" in all men (1.19.10 [317]). (Hear! Hear!) Laban searches Jacob's belongings for the missing gods. Rachel has them in the tent in the saddle bags of her camel saddle, which she sits on, saying she cannot get up because she is menstruating. We are then told that Laban suspects nothing because he cannot imagine "that his daughter in such circumstances would approach to those images" (1.19.11 [323]). (That is, how could an "unclean" woman possibly be sitting on "sacred images"?)

When Jacob hears that his brother Esau is approaching with four hundred men, he organizes "his company into parts" so that if the first rank is overpowered, the second rank will supply support and refuge (1.20.1 [328]). (This sounds like good military strategy!) The women and children are sent to the front "that they might see the actions of the men as they are were fighting, if Esau were so disposed" (1.20.3 [335]). But Esau did not fight Jacob; he "saluted him" (1.20.3 [336]). (Another nice military touch!) At the end of the story we are told that Rebekah died during Jacob's absence (1.22.1[345]). (The book of Genesis does not record when she died.) Other items are omitted or rearranged. Many things are condensed, or a narrative account is turned into a soliloquy. The final result is remarkable.

As one who has published a number of plays and written the scripts for two professionally produced feature-length films, I am impressed. There is good dialogue. Long tedious scenes are shortened. The identifications of motives are thoughtful. The entire "drama" is shaped to appeal to a significant recognizable audience. Well done! Impressive, yes, and amazing!

Granted, Josephus's major target audience consisted of Gentiles. Yet, no one disputes the fact that he was also trying to defend his actions before his fellow Jews. So, even though he had a Jewish audience partially in mind, he took the liberty to reshape the Jacob saga. He clearly felt he had the freedom to do so. It is true that, as in the case of Philo, it was the Christians rather than the Jews who preserved his writings. But the fact that he took so much liberty to rewrite the Jacob saga is still remarkable in itself, along with being significant for our subject. These two Jews wrote primarily for Gentiles. What about the Jew who wrote exclusively for Jews? For this we turn to *Jubilees.*

THE *BOOK OF JUBILEES*

Jubilees was composed in Hebrew by a Hasidic Jew from Palestine or an Essene

sometime between 161 and 140 B.C. As a work, it claims to present what the
Lord told Moses during the forty days he was on Mount Sinai to receive the
law. It opens with an account of creation and continues on through the stories of Adam, Noah, Abraham, Jacob and Moses. Jacob is the "central figure."[11] As O. S. Wintermute succinctly affirms, the biblical accounts are
condensed, omitted, expurgated, supplemented, explained and occasionally
radically recast.[12] The material on Jacob that covers Jacob's exile and return
fills ten of fifty chapters. The rewrite of the biblical account is too extensive
to summarize. Only a few high points can be noted.

Initially, after Abraham blesses Isaac, he calls Jacob to him and also gives
Jacob an extended blessing that includes a stern warning to separate himself
from the Gentiles. The blessing commands him not to deal with them, perform deeds like theirs or become their associates. The reasons for these stric-
tures are "because their deeds are defiled, and all of their ways are
contaminated, and despicable, and abominable."[13]

Jacob then sleeps "on the bosom of Abraham" and receives a second blessing. Later, Rebekah instructs Jacob about the importance of not marrying a
Canaanite woman, whereupon "a spirit of truth" descends on her mouth, she
places her hands on Jacob's head and then gives him an extended blessing.[14]
Only after this description of an inspired pious woman blessing her "pure
son"[15] do we read about Jacob's and Rebekah's deception of Isaac and Esau.
During the deception, when Isaac touches the hands of Jacob (now covered
with goat hair) and hears Jacob's voice, we are told, "And he [Isaac] did not
know him because the change was from heaven."[16] When Esau realizes that he
has been "defrauded" and cries out for a blessing, the blessing given him includes the promise that "you will surely sin completely unto death, and your
seed will be rooted out from under heaven."[17] Jacob is obliged to flee for his
life, and his mother Rebekah is disturbed and afraid. Her husband Isaac encourages her as he says, "Do not fear on his account, my sister, because he is upright

---

[11]O. S. Wintermute, *"Jubilees:* A New Translation and Introduction," in *The Old Testament
Pseudepigrapha,* 2:36.
[12]O. S. Wintermute, *"Jubilees:* A New Translation and Introduction," in *The Old Testament
Pseudepigrapha,* 2:35.
[13]*Jubilees* 22:16.
[14]*Jubilees* 25:15-23.
[15]*Jubilees* 25:12.
[16]*Jubilees* 26:18.
[17]*Jubilees* 26:34.

in his way and he is a perfect man. And he is faithful. And he will not perish."[18]

Jacob has his famous dream at Bethel, travels to "the land of the East," eventually acquires two wives, begins his return journey and is pursued by Laban. On meeting, they swear not to harm one another. Then Jacob "crossed over the Jabbok," and "on that day Esau, his brother, came to him and was reconciled to him and he went away from him to the land of Seir; but Jacob dwelled in tents."[19]

Amazingly there is no angel in the night, no struggle with the divine visitor, no new name and no dramatic meeting with Esau. Jacob does not go home, but he does send "clothing and food, meat and drink, and milk, and butter, and cheese, and some dates of the valley" to his parents in Hebron four times a year.[20] Since he was meeting "all their needs," they "blessed Jacob with all their heart and all their soul."[21] The story of the rape of Dinah is intensified by describing her as a little girl only twelve years old.[22] What can be made of all of this?

A careful analysis of the whys and wherefores of this radical rewrite of the Jacob saga is beyond the scope of our subject. Clearly, Jacob becomes larger than life, as does his mother. The keeping of the law and a rigorous separation from all Gentiles is prominent throughout. The remarkable omissions of the wrestling with the angel and the giving of a new name are not explained. Much more could be said, but for our purposes it is enough to note that in this text a conservative, pious, Palestinian Jew, composing in Hebrew for other pious Jews, freely rewrites critical sections of one of the primary stories that formed the identity of the community. Thus, in the tradition, rewrites of the Jacob saga are not only carried out to commend Judaism to Gentiles (Philo and Josephus) but are also used to promote a particular brand of Judaism to pious Jews![23] This is a critical precedent for our subject. We turn now to our fourth text.

GENESIS RABBAH

Thus far we have looked at philosophical fragments based on the Jacob saga (Philo), a rewrite of that same saga for Gentiles (Josephus) and a prior

---

[18]*Jubilees* 26:17.
[19]*Jubilees* 29:13.
[20]*Jubilees* 29:15-16.
[21]*Jubilees* 29:20.
[22]*Jubilees* 30:2.
[23]Fragments of the book of *Jubilees* were found among the Dead Sea Scrolls.

rewrite for Jews *(Jubilees)*. Finally, we now observe a deliberate effort at commentary, in which the story is not rewritten, but rather the biblical text, along with commentary on it, is presented to the reader. This is the *Genesis Rabbah*.

In the first century and beyond, the sages of Israel as a community were developing their own styles of dealing with the Hebrew Scriptures. Their work on Genesis was passed on orally and finally reduced to writing in the fourth century. A brief look at those styles is the fourth stop on our journey of understanding how the early Jewish tradition dealt with the Jacob saga.

The distinguished American Jewish scholar, Jacob Neusner, has ably described the rabbis as "writing with Scripture."[24] Neusner makes the point that the sages of Israel were not modern historical critics. They were not focused on what the text meant in the times and circumstances of its authors. They had their own system of thought, and, to employ Neusner's illustration, the rabbis/sages used the Hebrew Scriptures as "colors on a palette." He writes, "They used scripture as an artist uses the colors on the palette, expressing ideas through and with scripture as the artist paints with those colors and no others."[25] Although they created *their own pictures,* they used the Scriptures as paints with which to produce those pictures.

Neusner argues for more than "proof texting." The sages "wrote with scripture." To change the metaphor, the Scriptures were the building blocks for the new building. Yes, the blocks were reused for a different purpose, but the materials for the new structure were "recycled" from the Hebrew Scriptures. The sages did not generally comment on the Scriptures with the goal of understanding what the original authors were saying to their contemporaries; rather they radically contemporized the material for their own new purposes, purposes that gradually became more important than Scripture itself. The Babylonian Talmud records:

> Our Rabbis taught: They who occupy themselves with the Bible [alone] are but of indifferent merit; with Mishnah, are indeed meritorious, and are rewarded for it; with Talmud—there can be nothing more meritorious.[26]

Another rabbinic saying reads, "[The Sages], however, said: Scripture has

---

[24]J. Neusner, *Writing with Scripture.*
[25]J. Neusner, *Writing with Scripture*, p. 4.
[26]Babylonian Talmud, *Bava Metzi'a* 33a; *Shabbat* 16c.

been compared to water, the Mishnah to wine, and the *Shas* [Talmud] to spiced wine."[27]

One generation before Jesus, the famous rabbi Hillel set forth seven principles for biblical interpretation. These have to do with "inference drawn from a minor premise to a major" and "inference drawn from a similarity of words or phrases," and the relationship between general principles and a "specification," and such matters.[28] Trying to understand what the original author was saying, in his day, to his people, was not on Hillel's agenda.

The result of rabbinic exegesis can be seen in an early commentary on the Song of Songs. The Songs have long been identified as wedding love songs. In Song 2:6 the bride says, "O that his left hand were under my head, / and that his right hand embraced me!" For each of these lines a variety of interpretations is offered in the *Midrash Rabbah*. Assembled and summarized, they are:

LET HIS LEFT HAND BE UNDER MY HEAD:
This refers to the first tablets, or the fringes, or the recital of the Shema' or to the sukkah (booths), or the Mezuzah.

LET HIS RIGHT HAND EMBRACE ME:
This refers to the second tablets, or the phylacteries, or the Prayer, or the cloud of the divine presence in the time to come.[29]

Clearly, there is no attempt to connect the original meaning of the text to the new use the rabbis make of it. This same exegetical style is evidenced in the *Genesis Rabbah* on the Jacob saga under discussion.

Unlike Philo, Josephus and *Jubilees,* the *Genesis Rabbah* deals with many commentators who wrote over a number of centuries. A wide variety of interests is to be expected, as seen in the two examples below.

When Jacob, dressed in Esau's best robe, appears before Isaac in Genesis 27:27, Isaac says, "See the smell of my son is as the smell of a field which the LORD has blessed." The *Genesis Rabbah* reads:

This teaches that the Holy One, blessed be he, showed him the house of the sanctuary as it was built, wiped out, and built once more.

"see the smell of my son." This refers to the Temple in all its beauty, in line with this verse: "A sweet smell to me shall you observe" (Num. 28:2).

---

[27]Babylonian Talmud, *Soferim* 41a(2).

[28]Babylonian Talmud, *Avot of Rabbi Nathan* 32a(2); also cf. Tosefta, *Sanhedrin* 7:11(B) (J. Neusner, *Tosefta,* 4:222).

[29]*Midrash Rabbah, Song of Songs* 2.6.1, ed. Freedman and Simon, 9:111-12.

". . . is as the smell of a field." This refers to the Temple as it was wiped out, thus: "Zion shall be ploughed as a field" (Mic. 3:12).

". . . which the Lord has blessed." This speaks of the Temple as it was restored once more in the age to come, as it is said, "For there the Lord commanded the blessing, even life for ever" (Ps. 133:3).[30]

In this case, Isaac's comment on the smell of Esau's robe (now worn by Jacob) is read as referring to the temple throughout its history, as Neusner observes.[31]

Later in the saga when Jacob wrestles with the angel and dawn approaches, the angel says to Jacob, "Let me go, for the day is breaking" (Gen 32:26). The commentary on this particular phrase continues on for pages. It begins with:

"They are new every morning, great is your faithfulness" (Lam. 3:23):

Said R. Simeon bar Abbah, "Since you renew us morning by morning, we know for certain that your faithfulness is great to redeem us."

Said R. Alexandri, "Since you renew us morning by morning, we know for certain that your faithfulness is great to resurrect the dead."[32]

Here a bit of pastoral encouragement is offered to the readers on the basis of the phrase in Scripture. The idea of the breaking of day triggers some devotional reflection on the idea of morning as it appears in other texts and as the author contemplates resurrection from the dead.

Throughout the relevant sections of the *Genesis Rabbah,* the freedom to reuse the text of the Jacob saga is almost total. Indeed, a new picture is painted from the colors taken from Scripture, often with little or no reference to the scriptural scene itself.

Jesus' New Story

This same freedom with the biblical text is already seen in Matthew's Gospel, where the author quotes the Hebrew Scriptures as an important part of his overall goal of presenting Jesus as the long awaited Messiah of Israel. This brings us to reflect on what Jesus does with the Jacob saga.

In Luke 15 a discernible fifth alternative emerges. Jesus is neither com-

---

[30]*Genesis Rabbah,* trans. J. Neusner, 2:401.

[31]*Genesis Rabbah,* comment by J. Neusner, 2:402.

[32]*Genesis Rabbah,* trans. J. Neusner, 3:121

menting on the text of Scripture (Philo and the rabbis), nor is he retelling the story with his own slant (Josephus and *Jubilees*). Isaac, Jacob and Esau do not appear and are not named. Earlier, in the story of the lost sheep and the good shepherd, Jesus starts with Psalm 23, and, as observed, rewrites it with himself at its center.

Here, in the parable of the prodigal son, this same methodology appears. There is neither "text and commentary" nor a retelling of the old story such as appears in *Jubilees*. Instead, Jesus tells a *new story,* but *the new story follows the outline of and interacts with the old story*. The old story is the saga of Jacob. As in the cases of the good shepherd and the lost sheep, the new exile-and-return story *has Jesus at its center*. The former building blocks are not always reused in the same way. I have tried (imperfectly) to classify the points of comparison and contrast between the two stories into the following three types:

A. Dramatic content that is nearly identical. Both the overall outline and many dramatic elements within it are *nearly identical* (in each account). For example, in both stories the younger of two sons obtains his inheritance using dishonorable methods and leaves for a far country. Many other examples of this variety will appear.

B. Dramatic content that is reused with some changes. A clear example of this is the question of the father's death. In the Jacob saga Isaac says, "I am old; I do not know the day of my death" (Gen 27:2). As we have seen, the prodigal indirectly broaches the subject of his father's death by asking for his inheritance. The same subject appears in both accounts, and in each the story opens with it, but it is dealt with differently in the parable. The Jacob story is an example of what is *expected to happen*. The parable illustrates what is *not expected to happen*. Many cases in this category will be examined.

C. Radical reversals. Finally, a third list comprises items that appear in both stories but are *radically reversed* in Jesus' parable. For example, Jacob begins his sojourn in the far country as a *poor man* and in time becomes *rich*. The prodigal begins as a *rich man* and descends into *poverty*. The theme of "poverty/riches and the younger son" appears in each story. But the second story reverses the first. This list is also long.

In summary, certain items are accepted and endorsed in the new story as unchanged from the old (A). Others items are reused with some changes (B). The final category is made up of dramatic/theological content that appears in both stories but is reversed in the parable or radically changed for inclusion in the new story (C).[33] What then is Jesus doing with this remarkably distinctive and creative effort?

TRANSLATION AND EVANGELISM

Andrew Walls, a Scottish church historian and specialist in non-Western Christianity, has described the relationship between translation and evangelism, which begins with the incarnation. He writes:

> In the Incarnation, the Word becomes flesh, but not simply flesh; Christian faith is not about a theophany or an avatar, the appearance of divinity on the human scene. The Word was made *human.* . . . Christ was not simply a loanword adopted into the vocabulary of humanity; he was fully translated, taken into the functional system of the language, into the fullest reaches of personality, experience, and social relationship. The proper human response to the divine act of translation is conversion; the opening up of the functioning system of personality, intellect, emotions, relationship to the new meaning, to the expression of Christ.[34]

This divine translation from heaven to earth becomes the starting point and model for evangelism. The Word has come to us from God, and that same Word is then taken to other peoples and cultures. Incarnation is the model for a new "translation" from one culture and system of understanding of the world to another. Again Walls writes:

> Similarly, conversion implies the use of existing structures, the "turning" of those structures to new directions, the application of new material and standards to a system of thought and conduct already in place and functioning. It is not about substitution, the replacement of something old by something new, but about transformation, the turning of the already existing to new account.[35]

Putting the two ideas together, Walls says, "Following on the original act of translation in Jesus of Nazareth are countless retranslations into the thought

---

[33]To preserve the integrity of the flow of the story, I will discuss these items following the unfolding of the parable itself. But each dramatic element studied will be given a letter designation (A, B, or C) at the beginning of the discussion to indicate a suggestion for classification of the material along these lines. The three types are listed together in an appendix for convenience of comparison.

[34]A. F. Walls, *The Missionary Movement in Christian History,* p. 28.

[35]A. F. Walls, *The Missionary Movement in Christian History,* p. 28.

forms and cultures of the different societies into which Christ is brought as conversion takes place."[36]

Thus Walls sees a two-stage process:

- (Stage one) the word of God becomes flesh
- (Stage two) the resulting Gospel is "translated" into other cultures

Yet doesn't the New Testament present us with a three stage process? Between the word becoming flesh (stage one) and Paul's work among the Gentiles (stage two), we can observe Jesus' "translation" of who he was and what he came to do into the imagination and theological culture of first-century Judaism. This did not occur automatically. The new reality of God having visited and redeemed his people in the person of Jesus had to be presented in understandable forms within his own theological culture. Yes, the divine word of God was translated into *flesh* in Jesus of Nazareth. But that Word necessitated a further translation into the intellectual and theological world of which he was a part.[37] And in the three parables in Luke 15 it is possible to see that Jesus himself was the theologian who made that initial translation for "Israel according to the flesh" (1 Cor 10:18, literal translation; cf. KJV). Paul's efforts with the Greco-Roman (and the efforts of the author of Hebrews) then become the third (rather than the second) such translation. This "second translation," accomplished by Jesus, is often overlooked. These three can be seen summarized as follows:

1. The Word of God is translated into flesh in the person of Jesus.

2. Jesus "translates" the reality of who he is and what he has come to accomplish by reshaping the Old Testament stories of the Good Shepherd and the saga of Jacob into new forms with himself at their centers.

3a. Paul translates the resulting Gospel into concepts and metaphors that the Greco-Roman world can understand.

3b. The book of Hebrews does the same thing for that branch of Judaism that focused on the temple and its rituals.

Christian reflection on the New Testament generally moves from the first of these directly to the third. Granted, Christian witnesses across history have started with the "resulting Gospel" and labored to present that Gospel in un-

---

[36]A. F. Walls, *The Missionary Movement in Christian History,* p. 28.

[37]In a public lecture Andrew Walls has discussed what he calls "the conversion of memory." New Christians, argues Walls, should not erase their past but allow it to be converted to Christ. This is what Jesus is doing: "converting" the community's memory of the Jacob saga as he creates the new story of the compassionate father and the two lost sons.

derstandable forms to new cultures. But is the Gospel itself not better understood if the "second translation" is understood as well?

Yes, the author of the epistle to the Hebrews, was at work presenting the Gospel in the theological thought forms of first-century Judaism. But, it is my conviction that in the parable of the prodigal son, at the earliest point of the formation of the Gospel, *Jesus himself was at work on the same problem!*

This earlier, second stage is as profound, important and compelling as the first and the third. The community of which Jesus was a part took its name from the Jacob story. It was known as, *Israel,* the name given to Jacob in the great saga of his journey into exile and return, recorded in Genesis 27—35. His story was an important part of the community's story. The following chapters will focus on how Jesus took that great saga and mirrored it with a new story that presented himself as its center.

Finally, the Jacob story is selected not from the less venerated *Ketubim* (the Writings) as in the case of the reuse of Psalm 23 but from the *Torah* itself, and Jesus is expanding not a brief metaphor (the good shepherd) but an extended saga! Yes, *Jubilees* presents a new version of the Jacob saga. But its author did not write himself into the text as its hero. The freedom to offer a new version of the Jacob saga was already affirmed in the tradition. Jesus takes that freedom and exercises it in a new and daring way. Tracing the exercise of this freedom is the task to which we now turn.

11

THE GREAT REBELLION

The Family Before the Prodigal Leaves Home
(Lk 15:11-13)

This chapter will examine the parallels between the saga of Jacob and the parable of the prodigal son, focusing on the prodigal before he leaves home. The text of the parable and the parallel dramatic elements in the two accounts are as follows:

> And he said, "There was a man who had two sons; and the younger of them said to his father, 'Father, give me the share of property that falls to me.' And he divided his living between them. Not many days later, the younger son turned all he had into cash[1] and took his journey into a far country." (Lk 15:11-13, author's translation)

11.1 THE DEATH OF THE FATHER (B)

Each story opens with a reference to the father's death but does so in discriminatingly dissimilar ways. At the beginning of the Jacob saga, Isaac says to Esau, "Behold, I am old; I do not know the day of my death" (Gen 27:2). He then explains that he wants to bless Esau before he dies. It is the *father* who initiates the discussion, *not the son,* and the father refers to *his own* death.

In traditional Middle Eastern society (as in many cultures in the world), this is assumed to be the natural way to deal with the question of inheritance. Sensing that he is about to die, a father is expected to make his oral will. Abra-

---

[1]Rather than translating *synagō* as "gathered together," I have opted for the more literal "turned into cash," which appears in the New English Bible.

ham, at the approach of death, gives gifts to his children by Keturah, and "while he was still living he sent them away from his son Isaac" (Gen 25:6). Two verses later "in a good old age" he dies. The gifts to Keturah's sons appear to be a part of the settling of his inheritance. Her children do not initiate the exchange; Abraham does. In 2 Kings 20:1, Isaiah says to Hezekiah, "Set thine house in order; for thou shalt die" (KJV). Such is the normal pattern of traditional life assumed also in Hebrews 9:16. The idea that one of the sons might initiate such a discussion is unknown among both Jews and Arabs.[2] Ben Sirach specifically affirms that inheritance should not be transferred during the life of the donor (Sirach 33:19-23). Esau does not begin such a discussion.

By contrast, out of the blue, in the parable, the prodigal (the younger son, no less) bluntly asks for his inheritance from his father, who is assumed to be in good health. By broaching this subject, the prodigal implies that he desires his father's early death.[3]

Thus, in each story, the opening scene focuses dramatically on the subject of the father's death. The difference between the two accounts is that the prodigal, with no warning, *initiates* the discussion. Given the symbolic identifications of the three major characters in the parable, this request takes on great theological significance. For Jesus, sin is desiring the death of God and wanting to take his gifts without reference to the giver. This theme will reappear as we proceed.

11.2 THE YOUNGER SON BREAKS RELATIONSHIP WITH THE FATHER (B)

Both Jacob and the prodigal sever relationships with their fathers, but in different ways. Jacob does so by deceiving his father into thinking he is Isaac. Esau is understandably furious, but, strangely, there is no record of Isaac's reaction. Disappointment at the betrayal can be assumed. Upon returning home, however, Jacob seems in no hurry to see his father. Finally, he "came to his father Isaac at Mamre" (Gen 35:27), but there is no hint that it was an occasion of reconciliation, and there is no banquet celebration. The reader is left with the distinct impression that there was no critical break in relationship that needed healing. The author of *Jubilees* works very hard to make sure the reader knows that Isaac is always happy with his son Jacob[4] and that

---

[2]N. Levison, *Local Setting*, p. 156.
[3]K. E. Bailey, *Poet*, pp. 162-65.
[4]*Jubilees* 27:17.

after his return Jacob leaves no stone unturned to care for his father.[5] Such is not the case with the prodigal.

The prodigal breaks his relationship with his father by his blunt request. Inevitably, the split between them deepens when the prodigal sells the property given to him. As this happens, the unspeakable insult to his father becomes public knowledge in the community. At the end of the story the father engages in extraordinary dramatic actions to heal the broken relationships between himself and the prodigal and between the prodigal and the community.

If the two are compared, the broken relationship between the prodigal and his father is deeper and more painful than that which separates Isaac and Jacob. It is one thing to cheat the old man and grab more of the inheritance than the son deserves (all in private), but it is something else indeed to want one's father dead and to allow the village to discover this death wish. The parable opens with this powerful hand grenade exploding in the father's face. As this happens, the listener/reader goes into shock and anticipates anger and rejection on the part of the father.

As seen here, sin for Jesus is more than breaking the law. It is the breaking of a relationship. Indeed, the prodigal does break the law, but he does far more. He is, in fact, in total rebellion against his father. One of the Hebrew words for sin is *pesha* (rebellion). The prophet Amos thunders his judgments against the nations and against Judah and Israel using this freighted word (Amos 1:3, 6, 9, 11, 13; 2:1, 4, 6). In this story Jesus reflects this prophetic theological understanding of sin. Henceforth the listener/reader knows that the deepest issue that divides the father and the son is neither illegitimately acquired money (a broken law) nor the fact that he lost that money. Rather, it is a shattered relationship and the agony of rejected love that results from that shattering.

11.3 THE NATURE OF THE FATHER (C)

Archbishop William Temple has written:

> Every original genius is hampered by the terms which contemporary language offers as the necessary and sole medium of his self-expression. He must take the best terms available, and trust that his special use of them will gradually correct the suggestions attaching to them, which are alien from his thought, until at last he has imposed his own meaning on them.[6]

---

[5]*Jubilees* 29:15-20.
[6]W. Temple, *Readings in St. John's Gospel,* pp. xxv-xxvi.

This statement is profoundly true of Jesus' use of the word *father* as a name and metaphor for God. As seen in the parable of the prodigal son, the image of father is transformed from that of a tribal chief into a metaphor that can be used for God. The significance of this transformation is critical for an understanding of all four Gospels. In some theological circles it is assumed that Jesus and the apostles adopted an "Oriental patriarch" as an image for God. The traditional Oriental patriarch of the Middle East usually deals with his children with great tenderness. He may be gruff with the public, but he is rarely so with his own children. This is not generally known in the West. But at the end of the day, neither the reality or the perception is important.

What matters is that for the last two thousand years Christians in the East, West, North and South have at times allowed their understanding of human fathers to influence their understanding of God as Father of all. Such activity, wherever it occurs, is idolatry that surely must be identified, confessed as sin and rejected. The question that needs to be asked is, Does Scripture *define* the word *father* as it is applied to God? Because if it does, that definition *alone* should surely govern the way Christians understand God as Father.

Both the Old and New Testament authors and speakers make clear what they mean when they refer to God as Father. As a metaphor for God, the word *father* is overwhelmingly a symbol for tenderness and compassion. The Eastern and Western misunderstanding of this point is both colossal and pervasive. Thus, a brief examination of the use of the title Father for God in the Hebrew Scriptures is in order.

The title Father is applied to God sixteen times in the Hebrew Scriptures. Four of them speak of God as a father to David. The other twelve describe God as the father of his people. These twelve can be summarized in the following way:

- Father = redeemer/compassionate one/ merciful one (7)
- Father = creator (3)
- Father = honor (1), power (1)

Each of these three categories requires brief examination.

The following are the seven examples of God as a *redeeming/compassionate/merciful* father:

> Sing to God . . .
> Father of the fatherless and protector of widows. (Ps 68:4-5)

As a father has compassion on his children,
>   so the LORD has compassion on those who fear him. (Ps 103:13 NIV)

>   "The *yearning of* thy *heart* and thy *compassion*
>   are withheld from me.
> For *thou art our Father*,
>   though Abraham does not know us
>   and Israel does not acknowledge us;
> *thou*, O LORD, art *our Father*,
>   *our Redeemer* from of old is thy name." (Is 63:15-16)

>   "My Father, thou art the friend of my youth." (Jer 3:4)

>   "I thought
>   how I would . . . give you a pleasant land. . . .
>   And I thought you would call me, My Father." (Jer 3:19)

>   "I will make them walk by brooks of water, . . .
>   for I am a Father to Israel." (Jer 31:9)

>   Out of Egypt I called my son. . . .
>   It was I who taught Ephraim to walk,
>   I took them up in my arms; . . .
>   I led them with cords of compassion,
>   with the bands of love,
>   and I became to them as one
>   who eases the yoke on their jaws,
>   and I bent down to them and fed them. . . .
>   My heart recoils within me,
>   my compassion grows warm and tender. (Hos 11:1-9)

These seven texts make clear that for the authors of the Hebrew Scriptures the image of God as father was dominated with ideas of compassion, love, tenderness and redemption.

In addition to the above, three texts understand the fatherhood of God as including creator. These are:

> Do you thus requite the LORD
>   you foolish and senseless people?
> Is not he your father, who created you,
>   who made you and established you? (Deut 32:6; cf. also Deut 32:18)

> Yet, O LORD, thou art our Father;

> we are the clay, and thou art our potter;
> we are all the work of thy hand. (Is 64:8)

Have we not all one father? Has not one God created us? (Mal 2:10)

Finally, there is one text where the title Father refers to God's power and a second that identifies the name Father with honor. These are:

> Blessed art thou, O LORD, the God of Israel our father, for ever and ever. Thine,
> O LORD, is the greatness, and the power, and the glory, and the victory, and the
> majesty. (1 Chron 29:10-11)

> A son honors his father, and a servant his master. If then I am a father, where
> is my honor? And if I am a master, where is my fear? says the LORD of hosts.
> (Mal 1:6)

The title King implies autocratic rule, whereas the weight of the title Father, for God (as seen above), has to do with compassion and tenderness. Only in 1 Chronicles 29:11 is the title Father attached to power, glory and majesty.

God the Father at times behaves like a mother. As noted above, in Isaiah 63:10 and in 64:8, God is called Father, while a few verses later in Isaiah 66:13 that father is described with the following words:

> As one whom his mother comforts,
> so I will comfort you;
> you shall be comforted in Jerusalem. (Is 66:13)[7]

Female attributes are also applied to God in Deuteronomy 32:18, which reads:

> You were unmindful of the Rock that begot you,
> and you forgot the God who gave you birth.[8]

Psalm 131:2 follows in the same vein when it says:

> But I have calmed and quieted my soul,
> like a child quieted at its mother's breast;

---

[7]Granted, in Isaiah 66:7-12 Jerusalem is the mother, but by verse 13 the imagery shifts. In that verse Jerusalem is no longer the mother; instead Jerusalem becomes the *place* where the comforting occurs. The mother who does the comforting is God.

[8]In the Gospel of John this theme is highlighted and repeated in the conversation between Jesus and Nicodemus (Jn 3:1-15). Nicodemus is told that he must be born *anōthen* (again/from above). The intent of this language is spelled out further in 1 John 3:9, where the believer is said to be "born of God." Clearly, God acts like a mother who gives birth to the believers.

> like a child that is quieted is my soul.

Here the psalmist quiets his own soul, but while doing so he likens himself to a child quieted at his "mother's breast." The mother in this text is a simile for God.

Finally, Isaiah 49:15 reads:

> Can a woman forget her sucking child,
>> that she should have no compassion on the son of her womb?
>> Even these may forget, yet I will not forget you.

Here the compassion of God goes beyond the love of a human mother. Although like a mother's love, God's love is greater in its intensity.

Thus, the Old Testament offers its readers one metaphor and one simile. God is never called "mother" but is referred to as *a father* who acts *like a mother*. This carefully balanced language reappears in the Hymn Scroll *(Hodayot)* of the Dead Sea Scrolls, which reads:

> For Thou art a father
>> to all [the sons] of Thy truth,
> and like a woman who tenderly loves her babe,
>> so dost Thou rejoice in them;
> and as a foster-father bearing a child in his lap,
>> so carest Thou for all Thy creatures.[9]

Here God *is a father* who *acts like a mother* who tenderly loves her babe.

The understanding of fathers as people of compassion can be traced beyond the Old and New Testaments to Eastern (Semitic) Gnostic literature. In a collection of third- and fourth-century documents recovered from Central Asia there appears a commemorative hymn for Mar Zuku (c. A.D. 300) that includes

> O righteous Father, meek and merciful,
> magnanimous and generous,
> compassionate and kind;
> you brought joy to the oppressed;
> many souls did you save from misery,
> guiding them home.[10]

---

[9] *Hodayot,* in *The Dead Sea Scrolls in English,* trans. G. Vermes, 9:35-36 (182).
[10] H.-J. Klimkeit, trans. and ed., *Gnosis on the Silk Road,* p. 88.

Whatever the failings of many Middle Eastern (or Western) fathers may be, the above, like Hosea 11, is a rich tribute to the Middle Eastern understanding of father as a symbol of compassion.

Yet, in the Bible, the pinnacle of this understanding of father is reached in the parable of the prodigal son. At five points in this parable the father demonstrates compassion beyond what is expected of a traditional Semitic father.

(a) The father grants the original unprecedented and unreasonable request and gives the prodigal his share of the inheritance.

(b) He allows the prodigal to sell the property. This exhibits a generosity that goes beyond custom and Jewish law as set forth in the *Mishnah.*[11]

(c) He runs down the road welcoming his wayward son in a great drama of costly compassion, hoping to win the prodigal from servanthood to sonship, from being lost to being found, and from death to life.

(d) He endures the unspeakably painful public humiliation of leaving his guests, at a banquet in his own home, and offers more costly love to a publicly rebellious older son.

(e) After verbal insults from the older son, the father appeals for joy rather than resorting to judgment and punishment.

As Ebrahim Sa'id, a mid-twentieth-century Egyptian commentator on the book of Luke, has written in Arabic:

> The shepherd [in Luke 15] and the woman only do those things that we expect a good shepherd and a good woman to do. But the father in the story of the prodigal son carries out divine acts that we do not expect from any father.[12]

The pinnacle of the father's love in the parable is reached in the final appeal for joy (not in the embrace on the road). Ibn al-Tayyib, writing from Baghdad in Arabic in the eleventh century, comments on the father who goes out to meet his rebellious older son and says:

> Look at the heart of this father! It is full of tenderness and love in that he left the banquet, the guests, and his younger son to plead with his older son to come in. It is as if his own joy is incomplete as long as one of his children is grieving. He does not rebuke the older son on his hardness of heart or his inappropriate sensitivities. In like manner the heavenly Father desires the entrance

---

[11]K. E. Bailey, *Finding,* p. 114.
[12]I. Sa'id, *Luqa,* p. 396 (author's translation).

of the scribes and Pharisees into the kingdom of heaven as much as the tax collectors and sinners. Thus he demonstrated long suffering and intense desire for
them to come to him even as did this earthly father.[13]

Ibn al-Tayyib sees the father in the parable as a person full of "tenderness
and love" and clearly affirms that "in like manner the heavenly Father" exhibits the same characteristics. So much for the grim, authoritative patriarch
who can be found in real life in any culture but never appears in Scripture as
a model for God.

As noted, the Bible neither compares nor likens God to a human father. In
Hosea 11: 9 God speaks:

> For I am God *and not a human being,*
> > the Holy One in your midst,
> > and I will not come in wrath. (author's translation)

Scripture makes clear that God is not like *a father* but rather like *this father,* namely the father set forth in Hosea 11 and Luke 15.

In the Jacob story, Isaac is indeed an Oriental patriarch, and a poor one at
that. He is too proud to ask for help in his uncertainty about who is providing
his dinner. He offers Esau no apology. He seems unable to relate to his disloy-
al wife and makes no move to bring his dysfunctional family back together.
Eventually, at the end of the story, he passively fades away. Each story has a
father, but the differences between them are enormous!

It appears that Jesus of Nazareth took the picture of a divine father in Hosea 11, added the compassionate female side of God that appears in the Old
Testament and went beyond them as he created the figure of the father in the
parable. This new father is full of tenderness, patience, compassion, love and
a willingness to suffer in order to redeem.

As Henri Nouwen, the late Dutch Roman Catholic priest, wrote in his book
The Return of the Prodigal Son:

> The way the younger son is given robe, ring, and sandals, and welcomed home
> with a sumptuous celebration, as well as the way the elder son is urged to ac-
> cept his unique place in his father's heart and to join his younger brother
> around the table, make it very clear that *all boundaries of patriarchal behav-
> ior are broken through.* This is not the picture of a remarkable father. This is
> the portrayal of God, whose goodness, love, forgiveness, care, joy, and compas-

---

[13]Ibn al-Tayyib, *Tafsir,* 2:277 (author's translation); cf. K. E. Bailey, *Finding,* p. 173.

sion have no limits at all. Jesus presents God's generosity by using all the imagery that his culture provides, while constantly transforming it.[14]

Jesus did not merely teach his disciples to pray "Our Father." He defined his terms. Surely, no image of Father as a title for God should be allowed to inform the mind of any disciple of Jesus other than the one he created in the parable under discussion.

Islam has historically stood in opposition to using metaphors for God. For Muslims to call God Father is to liken him to a human being and thus to start sliding down the slippery slope to idolatry. Islam insists that adjectives be used to name God.[15] God is merciful, compassionate, creator, wise, all knowing, all powerful and so forth. But these are *names* not *attributes*. Regarding these "names," Islam developed the concept of *bila kayf* (without comparison). When the worshiper calls God "merciful and compassionate," those words have content shaped by the believer's experiences of people who are merciful and compassionate. But, Islam insists, this human experience of mercy and compassion is never to be used to understand what God is like. As Kenneth Cragg has written about the names of God, "[Muslims] use these names 'without knowing how' they apply and without implying any human similarity."[16] God's nature is totally unknown. Again Cragg writes, "God the Revealer remains Himself unrevealed."[17] He is "without comparison." We are given the *will* of God—the law, says Islam—but his nature is unknown. The believer is called on to obey God's *will* but *not to imitate his nature* because that nature remains unknown.

Naturally Islam looks with deep dismay at the Christian who prays "Our Father." For Muslims such a prayer inevitably leads to idolatry because the worshipers will be influenced in their understanding of the title Father by human fathers they have known. As Christians, we do well to listen carefully to this Islamic caution. Yes, throughout history we have often slipped into the idolatry of taking our understanding of God as Father from our culture or our personal experience, whatever that culture or that experience might be. The solution to this problem is not to set aside the title *Father*, but rather to carefully restrict its meaning to the definition Jesus gave it. The Islamicization of

---

[14]H. Nouwen, *The Return of the Prodigal*, p. 131 (emphasis added).

[15]The one exception that proves the rule is the word *malak* (king).

[16]K. Cragg, *The Call of the Minaret*, p. 55.

[17]K. Cragg, *The Call of the Minaret*, p. 47.

our understanding of and language about God is not the only alternative. We have this parable!

In passing, it bears noting that Jesus is also universalizing the inherited story. Rather than a tale about a particular clan in a particular place at a particular time in history, the new story is an account of the human predicament in all places and at all times. This universalization of the story will appear repeatedly as we move through the two texts under study.

11.4 THE MOTHER (C)

Jacob's mother, Rebekah, appears in a negative light when compared with saints such as Ruth, and with the good woman of Proverbs 31. Indeed, Rebekah deliberately deceives both her husband and her older son. After this double deception, she disappears from the text and is not mentioned again until she dies. It is a sad ending to the story of a marriage that began with the unspoken promise of better things. The author of *Jubilees* appears to be sensitive to this negativism. This may explain why *Jubilees* works so hard to present her as a saint.[18]

The parable of the prodigal son has no mother. Yet, when the father runs down the road to welcome the prodigal, he is doing what a mother would normally do. The father is the parent who is expected to remain aloof in the house, waiting to hear what his wayward boy has to say for himself. The mother is permitted, and even expected, to run down the road and shower the dear boy with kisses. Jesus gives us a portrait of a father who acts with the tender compassion of a mother—a father, if you please, who is a motherly father.

Later in the day, when the older son chooses the occasion of a public banquet for a shouting match with his father, the mother could have rushed to him to plead for reconciliation. Traditionally, the father should remain with his guests. Again, the father behaves like a mother.

In summary, what happens in Luke 15 regarding this particular point, vis-à-vis the Jacob saga? The negative image of Jacob's mother is quietly set aside. In its place, the clear, public, noble image of the good woman with her coin takes the stage, along with the presentation of a father who acts with the tender compassion of a mother. In the process, the unity of God is preserved without sacrificing the female aspects of God's nature available to Jesus in the

---

[18]*Jubilees* 25:11-23.

Hebrew Scriptures. God is spirit; he is neither male nor female. Yet God is a father who acts like a mother. This finely tuned theology is created in the Old Testament, reaffirmed in the Dead Sea Scrolls and comes to its finest expression in the mind of Jesus.

11.5 A FATHER AND TWO SONS (A)

Both accounts contain a father and two sons, an elder and a younger. The Jacob story does showcase minor characters. Rebekah, Laban, Leah and Rachel all appear along with four hundred armed men. Yet, they are the supporting cast. The story revolves around Isaac, Jacob and Esau.

In the parable, the prominent figures are clearly the father, the older son and the prodigal. The parable is not an extended saga, and the supporting cast is not identified by name. But there are people in the community who purchase the prodigal's inheritance. A citizen in the far country hires the prodigal. On the latter's return, there is mention of a class of craftsmen. House slaves and a young boy appear on stage and participate in the drama. A houseful of guests attend a banquet where musicians and dancers perform. And the older son says he has a circle of friends with whom he would like to enjoy a feast. These characters compose the parable's critical "extras."

As noted, some of these supporting actors appear on stage. The citizen in the far country hires the prodigal. Indeed, the prodigal "joined himself" (lit. "glued himself") to this citizen.[19] The servants/slaves are addressed by the father and told to bring the ring, robe and shoes and then to prepare a banquet. The musicians and dancers are heard but not seen. Only the young boy has a speaking part. The others in the supporting cast remain offstage or at its edge. In each story, center stage is dominated by a father and two sons.

The story of Abraham is also a tale of a father and two sons. Thus, the Pharisaic audience could initially wonder if Jesus was starting to draw parallels with the saga of Abraham. But as the story progresses, parallels to Abraham's traumas with Ishmael and Isaac fade, whereas points of contact with the account of Isaac, Esau and Jacob continue to expand.

Jesus' selection of these three major characters for his story alert his listening audience to the possibility that he is modeling his new drama after the structure of the saga of Jacob. As the parable unfolds they will be listening carefully to see if such an idea is plausible.

---

[19]K. E. Bailey, *Cross,* p. 44.

11.6 The Identity of the Two Sons (B)

In the Jacob saga, the two sons represent clan leaders. One heads Israel while
the other becomes the founder of Edom, and the hostility between them is
continuous. In the early centuries of church history, the two sons in the parable were allegorized to represent Jews and Gentiles. This identification cannot be sustained. If the prodigal were meant to represent the Gentiles, he
would have needed to be a Greek pig herder who was adopted by the father's
family. Instead, from the start the prodigal was a member of the family who
was estranged and then reconciled. The older son remained at home but was
also estranged, in his case from both his brother and his father. In the world
of Jesus and the text, they represent "tax collectors and sinners" (the younger
son) and "the Pharisees and the scribes" (the older son; cf. Lk 15:1-2). More
generally they are symbols of the human predicament. They might be called
the "ins and the outs" or "lawbreakers" and "lawless lawkeepers" or those
who follow the traditions of their community and those who do not.

By the ninth century, Musa bar Kepha, a Syriac scholar writing from Mosel
in Iraq, dismisses the Jew versus Gentile identification of the two sons. Musa
bar Kepha writes:

> And others say that he [Jesus] meant by "the older son" the Israelites, and "the
> younger one" the peoples [Gentiles]. . . . But we say that Christ referred to "the
> man" as his Father. He referred to "the older son" as the rank of righteous
> ones. . . . And he referred to "youngest one" as the rank of sinners. And he
> named him "youngest one" because careless, wanton, ignorant and wrong
> thought follows sinners.[20]

Clearly bar Kepha observes the universalizing of the parable. Jesus is not talking about two particular ethnic communities but instead is referring to well-
known types of people within any language and culture.

Henri Nouwen affirms these descriptive labels and takes them one stage
further. He notes repeatedly that both the younger and the elder sons are
within us, and if the older son enters the banquet hall, he must begin to treat
his brother the way the father treats both of his children. Nouwen writes,
"Being in the Father's house requires that I make the Father's life my own and
become transformed in his image."[21]

---

[20]Musa bar Kepha, *Luke,* trans. A. M. Saadi, fol. 78a.
[21]H. Nouwen, *The Return of the Prodigal,* p. 123.

Jesus said, "Be merciful, even as your father is merciful" (Lk 6:36). This parable defines both the nature of that mercy and of that father. Once again a story about one tribe, while not neglecting that tribe, becomes a story about all people.

11.7 THE NATURE OF THE BLESSING/INHERITANCE (B)

A blessing/inheritance is a critical component of each story, but there are some significant revisions in Jesus' version.

Jacob wants and receives his father's blessing, which relates directly to his personal wealth *and to his leadership of the family clan* (Gen 27:21-29). Esau first lost his birthright (Gen 25:29-34) and was then tricked out of his blessing. But losing his birthright was not nearly as serious a matter, and his father was not involved. Losing his birthright meant the loss of his opportunity to inherit the larger portion of the family's wealth (Deut 21:17). But to lose the blessing (as spelled out in what Isaac says to Jacob as he bestows the blessing on him) was to lose wealth *and* other very important things.

As noted, Isaac, in good Middle Eastern style, addressed his mind to this matter as he sensed his approaching death.[22] Clearly, he misjudged his state of health and, in fact, lived to see Jacob return twenty years later (Gen 31:38) from "the far country." But it is the threefold nature of the blessing/inheritance he gives to Jacob that is of special interest to us here.

Isaac blessed Jacob with wealth in the form of "the dew of heaven, and of the fatness of the earth, and plenty of grain and wine" (Gen 27:28). As Eugene Maly has written:

> This special blessing of the first-born is not otherwise recorded in Gn, but it might be presumed that such a blessing was given to indicate the right of inheritance (perhaps implied in 24:36b). [23]

Continuing, Isaac adds, "Be lord over your brothers, and may your mother's sons bow down to you" (Gen 27:29). Finally, a part of the Abrahamic blessing of Genesis 12:2-3 is rephrased. Abraham was promised, "And I will make of you a great nation, and I will bless you, and make your name great. I will bless those who bless you, and him who curses you I will curse." Isaac says to Jacob:

---

[22]In the late 1990s, shortly before he died of cancer, King Hussein of Jordan flew from America to Jordan to settle the matter of who was to be king after him.

[23]E. H. Maly, "Genesis," in *The Jerome Biblical Commentary*, p. 27.

Let peoples serve you,
>   and nations bow down to you. . . .
Cursed be every one who curses you,
>   and blessed be every one who blesses you! (Gen 27:29)

Jacob is offered three things: material prosperity, the servitude of his brothers (and the Gentiles/nations), and the invocation of curses on his opponents along with blessings for his supporters.

The question of *inheritance* is also central in Jesus' parable, but, as in the Jacob saga, the word itself is not used. The prodigal opens the first scene by saying, "Give me the share of property that belongs to me." As noted, this share is granted him, along with the implied right to sell, but the tribalism and nationalism are gone. The prodigal receives material wealth, but there is no promise that a Gentile, such as the citizen in the far country, will suffer harm if he dares send the prodigal off to feed pigs! Nor is there any promise that the older son will serve the younger.[24]

Indeed, the older son is angry when the prodigal returns, but there is no direct suggestion that the former fears servitude to his brother. To be sure, the older son is probably afraid lest the generous father give away more property to the vagabond younger son—property that is a part of the older son's rights. This would explain why the father pointedly tells him, "All that is mine is yours." A story of how leadership in a particular tribe was passed from one generation to another is transformed into a story of how a self-giving compassionate father offers costly love to a lawbreaker and a lawkeeper.

The question remains, What precisely did Jesus mean to signify in his reference to the *inheritance* that was given to the prodigal? We know what Isaac promised Jacob. But in Jesus' mind what did the inheritance symbolize?

The prodigal asks for his share of "the property." In all of the New Testament, the word, *property (ousia)* is found only here.[25] The father responds by "dividing his life" *(bios)* between them. What does this mean?

In a traditional Middle Eastern farming community a farmer's land is his life, not merely his livelihood. Land is central to his very identity. In the He-

---

[24]One tiny scrap of this aspect of the Jacob saga reappears in the parable. The prodigal is given "a ring" (Lk 15:22), which implies the signet ring of the house. Such a ring is expected to be passed to the older son. A. J. Hultgren notes in passing that "the younger son has in effect now supplanted his older brother" (*The Parables of Jesus,* p. 79). Hultgren does not connect this remark to the Jacob story. Perhaps this is parallel number fifty-two.

[25]The very avoidance of the word *inheritance* further ties the two stories together.

brew Scriptures, Naboth will *die* rather than sell his family's inherited land, *even to the king.* He tells King Ahab, "The LORD forbid that I should give you the inheritance of my fathers" (1 Kings 21:3). Americans proudly sing of their love for the land. Indeed, the characters in the musical *Oklahoma!* assert that they *belong* to the land. Such a perspective mirrors something of the traditional Middle Eastern attitude toward the family estate and what it means. By his actions, the father is giving the prodigal his very *life.*[26] Thus, symbolically, Jesus is saying to his Pharisaic audience that in some deep sense the children of God are offered both a natural world, which makes living possible, and God's very life as a free gift to his children. As the story develops, it is clear that both aspects of this twofold offering can be squandered. Yet the prodigal is offered no tribal authority, no curses for his enemies and no automatic blessings for his friends. Jesus' story is about a family, as was the old story. But in the new story, the bonds of race and tribe are not the critical factors that constitute the new family. Instead, the relationships between the members of the family are the central focus, and it is the life of the father (God) that is given to the two sons. Once more the parable speaks deeply to the entire human race and its needs.

To summarize, both stories turn on the issue of an inheritance, but the new story deals with the theme in a significantly different way. This shift in emphasis will reappear when the question of land is addressed. The father's very life is given to the prodigal. Will his son remember the giver and treasure the gift?

11.8 THE METHOD OF ACQUIRING THE BLESSING/INHERITANCE (B)

In each story the younger son seeks advantages (inheritance/blessing) from the father, using dishonorable methods, and succeeds.

Jacob's mother, Rebekah, hears of Isaac's plans to bless Esau and waits for him to depart on a hunting expedition before alerting Jacob to his father's intentions. She explains her plans for a major deception of her husband. Jacob is willing to be a partner in crime but is fearful lest they fail. Rebekah prevails; they proceed and are successful. Jacob manages to deceive his father Isaac into thinking he is Esau and obtains his brother's blessing.

---

[26]The Mount Sinai Arabic Gospels MSS 72 (A.D. 897) was translated from the Greek and survives in eight copies (cf. K. E. Bailey, *Finding,* p. 37) That important early Semitic version translated the Greek word *bios* as *'umr,* which literally means "the years of one's life." The translators caught something of the depth of the overtones of the word *bios* (life) that appears in the Greek text.

As noted, no son in a traditional Middle Eastern home has the right to ask
for his inheritance. Jewish law of the time was clear on this matter. If the father was under pressure when he made his will, the will was invalid.[27] To my
limited knowledge, this aspect of the parable is unique in all Middle Eastern
literature in any language.[28] In contemporary life, I have uncovered two accounts of a son requesting his inheritance from a living, healthy father—one
Persian and the other Syrian. In both cases, the fathers were deeply offended
and gave the young men nothing.[29]

Thus, although the *modus operandi* is different, in each story the younger
son is involved in acquiring his blessing/inheritance from the father using
dishonorable methods. Both succeed. Unmistakable connections between
the saga and the parable have now appeared. Theologically speaking, the
changes made by Jesus continue to move in the direction of a universalization
of the story. The tale of a particular clan becomes a profound story about the
human predicament.

11.9 THE NEED FOR HASTE (A)

In each story the wayward younger son is in a hurry. Because the nature of
the deception is different, the haste factor takes a different form.

In Genesis 27:5-20, the deception is planned and carried out. Coached by
his mother, Rebekah, Jacob takes the "savory food" of goat meat into Isaac,
who thinks he is being offered recently hunted venison and exclaims, "How
is it that you have found it so quickly, my son?" Continuing the deception Jacob answers, "Because the LORD your God granted me success." The reader
knows that the real reason for haste is that he wants to complete the fraud
and receive Isaac's blessing before Esau reappears and blows his cover. Jacob
has already expressed his fear of his father's anger if they are caught (Gen
27:11-12). He barely makes it. After receiving the blessing he "had scarcely
gone out from the presence of Isaac his father" (Gen 27:30) when Esau appears and the cat is out of the bag. So the need to rush, rush, rush is very
much a part of the dramatic tension of the story. The reader senses this tension throughout Jacob's interview with his father. The very nature of the operation requires haste.

---

[27]G. Horowitz, *The Spirit of Jewish Law*, p. 374.
[28]Jacob does not *request* his inheritance. Through deception he stole his brother's inheritance.
[29]K. E. Bailey, *Finding*, pp. 111-16.

There is also an element of haste in the parable. All that the prodigal had he "turned into cash" after "*not many days*" (Lk 15:13); i.e., he is in a hurry. The reason is clear. He has violated his family's honor, and as he begins to sell his newly acquired assets, the village becomes privy to the deeply humiliating split that has suddenly erupted in the family. As he moves around the community trying to make sales, public hostility against him rises. Self-respecting land owners will have nothing to do with him knowing that what the prodigal is engaged in is a deep insult to his father. Someone will buy, but, in the process, community displeasure inevitably arises and gradually intensifies.[30] The reader is also left to reflect on the older son's anger, which, like Esau's displeasure, is no doubt also rising. The very nature of the prodigal's request requires that he complete his betrayal of the family as quickly as possible and get out of town.

Jesus could easily have left out the phrase "not many days later" and simply stated, "He sold all that he had and traveled." But the short phrase "not many days" opens a window for the listener/reader into the hostile reaction of the community. This subtly expressed hostility against the prodigal becomes a critical part of the story when the prodigal returns. Thus, the element of haste is reused in the second story for a different purpose, but the need for speed assists in tying the two stories together.

11.10 DECEPTION AND BETRAYAL (B)

Rebekah and Jacob deliberately set out to deceive Isaac, the leader of the clan, and his oldest son, Esau. Isaac is old and half-blind. The mother-and-son duo achieve the desired goal. Both the father and older son are not merely deceived but betrayed.

On the other hand, the father in the parable is not deceived. He understands precisely what is happening. He is neither physically blind nor psychologically inept. The prodigal is no doubt aware that clever tricks will not work and thus does not resort to them. His call, "Give me the share [of the inheritance] that is mine," is blunt and heartless. The older son, in contrast, is conspicuous by his silence in this first scene. He also receives his inheritance at that time but says nothing. The text simply reads, "He divided to *them* his life/living" (Lk 15:12, author's translation).

---

[30]The prodigal's haste gives the reader an important hint about the attitudes of the community. As the story develops, that same community becomes even more important.

So Jesus presents a father who is not deceived and yet accepts betrayal. Once again, the image of the Oriental patriarch is transformed into a metaphor for God. While it is possible to betray God through sin, we can never deceive him.

11.11 ESTRANGEMENT FROM THE OLDER BROTHER (A)

In both stories the younger son is estranged from the older brother. Jacob, with the encouragement, coaching and assistance of his mother, cheats his older brother. The deception is quickly brought to light, and domestic violence becomes a life-threatening possibility. Esau plans to kill Jacob.

In the opening scene of the parable, the older son is quiet. He too has his share of the inheritance assigned to him as noted above. The listener/reader expects him to refuse, but he does not. His silence alerts the reader that the older son's relationships with both his brother and his father are unhealthy. Even if he dislikes his brother, for the sake of his father he will intercede and accept the traditional role of mediator—an important aspect of traditional culture across the Middle East. When a break in relationships occurs in a family, the closest kin is under enormous cultural pressure to intervene as the mediator. The original listeners to the story expect the older son to take up this responsibility.[31] Unlike Esau, the older son cannot complain about losing anything that was due to him, but he can become very angry about the insult to the father, the disgrace the family has sustained in the community and the loss to the entire family of the income of a substantial portion of the estate. Because he is silent, the audience is left to imagine how mad he really is, and why.

In both accounts, the older son's anger lies buried like a ticking bomb ready to explode. The listener/reader waits for it to go off. This theme is yet another powerful thread that weaves the two stories together. On the human level, Jesus appears to be granting the Pharisaic audience their right, like Esau, to be angry. By so doing he draws them into the story. Because their view is authentically represented, they are on board as the story proceeds.

11.12 TO BURN OR NOT TO BURN THE BRIDGES (C)

As he departs, Jacob remembers his home and clearly intends one day to return. On his way to his uncle Laban in Haran, he spends the night in the open, where he experiences his famous "ladder dream" in which God appears and

---

[31]K. E. Bailey, *Cross*, pp. 33-35; *Poet*, pp. 168-69.

makes promises to him. In the morning he sets up a pillar and makes a vow that if God will help him "so that *I come again to my father's house in peace,* then the LORD shall be my God" (Gen 28:21). He has received promises but no saleable goods. He takes nothing with him, and thus the home community is not offended. The giving of the blessing and the deception involved occurred in private. He is only leaving because if his father dies suddenly his brother will kill him. If he can solve that problem, he can return home. In short, he keeps his options open, and all the bridges behind him remain intact.

The prodigal's situation is quite different. Having insulted his father and the community by requesting, receiving and selling his inheritance, he has offended everyone in his family circle and in the community, including the buyers of his inheritance. There is no hint that he contemplates returning. If he succeeds in the far country, it won't be necessary to return home. If he does not succeed, no self-respecting return is possible.

By revising this aspect of the story, Jesus is surely continuing to reflect theologically on the nature of sin. At this point in the story, sin is portrayed as wanting God dead, taking his gifts and demanding the right to use them with no thought of responsibility to the giver of those gifts or of one day needing or wanting to return home.

The two younger sons are now on their way. Scene two opens with each of them in the far country. How their experiences compare when they are far from home is the next stage of our journey.

12

THE EXILE

The Prodigal in the Far Country (Lk 15:13-19)

J acob's extended sojourn far from home in Haran was a grand success. The prodigal, however, journeyed to a far country and slowly descended into the abyss. We observe first the text and then a series of eight points of contact between the two accounts.

> [He] took his journey into a far country, and there he squandered his property in [expensive] living.[1] And when he had spent everything, a great famine arose in that country, and he began to be in want. So he went and joined himself to one of the citizens of that country, who sent him into his fields to feed swine. And he [longed to eat his fill with] the pods that the swine ate; and no one gave him anything. But when he came to himself he said, "How many of my father's hired servants have bread enough and to spare, but I perish here with hunger! I will arise and go to my father, and I will say to him, 'Father, I have sinned against heaven and before you; I am no longer worthy to be called your son; treat me as one of your hired servants.'" (Lk 15:13-19)

12.1 THE REBELLIOUS YOUNGER SON IN THE FAR COUNTRY (EXILE AND RETURN) (A)

In each account, the younger son, under a cloud, travels to a far country and remains there a long time. Jacob flees to Haran and stays for twenty years. The prodigal travels to an unidentified far (Gentile) country where people own

---

[1]The Greek word *asōtōs* literally means "expensive, wasteful." The word carries no hint of immorality (see the discussion on p. 102).

pigs. We are not told how long he remains there, but he begins his sojourn with a significant amount of money, which he wastes in "expensive living." He is certainly in the far country long enough to see good days and to experience a severe famine. Eventually, the famine catches up with him. A "great famine" means that at least a year's crops, but more likely two or three in a row, have failed. His descent to feeding pigs also assumes the passage of time. Finally, at the end of his rope, he decides to risk returning home. The story assumes an absence of several years.

Clearly, both stories deal with the topic of "exile and return." Exile from what and return to where or to whom? Jacob's life is a story of exile from his family and land and a return to both. In the process, Jacob becomes Israel. Looking backwards, Israel, as a nation, experienced exile and return in the sojourn in Egypt and passed through the same paradigm in the Babylonian captivity, which culminated in return to Jerusalem after the conquests of Cyrus. Thus, the two great occasions of exile and return are both instances of national exile away from the land of Israel and a return to it. Jacob's saga is the saga of Israel, and his story is its story even as his name, Israel, is its name. But precisely what "exile and return" does Jesus have in mind when he creates a new story patterned after the great Jacob saga?

The book of Isaiah contains four special songs called the "servant songs."[2] The second of these includes Isaiah 49:5-6, analyzed in figure 10.

1. And now the *Lord says*	LORD SAYS
who formed me from the womb to be *his servant*,	HIS SERVANT
2. to bring *Jacob* back *to him*	JACOB TO HIM
and that *Israel* might be gathered *to him*	ISRAEL TO HIM
3. for I am *honored* in the eyes of the *Lord*,	HONOR/STRENGTH
and my *God* has become my *strength* –	FOR ME
4. *He says*:	HE SAYS
It is too light a thing that you should be *my servant*	MY SERVANT
5. to raise up the tribes of *Jacob*	JACOB
and to restore the preserved of *Israel*;	ISRAEL
6. I will give you as a *light* to the *nations*,	LIGHT/SALVATION
that *my salvation* may reach to the *end of the earth*.	FOR THE NATIONS

Figure 10. The Servant Song of Isaiah 49:5-6

[2]Isaiah 42:1-9; 49:1-6; 50:4-11; 52:13—53:12.

The themes of the first pair of ideas in figure 10 match the fourth (God and his servant). Following this, the second pair of two lines (#2) centers on Jacob and *Israel,* as does the fifth. Finally, the third pair of lines (#3) focuses on how God has given *honor* and *strength* to his *servant.* In turn, the matching lines in number six tell of the *light* and *salvation* that God intends for *all peoples*—to the end of the earth. I have chosen to call this "step parallelism," and by observing the rhetorical form, the reader is helped to understand the author's intent. In the second pair of lines, a return of Jacob and Israel to *God, not to the land,* is envisioned. In the matching lines, national restoration is a part of the result in that Jacob and Israel will be "raised up" and "restored." The first of these parallel ideas (the *return to God*) is amazing.

As I have known them, exiled and oppressed people naturally and understandably have an intense focus on returning to the geographical places from which they were displaced. Returning to God is generally not on their agenda. They feel that their *oppressors* need to return to God. Inasmuch as they are the oppressed, such things are not required of *them!* But in this song the special servant is called on to tell Israel /Jacob that *they* are estranged/in exile from God and need to return to him. Is this theological vision a part of the outlook of Jesus of Nazareth?

In the parable of the prodigal son, the story focuses on a return to the person of his father and not to his tribe or land. The father is clearly a symbol for God, and thus the return to the father is a return to God. As we will observe, on the deepest level this can only be accomplished by the father going to the prodigal.

The suffering servant has the task of leading Jacob/Israel back to God, which is precisely the father's task as he seeks to restore the prodigal. It is possible to suggest that the theology of the suffering servant, formative in the New Testament generally, appears here as a part of the theology of Jesus. His task is to bring the exiles back to God, a mandate that includes exiles who live in Jerusalem and Galilee. Residing in the land of Israel does not mean that they have returned to the God of Israel.

12.2 The Older Son Stays at Home (Offstage) (A)

In each story the older son remains at home living under his father's authority for the entire period of his younger brother's absence. Both stories reveal nothing about what the older son does during those years. In both, the storyteller focuses exclusively on the younger son and what is happening to him in the far country. In each case, if and when the younger son returns, there is serious unfinished business with the older son that needs to be addressed and dealt with. Thus, one more parallel between the two accounts falls into place.

12.3 HONORABLE VERSUS DISHONORABLE ANIMAL HUSBANDRY (B)

While in Haran (Gen 30:1-36), Jacob works for a number of years herding cattle, sheep and goats, all of which are honorable tasks. Jesus is creating the story of the prodigal; he could have had the prodigal try to run a small shop or learn how to build stone terraces, but he doesn't. Like Jacob, he herds animals, but, alas, they are pigs! His very willingness to herd these unclean animals makes it abundantly clear that he is not in the process of becoming the hero of the story. That role is played by Jacob. Jacob is on his way up, while the prodigal is clearly on his way down. Pigs, versus cattle, sheep and goats, constitute a part of that descending spiral. But there is more.

The shift from honorable to dishonorable animals is also an important part of the interaction between Jesus and his Pharisaic audience. Luke 15:2 lists the Pharisaic complaint as "This man receives sinners and eats with them." In effect, they are saying to Jesus:

> Rabbi Jesus, we perceive that you do not take sin seriously. Your doctrine of sin must be superficial because you are willing to welcome and even sit down and eat with these defiled types.

Jesus replies:

> Gentlemen, I see that you think my doctrine of sin is shallow. Please allow me to explain my understanding of sin. I think sin is so heinous that it is like a young Jewish boy who demands his inheritance while his father is in good health. He sells his portion of the estate with his father standing on it. He goes away from the holy land of Israel and loses the money among the Gentiles. In the end he works for them *feeding their pigs!* In fact, his degradation is so profound that he longs to *become a pig* so that he might eat their food! This is my doctrine of sin!

The unspoken audience response is:

> Amazing! This young rabbi has a *magnificent* doctrine of sin. He understands our position. We could not have explained it better ourselves. He has not devised a straw man. This account reaches the depth of our revulsion against sinners. He understands the way we feel. No righteous person could possibly sit down and eat with such types. One would become defiled by so doing!

The continuity and contrast with Jacob is obvious. In both stories the main character herds animals. But the Jacob saga does not define sin, whereas the story Jesus tells does. This part of the story presents the first half of that definition. Jesus is in the process of reshaping the Jacob saga into a theological paradigm, and a clear definition of sin is an important part of that process.

12.4. COMMUNITY IN THE FAR COUNTRY (C)
Jacob lives with his family in the far country. In fact, he was sent there by his mother, and his entire sojourn abroad is under the auspices of his relatives.

The prodigal, on the other hand, is not sent anywhere by a family member. He alone chooses to leave, and he alone decides where to go. Once in the far country, he attaches himself to a nobleman who, because he owns pigs, is obviously a Gentile. Unlike Jacob, the prodigal does not work for his relatives.

This shift in the far country is important. The listeners know that if the prodigal dares return home he will face the *kezazah* ceremony discussed above in chapter nine. He has broken the rules and lost his inheritance among Gentiles. By making these contrasts between Jacob and the prodigal, Jesus is continuing to define his doctrine of sin.

12.5. SUCCESS VERSUS FAILURE IN THE FAR COUNTRY (C)
This parallel deals with sharp contrasts. The theme of wealth and poverty appears in each account. But they are reversed in the parable. Jacob begins life in the far country with nothing. He works hard, struggles and, with God's help, becomes rich. In short, he succeeds and returns home a wealthy man. Furthermore, he wins a struggle with a divine visitor on his return journey. That victory assures him even greater blessings.

In contrast, the prodigal arrives in the far country a rich man. Due to his own failures he loses everything, struggles, tries to make it and fails. In total desperation, after hitting rock bottom, he decides to play his last card by struggling home and volunteering for job training with the intent of recovering the money he has lost. He begins his sojourn in the far country as a rich man and returns home barefoot and in rags.

Once again Jesus has turned the Jacob story into a universal parable about the human predicament. The prodigal reaps the rewards of his own self-destructive decisions and lifestyle. Jesus is accused fairly of sitting and eating with these types. He does not apologize for them by saying, "These sinners are not as bad as you think." Rather, he paints a picture of their self-destructive degradation with all its gory details.

Jesus appears to be saying to the audience:

> We are Jacob/Israel. Like Jacob we began with nothing, worked hard, suffered, struggled and with God's help prevailed. This is a good record of which we can be justly proud. But there is a larger story, a universal story of which we are also a part, and this larger story exhibits a more profound aspect of who we are as God's children who have rebelled against him and squandered his gifts. In a larger sense we are still in exile.

In this reversal from rags-to-riches (Jacob) into riches-to-rags (the prodigal), it is possible to see even more clearly what Jesus is doing as he creates a new story that runs parallel to the well-known ancient story of Jacob.

12.6 FEAR ON THE EVE OF RETURN (A)

In each account, the younger son eventually decides to return home and does so with fear and trembling vis-à-vis how he will be received because of his estrangement. Jacob is "greatly afraid and distressed" (Gen 32:7) as he makes elaborate preparations, for he knows his entire company may be massacred. The prodigal prepares a speech calculated to give the impression that he has turned into a very humble man and is eager to work hard, pay his debts and earn his own way. Affirming that he is unworthy to be a son, he offers to become a paid craftsman. As noted, these moves are designed to placate the anger of the family and the community.[3] The plans are motivated by fear of starvation (which is expressed) and fear of the hostile reception he expects to receive from his father, his brother and the community (which is implied). Although the fear is expressed in different ways, its presence in each story further ties the two accounts together.

12.7. DIRECTION AND PURPOSE OF RETURN (B)

In the Old Testament, the verb *shub* (return) is used to describe both a return to the land and a return to God. Jacob returns to his family and to the land. The text discuses no return to God. Indeed, the saga does not so much as hint that Jacob feels he has done anything for which he needs to repent. God is with him at every turn with encouragement and blessing. Why then does he return home?

---

[3]K. E. Bailey, *Finding*, pp. 129-33.

Three reasons for Jacob's return are offered in the text. The first is because he senses jealousy on the part of Laban's sons, who are saying, "Jacob has taken all that was our father's" (Gen 31:1). Second, Jacob feels that Laban himself "did not regard him with favor as before" (Gen 31:2). And finally, God commands "Return to the land of your fathers and to your kindred, and I will be with you" (Gen 3).

The prodigal plans to return to his home community but intends to live independently as a self-supporting craftsman. With no promises from any source on which to base his plans, he returns to his father hoping, after all of his failures in the far country, to yet make it on his own. In the end, he is returned by God to God. There is no hint of a return to the land of Israel.

12.8 LACK OF REMORSE (A)

Jacob expresses fear but not remorse. Although he reflects on how to "appease" (Gen 32:20) his brother, he offers no apology to anyone.

As noted above, it is often assumed that the prodigal repents in the far country and that his prepared speech is an expression of sincere remorse. That remorse is thought to be an important, indeed necessary, aspect of his repentance. Such a view creates insoluble problems within the three parables of Luke 15. A full discussion of my study of this question is available.[4] Pages 103-10 above expand that material yet further. Here, only a brief note is necessary.

There are three clinchers to this topic. The first is the prodigal's motive, voiced in his soliloquy in the far country. He says, "My father's hired servants [craftsmen] have bread enough and to spare, but I perish here with hunger!" (Lk 15:17) He wants to eat. The second is the fact that his planned speech to his father, "I have sinned against heaven and before you" (Lk 15:18), is a quote from the mouth of Pharaoh when he is trying to manipulate Moses into lifting the plagues (Ex 10:16). The audience of scribes and Pharisees knows full well that Pharaoh is not repenting. Neither is the prodigal. The last is the fact that, after receiving the father's unqualified costly love at the edge of the village, the prodigal accepts being found and does not presume to tell his father how he, the prodigal, is going to solve the problem of their estrangement. Together these three keys alert the listener/reader to the fact that in the far country he is planning to work the system, hoping to fill his stomach.

---

[4]K. E. Bailey, *Cross*, pp. 37-62; *Poet*, pp. 169-90; *Finding*, pp. 129-62.

But in response to his father's costly love, he accepts being found and is brought back from death to life. Thus, on examination, it is clear that both Jacob and the prodigal start home without remorse.[5]

In summary, Jacob works hard, acquires wealth and prepares to return home as the successful hero of the saga. The prodigal loses wealth, feeds pigs and finally opts to return home a failure, hoping for job training and some form of sustaining employment. Through contrasts and comparisons Jesus continues to borrow from the old story as he creates a new saga that has meaning both for the children of Jacob and for the children of Adam. In the process, the themes of sin and repentance receive prominence. For Jesus' audience their views on both subjects are authentically represented.

The prodigal has failed. Now he must work and pay. Interest is heightened as the audience wonders how it will all turn out. The listener/reader looks forward eagerly to the next scene, to which we now turn.

---

[5]K. E. Bailey, *Finding*, p. 133.

13

PEACE FOR THE ONE WHO IS FAR OFF

The Father Finds the Prodigal (Lk 15:20-24)

The plot thickens, and the drama takes some surprising turns. Here we will follow Jacob and the prodigal on their journey home and try to understand the significance of the similarities and differences between the two stories.

> And he arose and came to his father. But while he was yet at a distance, his father saw him and had compassion, and ran and embraced him and kissed him. And the son said to him, "Father, I have sinned against heaven and before you; I am no longer worthy to be called your son." But the father said to his servants, "Bring quickly the best robe, and put it on him; and put a ring on his hand, and shoes on his feet; and bring the fatted calf and kill it, and let us eat and make merry; for this my son was dead, and is alive again; he was lost, and is found." And they began to make merry. (Lk 15:20-24)

Isaiah 57:17-19 reads:

> Because of the iniquity of his covetousness I was angry,
> ... I hid my face and was angry;
> but he went on backsliding in the way of his own heart.
> I have seen his ways, but I will heal him;
> I will lead him and requite him with comfort. . . .
> *Peace, peace, to the far and to the near, says the LORD;*
> *and I will heal him.*

The father has two sons. One is *far away* and the other is *near*. The father's task is to bring peace to both, and for each that peace will come at great cost to the father. In one sense the entire parable is a *midrash,* a commentary on these two verses in Isaiah. As in Isaiah, so in the parable "peace to the far" is presented first. To this peace of the compassionate we now turn.

13.1 DIVINE VISITATION/INCARNATION (C)

Both stories contain a divine visitation (incarnation). Jacob wrestles with "a man" who is quickly identified with God (Gen 32:22-32). By dogged determination Jacob wins the wrestling match and receives additional blessings as a result. He struggles "with God and with men" and prevails (Gen 32:24-32). In the process he is given the name Israel, which means "He who strives with God." The struggle involves bodily contact.

In the parable, the father (a symbol for God) leaves the house and in self-emptying love embraces and kisses his filthy son. The prodigal is the one who is overcome and surrenders, not to physical strength but to costly love. Once again there is bodily contact.

Thus, in each story, the returning younger son comes in bodily contact with the divine, incarnate in a person. But the nature and intent of that contact is very different. The first is a struggle; the second is a surrender within a sacrament of reconciliation. The prodigal surrenders to the costly love of his father, asking for nothing and receiving everything that really matters.

The father does not sit in the house in grand isolation waiting to hear what his wayward son has to say for himself. Instead, he gives himself in costly love. That love becomes incarnate on the road at the edge of the village.

The appearance of divine incarnation in each story is a powerful dramatic reality that further binds the two accounts together. As we will see below, the differences between them are of utmost significance.

13.2 RUN, FALL ON NECK AND KISS (A)

In all Scripture, only Jacob and the prodigal receive this threefold welcome. Granted, it is the prodigal's father who is the agent of this welcome rather than his brother.[1] But the change of agent does not lessen the effectiveness or importance of this dramatic incident as a tool for interlocking the two accounts in the minds of the listeners/readers of the parable.

In passing, it should be noted that Jacob and Esau were twins (Gen 25:24-26); for one to run down the road to welcome the other means that he is over-

---

[1]These dramatic actions will be revisited in chapter fourteen.

come emotionally and consequently rushes to embrace and greet his twin brother. Furthermore, they are out in the country where there are no witnesses other than their own traveling companions. But the father's running is a different matter. I have argued elsewhere that for a landed gentleman to run in public was to expose himself to public shame.[2] This aspect of culture is documented in early Greek and pre-Christian Jewish literature. Both Aristotle and Ben Sirach tell us that gentlemen do not run.[3] For the father, this extraordinary gesture is a *costly demonstration of unexpected love.*[4]

13.3 THE FAMILY AGENT (C)

In the Genesis story the agent of reconciliation is Esau, the older brother. The prodigal is welcomed by his father. This shift from brother to father is easily discernible as a critical component of Jesus' upgrading of the image of father, from an Oriental patriarch to a figure worthy of becoming an image for God. Again, Jesus is universalizing the saga into a parable with significance for the human predicament. He is saying "God is love, and this is a parable of how he acts even toward those who betray him."

13.4 THE MANIPULATIVE SPEECH (B)

Jacob is afraid his brother Esau still wants to kill him. Jacob has no army with which to defend himself. He has God's promise that "I will be with you" (if you return; Gen 31:3), and he has his wits. The flow of what Jacob has to say to Esau is as follows (Gen 33:10-17):

- Offering flattery: "To see your face is like seeing the face of God" (Gen 33:10).
- Giving gifts: If Esau accepts the gifts, he will be continuing to "stand down" in his apparent plan to murder Jacob.
- Getting rid of Esau: Jacob declines Esau's offer to travel together.
- Getting rid of all Esau's men: Jacob insists Esau take *all* his men with him.
- Promising to follow Esau to Seir: Instead, as soon as Esau is out of sight Jacob proceeds to Succoth.

Jacob wins all five rounds. He manages to manipulate Esau at every turn.

---

[2]K. E. Bailey, *Poet*, pp. 181-82; *Finding*, pp. 43-46.
[3]Sirach 19:30; Aristotle, *Nicomachean Ethics* 4.3.1125a (cf. R. McKeon, pp. 13-17).
[4]In Luke's Gospel, Zacchaeus runs, but he is running away from the crowd and climbs into a sycamore fig tree with large leaves. He does not want to be seen (Lk 19:1-10).

In the far country the prodigal prepares a speech for his father. The speech is made up of three elements (Lk 15:18-19, author's translation):

- I am wrong: "I have sinned before heaven and your sight."
- I am worthless: "I am no more worthy to be called your son."
- Here is what *you* have to do *for me!*: "Fashion out of me a craftsman."

With its three parts, this is a second manipulative speech. The first two affirmations are the set-up, and the third is the goal the manipulator (the prodigal) wants to achieve. But as seen, after accepting his father's costly love, the prodigal drops the third item on the list. As he does this, the entire tenor of the speech changes. It is transformed from an attempt to manipulate the father into an authentic confession of unworthiness. The first two items, standing alone, acquire the ring of sincerity.

13.5 Reconciliation with the Father (C)

Jacob's meeting with his father is almost an afterthought initiated by Jacob (Gen 35:27). The father is totally passive. Furthermore, neither Jacob nor his father expresses any need for reconciliation. Gifts are not involved, and there is no celebration.

In Luke 15, reconciliation is achieved through a gift of costly love offered by the father to his son. Once accepted, this love and reconciliation are sealed by the offer and acceptance of four gifts: the robe, the ring, sandals and the party. The reconciliation is deep and comprehensive. Jesus is unfolding yet further his understanding of salvation as a gift that the prodigal must recognize and receive.

13.6. The Location of the Meeting
with the Returning Son (B)

Esau does not wait for Jacob to come to him. Instead, Esau leaves "the land of Seir, the country of Edom" (Gen 32:3), and goes out to meet Jacob some distance away. The text offers no reason for Esau's movement. He does take four hundred men with him, which looks very much like he is planning some violent act. Perhaps he wants to meet the opposing forces in the open countryside. Josephus pictures Jacob anticipating a battle.[5] The biblical account allows us to imagine that Esau does not want witnesses to what he intends to

---

[5]Josephus, *Antiquities of the Jews* 1.20.3 (335).

do. In any case, he goes out from Seir and takes a small army with him, which says *something* about his intent.

The father does not wait for the prodigal to enter the village and the family home. Instead, seeing him "at a distance" the father runs out to greet him. His motive is stated in the text. He has *compassion.* This key word has generally been interpreted as meaning that he saw him in rags and felt sorry for him. This is no doubt correct, but, more than this, the father knows full well that the prodigal violated the customs and traditions of the village when he demanded his inheritance, sold it and left. The father also knows that if and when his son returns in failure he will be treated badly. From his side, the prodigal understands all of this. As he returns, he grits his teeth and steels his nerves for the gauntlet he is obliged to run on entering the narrow village street.

The prodigal arrives at the village during the day when his father is able to see him while he is "still far off" (NRSV). If the father can see him, so can the people in the village. On arrival at the edge of the village, to his surprise and shock, the prodigal witnesses his father *running the gauntlet for him!* Thus the action of "going out" from the home to meet the exhausted, humiliated son is transformed from a maneuver for some kind of advantage (military?) into a willingness on the father's part to accept upon himself the shame due the wayward lad. Jesus' redefinition of repentance/salvation, begun in the first two stories, now unfolds to its fullest extent.

13.7 THE RETAINERS AND THE
MOTIVE OF THE FAMILY AGENT (C)

Jacob sends messengers ahead to his brother Esau in "Seir, the country of Edom." Word returns to Jacob that Esau is on his way to meet him with a small army. Jacob is "greatly afraid and distressed" (Gen 32:3-8). Confident that Esau intends to kill them all, Jacob divides his people into two companies, hoping that the second may escape when the slaughter of the first begins.

With gifts, obeisance and some clever dialogue, Jacob manages to avoid his brother's murderous intent, but in spite of the initial embrace and kiss, the two brothers are never fully reconciled, as we have seen. Jacob smooth talks Esau into leaving with all of his men, and the threat is over. The implied orders to the retainers/army are an important part of the tensions of their meeting and conversation.

In the parable the father also has "retainers" with him. Although often overlooked, they are there. When the father leaves the house and runs down the road to reconcile his lost son, the servants/slaves[6] follow him. After the prodigal delivers his truncated speech, the father turns to the servants/slaves and gives orders for the robe, ring, shoes and a celebratory banquet. As is true in the saga, orders to the retainers, spoken or assumed, form an important part of the story.

Anthropologists tell us that "what everybody knows" is not explained. One learns "what everybody knows" by living with a particular community, learning its language and participating in its life. No foreigner is told that in the Middle East crossing one's legs while seated is an insult to everyone else in the room. Everybody knows such things! Time and time again Scripture confronts us with attitudes and actions that are a part of "the way things are." Such cultural attitudes participate in the "plausibility structures" discussed above. Looking for written explanations for the things that everybody knows because "that's the way things are" is nearly impossible. Sometimes one is lucky, as in the case, noted above, where both Aristotle and Ben Sirach assert that a gentleman is known by his walk. More often than not, crucial evidence is unavailable. The Scriptures do not tell us that the four hundred men with Esau are armed. Josephus and the rabbis add this detail in passing.[7] What is to be done when there is no evidence and when cultural patterns in the East and in the West clearly differ from each other?

Hosea 2:9-13 reports that God is fed up with his wayward wife (the nation Israel) and that he is going to "lay waste her vines, and her fig trees, . . . and I will punish her [for her worship of Baal]." The text then reads:

> Therefore, behold, I will allure her
>   and bring her into the wilderness,
>   *and speak tenderly to her.* (Hos 2:14)

A traditional Middle Eastern reader expects the text to read

> Therefore, behold, I will allure her,
>   and bring her into the wilderness,
>   *and kill her for her unfaithfulness!*

Evidence for this assumption is not available. The second is a mindset deeply embedded in traditional Middle Eastern culture. The first is the text of

---

[6]The Greek word is *doulos,* which was the common word for slaves.

[7]*Jubilees* fails to report the entire scene and only says, "Esau, his brother, came to him and was reconciled to him" (*Jubilees* 29:13).

Scripture that comes as an amazing surprise to the eyes/ears of the above-mentioned traditional Middle Eastern reader/listener. This is a case where one must ask whose "plausibility structure" should be used when two contrasting perceptions of the text, growing out of two different cultures (one of them Middle Eastern), are available.

The father's retainers in the parable present a similar case. Alfred Plummer, in his classical commentary on Luke, notes the speech to the servants and writes, "But the servants are not present. They would not run out with the father. Not till the two had reached the house could the order to them be given."[8]

I find no ancient literary evidence to prove or disprove this assertion, but "everybody knows" in a traditional Middle Eastern village that the servants would be expected to follow their master down the street (along with many other people). What is clear is that the father extends his unqualified love, hears the son's shortened speech and then, *with no mention of a time interval,* gives orders to his servants/slaves.[9] The story, simply read, presents all of this as happening in public. The father badly wants to parade his son through the village streets wearing the father's best robe because such a display will speed the process of the son's acceptance by the entire village. Thus the reconciliation scene is deliberately staged to guarantee the presence of witnesses. Publicly announcing the party will assure that word of the reconciliation, and the father's reasons for the celebration will reach every home in the village within a few minutes. The village *will not* attend a banquet to congratulate *the prodigal.* They *will come to honor the father.*

The father's retainers are most certainly with him on the road, but they are not an army moving out to confront an opposing force. Instead, they are a spontaneous group of the father's servants who are ready to do his will and concretely extend his visible expression of costly love. Feared agents of potential vengeance are transformed into agents of reconciliation.

This transformation would be noted by reflective listeners who knew the earlier story and were following the revisions that appear in the new account. Salvation, as understood by Jesus, is still in the process of being revealed.

---

[8]A. Plummer, *Luke,* p. 375.
[9]It seems only fair to suggest that the burden of proof is on Plummer.

13.8 THE KISS (C)

Jacob masquerades as his brother and manages to deceive his father. During their interview Isaac requests that Jacob draw near and kiss him, and Jacob does so (Gen 27:26). It is Jacob who must "come near" to his father, and Jacob must deliver the kiss. The kiss itself occurs just before the blessing is given. Thus it is the climax of the act of deception.

Multiple kisses[10] take place in the story of the prodigal, between the father and the prodigal. But the surrounding circumstances differ in the following ways:

- The *father* draws near to the prodigal instead of the prodigal drawing near to the father.
- The father, not his son, initiates the kissing.
- The kiss takes place upon the prodigal's return, not when he acquires his inheritance prior to leaving.
- The kiss that Isaac receives from Jacob is a final act of deception. The father is not deceived and never was. The delivered kisses are an unqualified offer of reconciliation by means of costly love.

Thus, the kiss between the father and the wayward son is radically transformed and becomes a critical symbol for the depth of the reconciliation the father offers his son.

Granted, Esau also kisses Jacob on their first encounter as a part of the "run, fall upon the neck and kiss" trilogy. Once again there are differences between the two accounts. Jacob's reconciliation with Esau is brief in that the two brothers immediately set off in different directions and do not appear together again in the story until they gather to bury their father. After that meeting, they separate permanently. By contrast, the reconciling kiss between the father and the prodigal is a prelude to a celebratory banquet and an assumed reconciled life together.

13.9 GIFTS ON RETURN (C)

Jacob returns a rich man. Thus he is able to shower Esau with gifts of flocks of expensive animals (cf. Gen 32:13-15).[11] These gifts are an attempt to stave off slaughter. Initially Esau refuses. He knows that to accept will com-

---

[10]The verb for "to kiss" *(kataphileō)* in the Greek text of Luke 15:20 suggests the repeated kissing of a standard Middle Eastern greeting; cf. K. E. Bailey, *Poet,* p. 183.

[11]The list is impressive. It includes hundreds of goats, sheep, camels, cows and donkeys.

promise the apparent plan to kill his brother because it would be seen as dishonorable to accept gifts from his brother and then proceed directly to kill him. Knowing this, Jacob presses Esau to accept, and reluctantly Esau does so.

The prodigal returns home with nothing for anyone.[12] Gifts *are in-volved,* but the prodigal is the *receiver* rather than the *giver* of the robe, the ring and shoes. The robe is his father's robe. The ring is most likely the signet ring of the estate,[13] and servants/slaves do not have shoes. Sons of a wealthy family do.

Because Jesus is turning a tribal saga into a drama of salvation, this reversal of wealth and poverty is critical. He is clearly affirming that sinners return to God empty-handed. The words of the well-known hymn, "Nothing in my hand I bring," apply.

13.10 DRESSED IN THE BEST ROBE (C)

Throughout Scripture, the theme of "the best robe" appears only in these two stories.[14] Furthermore, in both stories this "best robe" is taken from the pos-sessions of one member of the family and placed on another.[15] Once again, however, the two stories handle this theme quite differently.

In the Jacob saga Esau's "best robe" is stolen from him by his mother and then "put on" Jacob as important costuming for the deception. By contrast, the father in the parable willingly and enthusiastically orders the servants to take "the best robe" in the house (assumed to be his robe) and to "put it on" the prodigal. In short, the servants are ordered to dress the prodigal. Such a deliberate act symbolizes the comprehensive nature of the reconciliation that is occurring. As noted above, the robe virtually guarantees the community's acceptance of the reconciled son both on the road as they return to the house and in the banquet that night as the guests greet the prodigal.[16]

---

[12]Traditional custom requires that the traveler to a distant land return with gifts for the entire family. This is universal across the Middle East and beyond.

[13]Cf. K. E. Bailey, *Poet,* p. 185.

[14]A. J. Hultgren notes that Joseph receives a robe from Pharaoh in Gen 41:42 (*The Parables of Jesus,* p. 79). This is correct. However, the robe is described as "garments of fine linen," and it is not identified as "the best robe." Nor is it Pharaoh's robe.

[15]The "best robe" in the house is the father's robe. Who in the house would have a better one?

[16]On a different theological level, this same robe can be understood to reflect the "robe of right-eousness" of the Messianic age. Cf. J. Jeremias, *Parables,* p. 130 (cf. Is 61:10).

13.11 THE PROMISE OF LAND (C)

The Jacob saga is profoundly related to the promise of land. This promise appears at three points in the saga. The first instance is Isaac's speech to Jacob just before Jacob leaves. In that speech, Isaac says, "May he [God] give the blessing of Abraham to you and to your descendants with you, that you may take possession of the land of your sojournings which God gave to Abraham!" (Gen 28:4).

The second promise of land occurs on Jacob's journey to Haran, his first night away from home. In his famous ladder dream, God promises land to Jacob and his descendants (Gen 28:13-14). The third is given after Jacob's return, but before he meets his father Isaac. Once again, God appears to Jacob, and the promise of land is repeated (Gen 35:12).

The parable deals with the subject of an inheritance, but that inheritance is never identified with any particular piece of geography. This continues the already noted de-Zionizing of the tradition. Like other themes in the list, this idea first appears in the parable of the lost sheep.

As seen, the parable of the lost sheep has its roots in Psalm 23. In that psalm a good shepherd "brings back" a *single sheep* (presumed lost). Jeremiah and Ezekiel turn that lost sheep into *a lost flock*. The story of a lost person is rewritten as an account of a lost nation and its return to the land. As mentioned, Jesus incorporates elements from each account into his version of the lost sheep. With David, Jesus discusses a lost individual (like the prodigal), and following Jeremiah and Ezekiel he reintroduces the flock. The ninety-nine are last heard of "in the wilderness." In like manner the older son is not yet in the house when the parable closes. He is also lost in a "far country." Only in his case, that country is his isolation from his father and family, created by his own attitudes and actions. He is "in exile," and he embodies the ninety-nine sheep still in the wilderness in the first parable. Those ninety-nine are a part of the shepherd's responsibility; they remain a part of his flock. In like manner the older son is addressed as "my dear son" *(teknon)* even though in rebellion outside the house. Concern for the entire family remains, but the necessity for land is gone.

The prodigal is an exile from *God* rather than from the *land,* and his return is to *God,* not to *Jerusalem.* In his book *The Parting of the Ways,* James Dunn argues that this unwillingness to affirm the importance of the temple and the land is one of four main reasons for the division between the church and the synagogue in the first century.[17] Finding this concern for the community

---

[17]J. D. G. Dunn, *The Parting of the Ways,* pp. 37-74.

without an accompanying concern for a particular building or any particular geography in two of the three parables in Luke 15 is significant for understanding both Luke and Jesus. For Jesus, returning to God requires no particular geography.

13.12 THE HERO OF THE STORY (C)

Jacob endures trouble, prevails, acquires wealth and is given a new name. He triumphs over numerous obstacles in his exile and return and is the hero of the saga.

The prodigal, on the other hand, is the *heel,* rather than the *hero* of the parable. The role of hero shifts to the father. The one who finds and restores the lost is the champion. This theme runs through all three parables in the trilogy.

The shepherd finds his sheep, calls his friends together for a party and says to them, "Rejoice with *me,* for *I* have found my sheep" (Lk 15:6). The lost sheep is not the hero of the story—the shepherd is. In the second parable, the woman finds her coin and calls in her friends. In like manner, she says to them, "Rejoice with *me,* for *I* have found the coin" (Lk 15:9). The woman, not the coin, is the center of attention. In the third story, the father finds his lost son and orders a banquet. The celebration itself is a way of saying, "Rejoice with *me* for *I* have found my son!" He is the hero of both the story and the banquet.

For Jesus, both brothers are sought by the father at great cost. He alone is the hero of the story. Neither of the sons qualifies for that honored position. Commitments and lifestyles are to be modeled after the father, not after either of the deeply flawed sons. "Be merciful, even as your Father is merciful" (Lk 6:36).[18]

13.13 CHARACTERISTICS OF THE TWO SONS (A)

Esau does what is expected of him, whereas Jacob is a rebel who deceives his father and leaves town. In Luke 15 the older son remains at home, and, as far as we know, is a lawkeeper. The prodigal is a lawbreaker. This particular set of parallels is close, and it contributes significantly to the linking of the two stories.

---

[18]Cf. H. Nouwen, *The Return of the Prodigal,* p. 123.

13.14 COSTLY LOVE (C)

In the Jacob story there is no self-emptying love exhibited between any of the three major players in the saga.[19] Jacob does send costly gifts to his brother Esau and bows to him seven times, but the motive expressed in the text is fear, not love. Esau runs down the road and kisses his brother. Yet as observed, their reconciliation is short-lived. Esau returns to Seir, and Jacob, breaking his promise to follow him, heads for Succoth. As soon as their father Isaac dies, the brothers part company and never see each other again. Their descendants become bitter enemies.

The father demonstrates costly love to the prodigal. He does *not* take four hundred armed men with him as he runs down the road! A few hours later, even more costly love is offered to the older son. The two brothers are equally estranged from their father and in need of his love if their relationship to him and to one another is to be restored. Without those demonstrations of love, hope for reconciliation dies.

13.15 REPENTANCE/SALVATION (B)

Repentance and salvation are closely linked in biblical theology, and both need to be traced through the two accounts. Together they form a great diamond that sheds light in a variety of directions. This parable showcases one facet of that diamond.

Chapter twelve touched on the lack of remorse exhibited by both Jacob and the prodigal. The focus here is on the related, yet distinct themes of repentance and salvation.

Jacob does not repent of anything. He works hard and, with God's help, prospers. His attitudes toward his brother and his father show no awareness that he has done anything for which he needs to repent. He returns (*shub*) to his family and to his country—no more (cf. Gen 28:21; 31:3, 13).

Salvation comes to Jacob and to the prodigal in different ways. Jacob, with God's help, solves his own problems. The prodigal is found and restored by his father. This pivotal distinction requires further explanation.

---

[19]Jacob does place himself in front of his family as Esau approaches. Jacob thereby demonstrates a willingness to be the first killed with the hope that some of his family may survive. No doubt this is a sincere demonstration of potentially costly love, an offer that proves to be unnecessary. But this has little to do with his long-term relations with his brother and father. It is a part of his strategy for survival. He knows he is destined to rule over his brother, and, by bowing to him, Jacob is surely not surrendering that part of his blessing.

Earlier I argued that the prodigal in the far country works out a plan, his last option, to put food in his stomach. Responding to his father's love at the edge of the village, he accepts being found by costly love. Thus, at the edge of the village he is still lost and dead.

The 1980 Church of England Holy Communion liturgy includes a post-Communion prayer, which opens with "Father of all, we give you thanks and praise that when we were still far off you met us in Your Son and brought us home." In this prayer, David Frost is intentionally interpreting the parable of Luke 15.[20] The father saw his son and offered peace/reconciliation to him "while he was still far off" (cf. Is 57:19).

The prodigal "accepts being found," and that acceptance is his repentance. What he accepts is a free gift of unearned grace. Such a definition of repentance is already affirmed in the parables of the lost sheep and the lost coin. Here it flowers to its fullest expression.

In summary, Jacob makes it home on his own and needs no help from anyone on arrival. This contrasts with the prodigal who, at the edge of the village, is lost, dead, penniless, barefoot and smelling of pigs. Yet, he still believes he can solve his own problems. At that point, the father's love becomes incarnate, and, as a result, resurrection and restoration are freely offered to him. He accepts, and his exile that began before he left the house is—at long last—over.

The party is ordered, and the parable moves to its second climax. The listener/reader knows that the older son (like Esau) is angry and waiting ominously in the wings and that his appearance will be critical for the story as it continues to unfold. To that unfolding we now turn.

---

[20]R. C. D. Jasper and P. F. Bradshaw, *A Companion to the Alternative Service Book,* p. 243.

14

PEACE FOR THE ONE WHO IS NEAR

The Father's Search for the Older Son (Lk 15:25-32)

After his return Jacob interacts with both his brother and his father. These same three are on stage in the last scene of the parable as well. The comparisons between these two final scenes now need to be examined.

> Now his elder son was in the field; and as he came and drew near to the house, he heard music and dancing. And he called one of the young boys[1] and asked what this meant. And he said to him, "Your brother has come, and your father has killed the fatted calf, because he has received him with peace."[2] But he was angry and refused to go in. His father came out and entreated him, but he answered his father, "Lo, these many years I have served you, and I never disobeyed your command; yet you never gave me a kid, that I might make merry with my friends. But when this son of yours came, who has devoured your living with harlots, you killed for him the fatted calf!" And he said to him, "My dear son,[3] you are always with me, and all that is mine is yours. It was fitting to make merry and be glad, for this your brother was dead, and is alive; he was lost, and is found." (Lk 15:25-32)

In this scene the audience (the scribes and Pharisees) appears on stage in the person of the older son, who voices their point of view. Symbolized by

---

[1]The Greek word *pais* can mean "young boy." This translation, universal in Middle Eastern versions, is in harmony with the culture and with the story. Servants are in the house busy with the banquet. Young boys are gathered outside playing among themselves.

[2]*Hygiainō* translates the Hebrew word *shalom* in the Greek Old Testament. It can be translated "peace" as we have seen above.

[3]*Teknon* (son) carries the meaning of "beloved son."

the father in the courtyard, Jesus is also on stage seeking reconciliation with the older son. The compassion the father demonstrates on the road with the prodigal is the first climax of the story. This scene with the older son forms a second climax that is more intense, more costly for the father and more important for the larger scene because Jesus and the listeners (the scribes and Pharisees) are both symbolically on stage. Parallels between the saga and the parable continue. The following are worthy of note.

14.1 THE OLDER SON COMES IN FROM THE FIELD (A)

Early in the saga of Jacob, the father (Isaac) summons his older son Esau and tells him, "Go out *to the field,* and hunt game for me" (Gen 27:3). A few verses later, the text reads, "So . . . Esau went *to the field*" (Gen 27:5). When Esau returns we are told, "Esau his brother came in from his hunting" (Gen 27:30). The "field" is not mentioned, but it is presupposed. Because he went "to the field" to hunt, when he returns from his expedition he is naturally returning "from the field."

The last scene of the parables opens, "Now his elder son was *in the field;* and as *he came and drew near* to the house" (Lk 15:25). Familiarity with the parable has a tendency to dull the imagination, and it is easy to overlook that the original composer of the parable, at each turn, had to make a choice. Jesus could have had the older son come in "from the outside," or simply "from the village" or "from the gate." None of these was chosen. Instead, the older son came in from "the field."

In the modern period, commentators have noted that, in the parable, the phrase "in the field" helps tie the two brothers together.[4] Actually, a series of similarities between the brothers can be noted. Indeed, they both start "from the field." Each makes a journey to the house. Each son is welcomed by a father who goes out to each in turn. Both are estranged from their father. Each needs to accept being found.[5] These comparisons are valid and important. Anyone who focuses exclusively on the parable will no doubt observe this list.

But references to "the field" also connect Jacob and the prodigal. As noted above, Esau was sent by his father *to the field,* and the older son came in to the father *from the field.* Esau came in from the field just after his father had dealt with Jacob in a way that Esau did not like. In the parable the older son

---

[4]P. Perkins, *Hearing the Parables of Jesus,* p. 55.
[5]K. E. Bailey, *Finding,* p. 182.

approached the house from "the field" just after his father had dealt with the prodigal in ways that the older son did not like. This parallel provides one more link in the chain that binds Esau and the older son together in the minds of the original audience.

14.2 THE YOUNGER SON'S RETURN AND THE QUESTION OF SAFETY/PEACE (B)

Each story expresses concern for the younger son's safety/peace as he returns. Jacob hopes to go home *be-shalom* (in peace; Gen 28:21). The Greek Old Testament (LXX) translates this phrase "bring me back *in safety.*" Safety is a part of what defines *shalom,* but only a part. Granted, returning home alive is the focus of Jacob's speech, but *shalom* denotes far more than *safety.* Naturally, Jacob also wants to reach some kind of an accommodation with Esau because without it he cannot return. He also mentions bread and clothing, but there is no word about any strained relations with his father. He is certainly not estranged from his mother, and there is no hint that the clan is unhappy. The text focuses on his efforts at staying alive during his absence.

As has been observed, in the parable the older son approaches the house and summons one of the young boys in the courtyard to explain things to him. The *pais* (young boy) tells the older son the truth: The party is a celebration of the father's successful efforts at creating peace/*shalom.* Once this piece of the puzzle is in place, the older son's response is clarified and becomes credible. He is not angry over a *health report.* If the party is merely a celebration of the fact that the prodigal is home unharmed, it would mean that the father had not yet decided what to do with him. In such a case the older son would enter the house immediately to be sure his point of view was represented when the critical discussion took place (perhaps later that night). He wants no reconciliation without compensation. And he would not insult his father publicly over a health bulletin!

But if the party is in celebration of the success of the father's costly efforts at creating *shalom,* then it is too late to argue for restitution as a prerequisite to reconciliation. Only in this light does the older son's anger make sense. In short, *shalom* is a key factor in each story.

As seen, *shalom* for Jacob focused on food, clothing and safety. Jesus takes the same theme (which includes the idea of making it home alive) and emphasizes "he [the father] received him [the prodigal] in peace" (Lk 15:27, author's translation). The new focus is on reconciliation, not good health/safety.

14.3 ON ARRIVAL AT THE HOUSE BOTH OLDER SONS FACE "INJUSTICE" (B)

Esau entered into the presence of his father to face the stunning and shocking news that he had been cheated out of his blessing. He then "cried out with an exceedingly great and bitter cry" (Gen 27:34). Having been swindled, he is naturally angry.

Unexpectedly, the older son in the parable is also confronted with bad news, which he understands to be a great injustice. The details are given to him by the above-mentioned young boy. The lad announces that the banquet is in celebration of the father's successful efforts at creating *shalom.*

Once more, there is a slightly different take on the older son's response when looking strictly at the parable by itself, as opposed to examining the parable in the light of the Jacob saga that stands behind it. The older son's speech will be examined below. Here our focus is on the sense of injustice. Esau had the right to cry out with the pain and anger of great injustice. But, in the parable, is the father's banquet celebrating the *shalom* he has created an injustice to the older son? The older son certainly thinks so and verbally attacks his father for ordering it. Although Esau is mad and in pain, he does *not* attack his father. He could have. The loss of Esau's blessing is partly his father's fault.

By contrast it must be asked: Is the attitude of the older son fair? Not really. The older son *thinks* he is facing injustice, but as the father points out to him, all his rights are preserved: "all that is mine is yours" (Lk 15:31), his father tells him.

Thus the attitude of "I am being treated unjustly" appears in each account but with an important difference. Esau cannot be blamed for feeling he has been treated unfairly, but the older son's sense of injustice is unfounded.

On the other hand, if the older son's mistaken understanding of the purpose of the party is accepted at face value, then his complaints take on a certain validity. If, as the older son insists, the banquet is "for the prodigal," then perhaps he has a point. On the popular level across the church, most people accept that the banquet is indeed for the prodigal. But as we have seen, the older son deliberately chooses to *ignore* the reason for the banquet just given him by the little boy in the courtyard. His outburst is therefore built on his own self-deception, not on the reality of what is taking place in the banquet hall. The celebration is *for the father,* not *for the prodigal.*

Clearly, Jesus is telling his audience that their complaints are also unfounded. Yes, he is eating with sinners. But this does not lessen the Pharisees' rights and privileges before God. They have no legitimate reason to complain about his gracious acts.[6] Jesus does not eat with sinners to *celebrate their sin*. He does so to *celebrate his grace*.

14.4 THE OLDER SON BECOMES ANGRY (B)

The older brother's anger is, obviously, a key factor in each story. It is what both older brothers do with their anger that must be traced in each account.

In both stories the older son's anger appears twice. In the Jacob saga Esau's anger shows itself when he is cheated out of his blessing. On that occasion he becomes so enraged he plans to murder his brother Jacob. As noted, there is no expressed resentment of Isaac, who allowed himself to be deceived.[7] All Esau's anger is directed at his younger brother.

The second case of older-brother anger occurs when Jacob returns and Esau goes out to meet him with a small army of four hundred (presumably armed) men.[8] Jacob's terror reveals that he believes Esau is coming to kill him and his entire party (Gen 32:17-21).

Esau's anger is never resolved. He simply sets it aside temporarily for their brief, tense parley. But, as noted, the two brothers continued to live apart. Their reconciliation is superficial, and a long-term relationship fails to materialize.

In the parable, the older son's anger also occurs twice, once in an action and the second in a speech. Unlike Esau, the older brother's anger has a double edge. He is mad *both* at his brother *and* at his father.

At the beginning of the parable the older brother remains silent, and we do not know what that silence means. Only in the final scene does the older son give vent to his feelings. From the sound of music and dancing, he discov-

---

[6]The parable of the laborers in the vineyard in Matthew 20:1-15 deals with the same topic. The laborers who toiled all day are upset at the grace given to those who came late in the day. The householder then sharply criticizes the angry laborers, pointing out that he has treated them *justly* and that his grace to others is none of their business!

[7]The *Genesis Rabbah* consistently attacks Esau, but it grants that he had one point of merit: he honored his father. The same text claims that "Jacob carried out the whole of the Torah" (cf. *Genesis Rabbah*, trans. J. Neusner, 3:176).

[8]The *Genesis Rabbah* refers to these four hundred men as "armed warriors" (cf. *Genesis Rabbah*, trans. J. Neusner, 3:105). Josephus also assumes that they are armed. He mentions Jacob's fear of the likelihood of armed conflict (*Antiquity of the Jews* 1.19.3 [335]).

ers that a party is in progress in the family home. Thunder rumbles in the distance as he stands aloof and asks for an explanation from a young boy. The natural and expected reaction is to enter the house with joy and participate in the party. On discovering that his brother has arrived and has been reconciled by their father, he becomes angry over the fact of reconciliation without compensation. This anger is best understood as directed against both his brother and his father, but the father takes the brunt of his wrath.

The older son decides to punish his father in public by refusing to enter the banquet hall and to congratulate his father, welcome his brother and greet his father's guests. This is a calculated, serious public insult, and all the guests in the parable (and the listeners/readers) know it. The father then humiliates himself publicly by leaving his guests and going out to the older son, pleading (*parakaleō*) with him to be reconciled. At this point in the story we are not told what the father says. We only know the purpose of his self-emptying actions.

The older son responds to the father's love by delivering a bitter attack on both his brother and his father. The older son begins by accusing his father of favoritism, which can be summarized as "He gets a fatted calf, I don't even get a small goat!! You love him. You don't love me!"

He then refuses to call the prodigal "my brother" but instead refers to him contemptuously as "this son of yours" (Lk 15:30). Finally he accuses the prodigal of wasting the father's money "with harlots." Middle Eastern villagers kill each other over public accusations this strong. In fact, the older brother has just returned from the field and does not even know that his brother has appeared. How can he know such details? He is raging out of control.

But it is the banquet that truly sticks in his craw. As noted, the little boy has just told him that the party is in celebration of the success of the father's efforts at reconciliation. He is deaf to this message. This deafness leads him to the climax of his speech, which is the false claim that the banquet is in honor of the prodigal. "You killed *for him* the fatted calf!" he shouts (Lk 15:30). The unbiased listener knows that this is not true. The guests would not be there if the banquet were in honor of the prodigal. This climactic claim that the banquet is for the prodigal is the final thrust of his public attack on his father's integrity.

The wording and intensity of this angry barrage suggest that the older son is trying to define the prodigal as a "rebellious son." If he can make that accusation stick, the prodigal will be stoned as required by the law set forth in Deuteronomy 21:18-21.[9] Such a prospect brings Esau and the older brother even closer together. Both are *so angry* at their younger brothers that Esau contemplates murder while the older brother may be trying to build a case for capital punishment.

In summary, the unresolved anger of the older son is a critical aspect of each account, and it cements the connection between the two. Esau is never permanently reconciled to Jacob and, as the parable closes, the father's call to the older brother for reconciliation hangs suspended in the air. What will the father do?

14.5 THE FATHER RESPONDS TO HIS ANGRY SON (C)

Each father must respond to his older son's anger. Jacob deceives Esau. Esau asks for a blessing and is given one that tells him he will live by the sword far from "the fatness of the earth" (Gen 27:28) and that he will serve his brother but finally manage to "break his yoke from your neck" (Gen 27:34-40). These are the last recorded words between Isaac and Esau. It is a speech that says, "There is really nothing left, but here take this—you will spend your life fighting, become a servant of your brother and eventually break free of his yoke." When Jacob returns, the father has nothing to say to either of them.

In the parable the father *must* respond to the older son's rude behavior. With a large banquet spread, a houseful of important guests and hired entertainers already performing, the father cannot pretend his older son is not on the property. Some response is unavoidable.

I have been told by American Roman Catholic Maryknoll priests who spent their lives in China that in that country a father can kill his son for such a public insult. In the Middle East the father would most likely proceed grimly with the banquet.[10] Later the older son would be severely punished, and perhaps beaten. As seen above, the father in this story is not an Oriental patriarch. He is a symbol for God that deepens and expands the fatherly image for God that appears in Hosea 11:1-9. His journey from the banquet table to the older son in the courtyard is very painful. The father faces critical estrangement in his relationships with both sons, and each evokes from him a costly demonstra-

---

[9]K. E. Bailey, *Finding,* p. 179.

[10]There is a story from fifth-century Yemen that is built on a father's declaration that he must kill his son after the son insults the father at a public banquet. In the story the guests grant the father's right to do so but prevent him from exercising that right (cf. K. E. Bailey, *Poet,* pp. 195-96).

tion of unexpected love. In fact, the father's journey from the banquet hall to the courtyard for the sake of his older son is more costly than the humiliating public run down the road for the younger son because the insult is fresh and it takes place at a formal public occasion.

The older son is not impressed with the love offered him. Instead, he delivers the attack that we have examined. After a string of insults, the father has the right to cry out in a loud voice, "Enough! I do not have to take this! Lock him up! I will deal with him later!" He doesn't do so. Instead he gently appeals for joy.

14.6 THE ANGRY, AGGRESSIVE SPEECH (B)

Some time after Jacob prospers in the far country, he begins to sense hostility from the sons of Laban (Gen 31:1-2). At the same time, God speaks to him and orders him to return to the land and to his family. He does so without telling his father-in-law, Laban. Jacob's wife Rachel steals her father's household gods on the way out and takes them with her. Three days pass before Laban discovers that Jacob, Rachel and the household gods are missing, at which time he pursues and in time catches Jacob and his band. Laban searches Jacob's possessions looking for the stolen property, but, thanks to a ruse pulled off by Rachel, fails to find them. Jacob then delivers an angry, in-your-face speech to Laban. The essence of the speech is, "All these years I have served you . . . and you have not treated me justly" (Gen 31:36-42).

The older brother delivers a similar in-your-face speech to his father, of which a significant number of elements are borrowed from Jacob. Among these are:

- Hard service: All these years I have served you.
- Innocence: I am innocent of any wrongdoing.
- Injustice: I have been treated unfairly.
- Honor: My personal honor has been violated.
- Flawed self-understanding: Jacob's wife stole from her father, so Jacob's berating of his father-in-law is unfair.

Likewise, at the beginning of the parable, the older son also received his inheritance ("He divided his living between *them*"); thus, his complaint that he never received anything is also grossly unfair.

These five items strongly suggest that the older son's speech in the parable is deliberately shaped after Jacob's outburst. Yet there are important differences. In the saga, Jacob, the younger son, delivers the speech, whereas in the parable it is the older son. Jacob talks to his father-in-law, while in the parable the older son speaks to his father. There are no comparisons between one person and another in Jacob's speech. In the parable the older son compares the way he has been treated vis-à-vis the way he perceives his younger brother is being treated.

In spite of these differences, each speaker's central stance it the same. Both Jacob and the older son express anger that grows out of a sense of affronts to personal honor. Jacob's position is, "You have unjustly accused me of being a thief!" The older son's view is, "The prodigal is an immoral spoiler, and you have made a fuss over him. I am obedient and hardworking and get nothing!"

The similarity with Jacob's speech not only ties the two accounts together; the repetition of the "flawed self-understanding" theme in the parable encourages the Pharisees to look for self-deceptions in the older son's attack on his father. If that happens, they may be able to see the flaws in their attack on Jesus!

14.7 A YOUNG GOAT (KID) FOR A MEAL (A)

Both accounts contain the theme of kid meat for a meal. Rebekah orders Jacob to bring "*two good kids*" from the flock to feed Isaac (Gen 27:9). The older son voices his desire to have *a kid* to "make merry" with *his* friends (Lk 15:29). The first meal takes place. The second does not. Yet both feature kid meat on the menu, and both are set in the context of broken relationships.

Kid meat was occasionally used for sacrifices. But in the entire Bible, kid meat as food for people only appears in these two stories. I sense no theological reason for the mention of kid meat. The older son could have said "You never gave me a lamb!"[11] The reference to kid meat provides one more dramatic link between the two texts.

14.8 "ALL THAT YOU SEE IS MINE" VERSUS "ALL THAT IS MINE IS YOURS" (C)

Laban replies to Jacob's angry speech by stating, "The daughters are my daughters, the children are my children, the flocks are my flocks, and *all that you see is mine*" (Gen 31:43). He is saying, "All that is yours is mine." But Laban knows that he cannot expect his daughters to abandon their husband Jacob and return to him. He says in short: It is all mine—but I cannot acquire

---

[11] Abraham offers "a calf, tender and good" to his angelic visitors (Gen 18:7).

my rights. So Laban offers to make a covenant with Jacob that is a pledge to honor a cease-fire. To seal the covenant, Jacob offers a sacrifice, and they eat a meal together.

In the morning Laban arises early, blesses his daughters and their children (but not Jacob), and slips off stage never to appear again in any Old Testament story. The reader is left to conclude that both Jacob and Laban honored this covenant and in so doing finalized their *separation* (not their reconciliation) from each other.

Is there a reply to the angry speech in Jesus' parable? In the parable, the father listens to the older son's verbal attack and knows that he must respond. As he does so, he reverses Laban's stance. Rather than, "All that is yours is mine," he says, "All that is mine is yours" (Lk 15:31). In the story line the father is saying,

> I am not going to violate your rights. Your share is safe. Relax! I won't take a part of what I have already pledged to give to you and transfer it to your brother.

The great Syriac scholar Musa bar Kepha emphasizes this point as he reconstructs what the father is actually saying to the older brother. As a speech delivered by the father, bar Kepha writes:

> O my son, did I strip you and clothe him? Did I take off your ring from your finger and put it on his finger? Or did I pull off shoes from your feet and put them on his? Was it not from mine that I gave him, just as I gave even to you?[12]

On the theological level, Jesus is reassuring his Pharisaic audience that their rights and privileges before God are not reduced or compromised when sinners are welcomed into the kingdom of God by means of a costly act of grace. There is ample grace for all. Clearly, Jesus is "ringing the changes" of the earlier story as he constructs the parable.

14.9 RECONCILIATION WITH THE OLDER BROTHER (B)

Once again similarities are discernible and striking differences are evident. In the Genesis story, Esau is the family's contact man. Although formally reconciled, the reconciliation is shallow (Gen 32:20). On meeting his brother, Esau does run, fall on Jacob's neck and kiss him. But the rabbinic tradition was very skeptical about what the kiss meant.

---

[12]Musa bar Kepha, *Luke*, trans. A. M. Saadi, fol. 80b.

From the *Genesis Rabbah* we know that as the rabbis witnessed this kissing scene some of them noted that the Hebrew word for "kiss" and that for "bite" have the same consonants.[13] So, depending on the vowels added by the reader, the text can be read "he kissed him" or "he bit him."[14] *Genesis Rabbah* records that R. Simeon b. Eleazar (second to third century) pointed the Hebrew in the text in a way that affirmed "He kissed him in all sincerity." But R. Jannai[15] said:

> Rather, it teaches that he wanted to bite him. . . . But our father Jacob's neck
> became stone, and hurt the teeth of that wicked man [Esau]. [In line with the
> view that Esau bit his neck, but that Jacob's neck was turned to stone,] this one
> wept on account of his neck, and that one wept on account of his teeth.[16]

The *Midrash Rabbah* on Song of Songs compiles material from the Jerusalem Talmud and other early Jewish sources. Song of Songs 7:4 reads, "Your neck is like an ivory tower." The *Midrash Rabbah* understood this text as referring to the meeting of Esau and Jacob and explains the scene as follows:

> It teaches us that he (Esau) came not to kiss him (Jacob) but to bite him, and
> the neck of our father Jacob became marble and the teeth of that wicked man
> were set on edge and melted like wax. Why then does it say "and they wept"?
> One wept for his neck and the other for his teeth.[17]

These two early rabbinic traditions did not see the two as reconciled. These imaginative interpretations do tell us how the community understood the tale, but the story itself makes the same point clear. Jacob's language betrays his continuing fear. He says, "To see your face is like seeing the face of God" (Gen 33:10; he is still afraid lest Esau kill him; hence this gross, yet flattering, overstatement). Esau, however, refuses to accept the gifts. A refusal would have eased the path to the murder of his brother, while accepting them is to begin to back down from his murderous plan. Jacob, who is well aware of this, presses Esau to accept those same gifts and, once again, prevails.

---

[13]In Hebrew as in Arabic the consonants are written, and the reader is expected to supply the vowels.

[14]J. Neusner comments, "The words for bite and kiss share consonants in common," in *Genesis Rabbah*, 2:129.

[15]More than one rabbi had this name. The first is a Tanna (first to second century) and the second is a Palestine Amora (second to third century). It is impossible to determine which one is here quoted.

[16]*Genesis Rabbah*, trans. J. Neusner, 2:129-30.

[17]*Midrash Rabbah, Song of Songs 3.5.1*, ed. Freedman and Simon, 9:284-85.

Esau's next strategic move is to offer to travel with Jacob, but the latter refuses. Hovering between the lines of the story is Jacob's fear that Esau is still plotting violence against him. Finally, Esau suggests leaving behind some of his armed men. Jacob knows that Esau can easily give secret orders to his troops to kill them all once the big man is over the first hill. Esau will then deny any responsibility for the slaughter and claim that his men acted without orders.[18] Knowing how this game is played, Jacob presses Esau to leave *with all of his men.* Finally, Jacob promises to "come to my lord in Seir" (Gen 33:14). Seir is in Edom. As soon as Esau leaves, Jacob heads for Succoth on the other side of the Jordan valley. Having finally gotten rid of his brother and his dangerous army, he clearly has no intention of following him to Seir. As noted, at the conclusion of the story the father dies and the two brothers permanently part company.

In Luke 15 reconciliation with the older son hangs in the balance, awaiting his response to his father's costly demonstration of love for him! Jesus appears to be dissatisfied with the conclusion to the Jacob saga. He hopes and works for more, striving mightily to bring both the righteous and the sinners to repentance as he reaches out to find both kinds of lost people in the yearning hope that each might accept being found. The story ends with an uncertain conclusion.

14.10 A BANQUET CELEBRATION (C)

Shortly before meeting Esau, Jacob makes a covenant with his father-in-law, Laban. Their agreement is sealed with a sacrifice and a meal (Gen 32:54). Jacob offered the sacrifice. But Jacob's "reconciliation" with Esau was neither sealed nor celebrated with any form of symbolic feast.

In contrast, the father of the parable urges the older son (after his angry speech) to come in, join a celebratory banquet and participate in sealing their *reconciliation,* not their *separation.* The one who extends the invitation (the father) is the one who has ordered the sacramental meal (the fatted calf) and the festivities. The older son is urged to join the banquet, and a decision on his part is inevitable. He must either accept or refuse to participate.

---

[18]A well-known Middle Eastern proverb says, "When the wolf came, the sheep dog went behind a bush to relieve himself." The point is: If you are out of sight, no one can blame you for what you did not witness. Never mind the details. Herod the Great married into a powerful prominent Jewish family. His wife's brother was popular and good looking. Herod felt threatened. The brother-in-law "drowned" in the palace pool at a party. Such a shame! Herod was not there.

In summary, the Jacob saga tells of sacrifice that seals *separation.* Jesus takes this dramatic element from the saga and fashions out of it a banquet/ celebration scene that is intended to create and seal *reconciliation.*

As discussed above, table fellowship with Jesus is an important theme that runs throughout the Gospel of Luke. It is an integral part of the ministry of Jesus and an important focus of Luke's understanding of that ministry. Overtones of the theology of the Lord's Supper (the Eucharist) can be heard.

14.11 JOY (C)

Jacob returns home and is met by Esau. On meeting, Esau kisses Jacob, and the two of them weep. Almost immediately they separate, and they are never seriously reconciled. There is no indication of any form of joy in the account of Jacob's return, not even on the occasion of Jacob's finally meeting with his father, Isaac, at Mamre (Gen 35:27).

In all three parables, the theme of joy at finding the lost rings out "loud and clear." This theme appears as follows:

- The shepherd picks up the lost sheep with *joy.*
- The shepherd *rejoices* with his friends at a party.
- Heaven *rejoices* over the finding of the lost.
- The woman *rejoices* with her friends.
- Heaven again *rejoices* over the finding of the lost.
- The father orders a banquet where all can "*make merry.*"
- The entire company begins to "*make merry.*"
- The father defends his *joy* as he urges the older son to join the party.

Clearly, this theme is an exceedingly important new element that Jesus has introduced into his new story, built on the old. Joy flows from the one who *pays the price* to find and engulfs the one who *accepts* being found. That same joy echoes in heaven before the angels of God.

14.12 THE EVOLUTION OF THE SYMBOL OF THE FATHER TO A SYMBOL FOR JESUS (C)

As noted above, Isaac in the Jacob saga is an inept Oriental patriarch and no more. In the parable, the father is a symbol for God, but by the end of the story this symbol has quietly evolved into a symbol for Jesus. This transformation is evident from the text itself. The Pharisees complain, "This man *receives sinners and eats with them*" (Lk 15:2). Jesus replies by saying, as it were,

> Things are much worse then you imagine. I not only eat with sinners; I run
> down the road, shower them with kisses and drag them in that I might eat with
> them. Let me tell you a parable in three parts to explain how this works.

Furthermore, the little boy in the courtyard, when talking to the older son, affirms this identification between Jesus and the father. He says, "Your brother has come, and your father has killed the fatted calf, because *he received him* [with peace]." The key words here are "he received him." The father received the sinner/prodigal and plans to sit and eat with him. As observed, this is *precisely what the Pharisees accused Jesus of doing*. Thus, from the text itself, it is clear that by this point in the story, the father has quietly evolved into a symbol for Jesus. In the ninth century, Musa bar Kepha of Mosel in northern Iraq noticed this evolution.[19] He observed first that the woman is the Word of God that became flesh "and searched for sinners who were lost in sin." Later bar Kepha fuses the love of God for sinners and Jesus' actions in reaching out to the same. He writes, "Christ composed these [three] parables through which *he* [Jesus] demonstrates the love for humanity of his Father towards people and his care for them."[20]

In the eleventh century, Abdallah Ibn al-Tayyib of Baghdad picked up and expanded bar Kepha as he focused on the father. Regarding the father's kiss, Ibn al-Tayyib writes:

> From this action we learn the extent and scope of the joy with which Jesus
> rejoices at the repentance of the sinner. . . . In this expression also is a sign of
> the sending by God of His Word from heaven to this world to redeem the hu-
> man race.[21]

In the twentieth century Joachim Jeremias of Germany came to this same conclusion independently when he wrote:

> Jesus vindicates his revolutionary conduct by claiming in the parable, "God's
> love to the returning sinner knows no bounds. What I do represents God's na-
> ture and will." *Jesus thus claims that in his actions the love of God to the re-
> pentant sinner is made effectual*. . . . Jesus makes the claim for himself that he
> is acting in God's stead, that he is God's representative.[22]

---

[19]Musa bar Kepha, *Luke*, trans. A. M. Saadi, fol. 77b.
[20]Musa bar Kepha, *Luke*, trans. A. M. Saadi, fol. 77b (emphasis added).
[21]Ibn al-Tayyib, *Tafsir*, 2:272 (author's translation).
[22]J. Jeremias, *Parables*, p. 132 (emphasis original).

Three times in Luke 15 symbols for God gently evolve into symbols for Jesus. This transformation is of the utmost significance. In the Jacob story the father is an honored patriarch but is unable to hold his family together. At the end of the story he barely appears and quickly fades away. The father in the parable, as he evolves into a symbol for Jesus, offers the listener/reader one of the New Testament's loftiest affirmations concerning the person of Jesus.[23]

14.13 THE TWO SONS AND THE INTENDED LISTENERS/READERS (C)

As Luke presents them, the three parables of the good shepherd, the good woman and the good father are all about those who keep the law and consequently see themselves as righteous and those who do not keep it and are called sinners. Tension naturally develops in any society between these two basic types of people, and such tension was known in the world of Jesus.

We have already seen that the *haberim* (the companions) and the *am ha-arets* (people of the land) coexisted in second-temple Judaism. The first were the law-keeping scholars, and the second were lawbreaking common people. The Babylonian Talmud includes an extended discussion about the tensions that existed between the *am ha-arets* and the scholars. Tractate *Pesahim* reads:

> R. Hiyya taught: . . . Greater is the hatred wherewith the ʿ*amme ha-arez* hate the scholar than the hatred wherewith the heathens hate Israel, and their wives [hate even] more than they.[24]

But the feeling was mutual. The same section also says:

> Our Rabbis taught: Six things were said of the ʿ*amme ha-erez;* We do not commit testimony to them; we do not accept testimony from them; we do not reveal a secret to them; we do not appoint them as guardians for orphans; we do not appoint them stewards over charity funds; and we must not join their company on the road.[25]

One generation before Jesus the great Hillel stated, "A brutish man dreads not sin and an ingorant man [note: *am ha-arets*] cannot be saintly."[26] Such hostility between the learned and the unlearned can be found in most

---

[23]In Colossians 1:15 Paul writes concerning Jesus, "He is the image of the invisible God." This language is in harmony with the symbolism of the parable before us.
[24]Babylonian Talmud, *Pesahim* 49b.
[25]Babylonian Talmud, *Pesahim* 49b.
[26]Mishnah, *Avot* 2:6, trans. Danby, p. 448.

communities, but Jesus gives this tension a special twist.

The scribes and Pharisees who came to Jesus identified themselves with Jacob (as did all of Israel). Jacob, the younger son, *was* Israel in the sacred tradition, and Esau, the older son, became Edom, the enemy of Israel. This identification runs throughout the Old Testament and through all the literature of rabbinic Judaism. In light of this, an amazing and daring reversal takes place in the parable.

In Luke 15 the lost sheep, the lost coin and the prodigal son symbolize the sinners whom Jesus accepts and with whom he eats. At the same time, in Jesus' trilogy, the ninety-nine sheep, nine coins and the older son represent the audience of Pharisees "who [think they] need no repentance" (Lk 15:7). This part is relatively nonthreatening.

But if Jesus is retelling the Jacob saga, in that story the older son is *Esau* (that is Edom). It then follows that *Jesus' audience,* if it rejects sinners, *becomes Esau* and thus *Edom.* In turn, the very repentant sinners, whom the Pharisees reject, turn into a Jacob/*Israel.* Put another way, if the prodigal (once reconciled) is Jacob reborn (that is Israel), then the older son (if he rejects his brother) becomes Esau, who in the end permanently separates from his younger brother.

All of this is within the family. We are still talking about lawkeepers (Pharisees) and lawbreakers (sinners). Except, in Jesus' story, Jacob (the good guy in the mind of the audience) is rewritten and appears as the prodigal (a bad guy). In Jesus' new story the older son represents a second bad guy. The two sons each break their relationship with their father. The Pharisees, who have always seen themselves as Jacob, suddenly find themselves portrayed in the parable in the person of the older son who, if he rejects his brother, becomes Esau.

In the saga of Jacob, the point in the story where Jacob returns is crucial because it was at that point that Esau and Jacob finalized their separation. Jesus is trying to bring the family together. The prodigal (sinners) and the righteous (the Pharisees and scribes) are each offered an extraordinary invitation to join the party. This symbolic connection between the two stories may explain why the father in the parable puts out so much energy "entreating," that is, pleading, with the older son to be reconciled with the younger. Jesus *does not want the separation that took place between Jacob and Esau to be repeated.* Rather, he longs for a single family celebrating together at a single banquet. This drama and its attendant longing have been played out repeatedly wherever the parable has become a part of the identity of the believing community.

At the same time, the picture in the parable of an older son who mirrors Esau contains within it a message of offered grace. In the parable, the father pleads with the older son not to follow Esau's example and withdraw to a separate party with his friends (Seir?). The potential new Esau (the Pharisees) does not need to remain outside the banquet hall. Then as now, lost righteous sinners and lost unrighteous sinners can each accept being found and join with the host at the same banquet. Exile is only really ended when both brothers enter the banquet hall and celebrate with their father.

14.14 THE GENTILES (C)

After his return, and before seeing his father, Jacob is in contact with the Gentile family of Hamor and Shechem. A son of that family rapes Jacob's daughter Dinah. Smooth promises are offered to Jacob, but they are marred with hints of robbery behind his back. By means of a ruse, Dinah's two brothers from the same mother, Simeon and Levi, manage to kill the perpetrator, his father and all the males of the town. The scene quickly disintegrates into plunder and pillage (Gen 34:1-31).

The picture of the Gentiles portrayed in the parable is less harsh. The prodigal goes into exile among the Gentiles and descends to feeding pigs for a citizen of that "far country." But there is no violence. This citizen is not criticized for sending the son of an obviously wealthy family off to feed pigs without a salary. The prodigal does not turn to violence at his unjust treatment. Nothing more is said about any Gentile. But is it possible for the imagination of the reader to go one step further? On returning home, the ragged boy, defiled by contact with the Gentiles and their pigs, discovers an open-hearted welcome awaiting him *in his defiled state.* Such a reality at least raises the question of the status of the pigs' owners in the mind of the self-giving father. Is there a welcome awaiting them as well? We are not told. But this question is somehow raised and left dangling. In the saga, after rape and retaliatory murder, further relationships between the two families is impossible, at least for a very long time. In the parable, the door for further contact between the two communities is somehow left open.[27]

---

[27]As noted, *Jubilees* allows for no such contact between Jews and Gentiles (*Jubilees* 22:16-22; 29:13).

14.15 THE ENDING: PRESENT OR MISSING? (C)

The Jacob story has closure; the story finishes, albeit with a final break-up of the family. The father (Isaac) dies and is buried by Esau and Jacob, who then permanently separate. "Esau is Edom" reads Genesis 36:8. The country was so despised that *Edom* became a code word in rabbinic literature for Rome.

Unlike the parable of the lost sheep, the story of the compassionate father and his two lost sons does not end; it stops. In the last scene the major actors are all on stage, and joyous reconciliation between the three of them is still a realizable possibility. The reality of "repentant sinners," "the righteous" and Jesus coming together at a festive banquet spread at great cost by the father/ Jesus can and does take place in countless cultures and settings.

14.16 THE IDENTITY OF THE REMEMBERING COMMUNITY (A)

Moving beyond the text to its listeners/readers, each story is critical for the identity of the community that recalls and tells it. The Old Testament community took its name, Israel, from the Jacob story. For the prophets and the rabbis, Jacob and his story helped form the community's self-understanding. The two words *Jacob* and *Israel* are often interchangeable, as noted above in Isaiah 49:5-6. Again and again the phrase "the house of Jacob" appears as a title for the entire community of faith. To invoke the name is to invoke the story. Israel is not only remembering its racial descent from this ancestor. Were this not the case, the "house of Abraham" or "the house of Isaac" could dominate the text. By invoking "house of Jacob," the community affirms his story to be its story.

Although it is necessary to go beyond the New Testament period to see it, for centuries the story of the father with his two wayward sons has been called "the gospel within the gospel" (*Evangelium in Evangelio*). Along with the famous text of John 3:16, this parable has been viewed as a summary of Jesus' message within which the community that bears his name discovers its identity. Understanding the parable as a new story patterned after the saga can perhaps help shed light on Jesus as a theologian and expose central aspects of his theology.

This brings the comparisons between these two great stories to an end. At this point in the discussion it seems appropriate to interact with the insightful interpretation N. T. Wright gives the parable of the prodigal son. To that task we now turn.

15

TWO DANCERS IN A SINGLE DANCE

Reflections on N. T. Wright's Interpretation of the Parable of the Prodigal Son

In his monumental work *Jesus and the Victory of God,* N. T. Wright discusses the parable of the prodigal son in a thought-provoking and stimulating manner.[1] Because of the broad scope of what he has written, it is difficult, if not impossible, to interact adequately with the many theological echoes that reverberate on numerous levels from his reflections. However, a few brief remarks may be useful to the continuing wider discussion.

Wright's main thesis, regarding the parable of the prodigal son, is that it is a story of "exile and return" that is "designed to blow apart the normal first-century reading of Jewish history and to replace it with a different one."[2] Israel's history in both the exodus and the exile was a story of "exile and return," and the prodigal is a symbol of that same classical movement. In the parable, Wright argues, the real exile and return occurs in Jesus' own ministry. I perceive that Wright and I are climbing (and describing) the same mountain but from different sides.

Wright's call for a "criterion of double similarity" needs to be taken with utmost seriousness. He argues that when an understanding of Gospel texts fits into the world of first-century Judaism and at the same time functions "credibly as the implied starting point (though not the exact replica) of something in later Christianity, [there] is a strong possibility of our being in touch with the genuine history of Jesus."[3]

---

[1]N. T. Wright, *Jesus and the Victory of God,* pp. 125-44.
[2]N. T. Wright, *Jesus and the Victory of God,* p. 126.
[3]N. T. Wright, *Jesus and the Victory of God,* p. 132.

As indicated in the preface, the concern of this work is the theology of Jesus in his first-century Jewish setting. This Jesuic starting point is demonstrably the foundation of early Christianity.[4] No one is more completely saved by grace (the message of the Epistle to the Romans) than the prodigal son. But the developing Christian theology of the Epistles and of the Gospel historians and theologians is beyond the focus of this inquiry. Yet, within the limits of this quest, it is appropriate to ask two related questions: (a) What does Jesus say in this parable to individuals and groups of listeners as he answers the Pharisees' complaint, "This man receives sinners and eats with them"? (b) Is Jesus also talking to Israel as a whole as he creates this parable, and, if so, what is he saying to the nation?

Throughout this book I have attempted to answer in detail the first of these questions. On the level of lawkeeping and lawbreaking sinners, Jesus presents two points of view:

- The prodigal (in the far country) says, "I will work and pay—and everything can thereby be made right."
- The older son says, "I have worked and I have obeyed, and everything is fine as long as my standards are maintained."

Both are wrong, and both are lost and in "exile." The father must pay a high price to restore each of his sons. This applies on the personal level and at the level of the various parties around Jesus, such as the scribes, the Pharisees and the "people of the land." Yet the parable also has a wider application as it depicts the crisis of the nation, as Wright has so ably argued.

But Israel is not merely *the prodigal* returning home from exile. Israel includes *two sons,* both of whom start "in the field." Each moves toward the house. Each, at some point, defines his relationship to the father as that of a servant. Each breaks his relationship with the father on a very deep level. The father suffers to reconcile each. Both must accept being found, for only then can the real return from exile be accomplished. Their exile is not from the land but from their father's heart. The prodigal is still in exile at the edge of the village while the older son is in exile in the courtyard of the house. The prodigal's return "from the field" with the pigs means nothing if, at the edge of the village, he insists on becoming a paid craftsman and thereby refuses to be found and brought from death to life. Likewise, the return of the older son

---

[4]Cf. C. H. Dodd, *The Founder of Christianity.*

"from the field" signifies nothing if he refuses to accept his father's love and continues his "exile" in the courtyard of the family home.

As noted, Jesus is addressing not only individuals and groups within the community, like the Pharisees, but the nation as well. Both the saga of Jacob and the parable of the compassionate father deal with a family. Genesis 27:1—36:8 focuses on a father and two sons, as does the parable. Each text is deeply concerned for the entire family. Thus the topic of the significance of Jesus' parable for the nation requires investigation.

Wright investigates the importance of the parable for the nation. He sees this story as applying both to the *exodus* (the sojourn in Egypt and the return from Egypt) and to the *exile* (the captivity in Babylon and the return from that captivity). He writes:

> The exodus itself is the ultimate backdrop; Israel goes off into a pagan country, becomes a slave, then is brought back to her own land. But exile and restoration is the main theme. This is what the parable is about.[5]

I readily grant that exile and return is the main theme of the parable of the two lost sons. But any attempt at finding too close a parallel (or a set of parallels) between the exodus, the exile and the parable creates problems for interpretation. Jacob and his family migrated to Egypt because of a famine. They did not leave their homeland under a cloud of sin related to tensions and ambitions within the family, as did the prodigal and Jacob. They were not driven into exile by God because of their worship of idols.

Too close a tie between the parable and the details of the exodus further complicates the overall interpretation of the parable. Wright suggests that the older son (who opposes the prodigal's acceptance at home) can be identified with Pharaoh (who tries to stop Israel from returning home).[6] But the older son did not try to stop the prodigal from leaving the far country as Pharaoh attempted to do with Israel. Such a part *could* easily have been played by the citizen in the far country who hired the prodigal to feed his pigs. That citizen could have come on stage and done his best to prevent the prodigal from starting home. Said citizen would understandably not want to lose a pig herder whom he does not have to pay, but unlike Pharaoh the citizen does not oppose the prodigal's return. In fact no one attempts to stop him.

---

[5] N. T. Wright, *Jesus and the Victory of God,* p. 126.
[6] N. T. Wright, *Jesus and the Victory of God,* p. 130.

Close comparisons with the exodus and the exile introduce other compli-cations. Among them are the following.

(a) A difficulty emerges with the exile in Babylon, where the older broth-er, in Wright's view, parallels the Samaritans.[7] The Samaritans oppose the re-turning Jews. There is no group that welcomes the Jews back. In contrast, the older son quarrels with the *father* and his actions. The reader knows that the older son does not like his brother, but the older son's anger is focused on the father's welcome, not the fact of the prodigal's return.

(b) Wright suggests that the prodigal is "brought back" like Israel out of Egypt. This is also problematic. Indeed, the tradition affirms that Israel was brought back by God, but there is no such hint in the account of the return of the prodigal. The prodigal is not brought back, or helped back from the far country, by his father or by anyone else.

(c) The authenticity of the prodigal's repentance in the far country is a fur-ther difficulty. Wright observes, "When, therefore, Israel comes to her sens-es, and returns *with all her heart,* there is an astonishing, prodigal, lavish welcome waiting for her."[8] This assumes that the phrase "he came to himself" (Lk 15:17), used to describe the prodigal in the far country, is authentic re-pentance as taught by Jesus. As I have argued at length in this study, if this be the case, then the parables of the lost sheep and the lost coin are false pre-sentations of Jesus' views. In both of those stories the key figure must work hard to find the lost. The lost do not come home of their own accord.

Does the third story (the parable of the prodigal son) contradict the two parables that immediately precede it? Surely not. Rather, the parable of the prodigal son presents two views of repentance. The first is the audience's view of repentance, which Jesus shows to be inauthentic. The second is the new, authentic view he presents. The audience's perception is demonstrated by the prodigal in the far country, who in effect says:

> I will solve my own problem. I will apologize, get job training, become a skilled craftsman, earn money and pay back what I have lost. My only problem is a cash-flow shortage and the resulting fact that I am starving.

The second view of repentance is presented at the edge of the village, where a costly demonstration of unexpected love breaks through to the prod-

---

[7] N. T. Wright, *Jesus and the Victory of God,* p. 130.
[8] N. T. Wright, *Jesus and the Victory of God,* p. 129 (emphasis added).

igal, who at long last realizes that money is not the issue. When he sees his father getting hurt for him, he suddenly discovers that he has a broken relationship that needs restoration. He "accepts being found" by costly love, and a new world opens that can only be adequately described with the language of resurrection. This resurrection does not take place in the far country. It happens at the edge of the village when he accepts the unqualified grace offered to him by his father. As he arrives at the edge of the village, *the prodigal is still in exile!*

Jubilees rewrote the saga of Jacob, as did Josephus. The rabbis commented on the fixed text. Philo chose to philosophize on it. Jesus writes a new story, but that new tale reuses, revises and reverses primary elements from the old. As regards "exile and return," I would suggest that Wright is correct in observing that Jesus' parable relates to that classical movement. Perhaps it is helpful to see four distinct journeys of exile and return, each with its own unique elements. These are:

- Out of fear Jacob goes into *exile to Haran* and *returns to Succoth.*

- Jacob's family *migrates to Egypt* because of famine, and centuries later, with God's help, *returns* at the time of *the exodus.*

- Israel is driven by God into *exile in Babylon,* and a part of the community *returns under Cyrus.*

- Jesus tells a new story about exile and return, and those around him hear this story as a *unique addition* to this series, an addition that is fashioned out of the saga of Jacob. They also understand this new story as containing a description of his own person and mission.

Naturally, the "unique addition" has a new twist. Wright correctly affirms, "The real return from exile . . . is taking place, in an extremely paradoxical fashion, in Jesus' own ministry."[9]

It is clear that for Jesus the problem for the nation is not simply a matter of unfulfilled "perks" of restoration promised by the prophets to the people on their return from exile. Rather Jesus sees the Essenes, Pharisees, scribes and indeed Zealots on one side taking the law very, very seriously. He also sees the "people of the land," who were slack about the law and thus despised, on the other side. Both groups assumed that their physical presence

---

[9]N. T. Wright, *Jesus and the Victory of God,* p. 127.

in the land demonstrated that they had already returned from exile. Jesus'
new "exile and return" vision thunders at them:

> Both of you are still in exile! Both of you are sinners! Both of you live unrecon-
> ciled to God! The divine presence of God is with you in me, and I am among
> you calling on you to be reconciled to him. I am eager to welcome and eat with
> both kinds of sinners. I will eat with Simon the Pharisee and in his presence de-
> fend a sinful woman who makes up for his mistakes. I will also eat with Mat-
> thew the tax collector and his friends. I am among you in the landowner who
> pays all workers a living wage irrespective of how long they have worked.
> When you accept being found by my costly love, you are authentically brought
> back from your real exile, and the lost are found and the dead brought to life as
> you are reconciled to God.

As Wright eloquently says:

> In telling this story, he [Jesus] is explaining and vindicating his own practice of
> eating with sinners; his celebratory meals are the equivalent, in real life, of the
> homecoming party in the story. They are the celebration of the return from ex-
> ile. What is more, Jesus is claiming that, when he does all this, Israel's god is
> doing it, welcoming sinners no matter whether they have passed all the normal
> tests for membership, as long as they will accept the welcome of Jesus.[10]

To this statement I would only suggest one emendation. The banquet in
the parable is perhaps better described as a celebration of *"restoration* from
exile." This "restoration from exile" occurs at the edge of the village and is
accomplished by the father (as the father and the young boy in the parable
make clear). Also, the parable affirms that the state of exile applies to the older son as much as it does to the younger. The extraordinary efforts of the father before and during the celebration are directed first to one son and then
to the other in heroic attempts at bringing both sons back from exile, and at
restoring each from death to life.

Jesus is indeed addressing the entire nation. As noted, both lawkeepers
and lawbreakers are in exile. He goes to them in their exile and is willing finally to pay the ultimate price of his own life to bring them back from exile.

The parable of the lost sheep has the same basic dynamics. There are three
elements in the story: a flock, a shepherd and a lost sheep. It is impossible to
imagine that the shepherd is indifferent to the fate of the entire flock. In the

---

[10]N. T. Wright, *Jesus and the Victory of God,* p. 130.

parable he carries the lost sheep back to the village. The story stops with the ninety-nine still "in the wilderness." The listener instinctively asks, "Isn't the shepherd going to go after them as well?" The answer to this question appears in the third story when the father first "brings back" the lost younger son and then does his best to rescue the older son. Together they are the flock/Israel/the family. Getting the family together/at home/at the banquet table with him is his goal. This is the authentic return from exile.

The looming battle with Rome is misguided. Among the twelve apostles Jesus includes a tax collector (the worst of sinners) and a Zealot (the most aggressive of the lawkeepers).[11] This is by choice! There is no hint anywhere in the Gospel tradition that these two were not reconciled. Jesus' new vision of exile and return can save the nation by redirecting its energies to its *real problem,* which is its *exile from God.* When his solution is not accepted by the majority, he knows the result will be tragic for the nation. He is fully able to "interpret the present time" (Lk 12:56). This awareness leads him to weep over Jerusalem, to prophesy against her and, on the way to his cross, to warn the women of the terrible inevitable consequences of the nation's rejection of his solution to its continued exile from God.

"Exile and return" is indeed a paradigm at the heart of Jesus' message—for the individual, for groups within the nation and for the nation itself. Jesus speaks to all three in this parable, which is newly created on the foundation of the saga of Jacob and is, at the same time, a new addition to the classical historical episodes of exile and return experienced in the exodus and in the exile.

I perceive that what I propose and what N. T. Wright has suggested are, to a large extent, complementary. Our separate studies perhaps supplement each other like two dancers in a single dance.

All that remains is to draw a number of conclusions and to summarize what these fifty-one parallels mean for a fresh understanding of Jesus as a theologian.

---

[11]Functioning between A.D. 6 and 70, the Zealots were founded by a scribe (Judas the Galilean) and a Pharisee (Saddok). Martin Hengel demonstrates that this movement was "firmly rooted in the Jewish and Pharisaical tradition" and "may be regarded" as the extreme left wing of the Pharisees. Part of their agenda involved killing Jews who cooperated with the Roman authorities (cf. M. Hengel, *The Zealots,* pp. 87, 76-145).

SIGNIFICANCE OF THIS STUDY FOR AN UNDERSTANDING OF JESUS' THEOLOGY

16

A Summary of the Significance of the Comparisons Between Jacob and the Prodigal for Aspects of Jesus' Theology

After reflecting on methodology and authenticity, this study began with an examination of the parables of the good shepherd, the good woman and the good father in the light of the cultural and theological world of Jesus. I then noted what Philo, Josephus, the book of *Jubilees* and the early rabbis did with Genesis 27:1—36:8. Finally, I compared the parable of the prodigal son and the saga of Jacob. Fifty-one common dramatic elements were discovered (in one form or another) in the two stories.

It is now appropriate to attempt a brief answer to the question: What difference does it make to our understanding of the theological content packed into the parable by Jesus when we observe that the Jacob story lies behind it? What fresh insights into the mind of Jesus are available when we stand with the scribes and Pharisees and hear Jesus answering their challenge by telling a new story built on the saga of Jacob?

It is not easy to contemplate a diamond from all angles at once. Nor is it possible to appreciate the full grandeur of a great mountain while climbing one face at a time. But we will try. Some dramatic elements that appear in each story seem to be theologically neutral. After a brief overview of these elements, I will concentrate on four themes that present themselves with particular force when observed in the parable with the saga of Jacob in the background. These are:

- Sin (How is sin defined in this parable?)
- The nature of God (What is Jesus saying about God?)
- Christology (What does the parable affirm about the person of Jesus?)
- Repentance/salvation (What is said in the parable about these two great interlocking themes?)

Initially, what dramatic elements appear in the parable and function primarily as threads to help weave the two stories together? Three of the four scenes contain these theologically relatively neutral ties.[1]

In the first scene it is immediately evident that each story has a father and two sons. The pattern of Moses, Aaron and Miriam will not do. Isaac had two sons. The parable duplicates the triangle of one father and two sons (11.5). In each account the younger son acquires the blessing/inheritance using underhanded methods. The differences are significant and will be summarized below. Yet each story opens with this theme (11.8). The need for haste is quite important in the first story. This element could have been omitted in the second. The linkage with Jacob appears to be the primary reason for its appearance in the parable (11.9).

In the second scene neither account provides any information about the older son during the absence of the younger brother in the far country. In both cases the older son is simply at home, presumably doing what he is told (12.2). Each of the younger sons is afraid on the eve of his return. They try to deal with their fears in different ways, but both are afraid (12.6).

In the last scene both older sons come in from "the field" (14.7). The appearance of goat meat for a meal in the two stories has no apparent theological significance. As a theme it merely helps bind the two stories together (14.1). Gentiles appear in each story. Although they interact with the main characters very differently, their presence forms a connection (14.13). Jesus appears to include these details to be *very sure* that his Jewish listeners know he is creating a new saga for Israel's life. This brings us to the four theological themes mentioned above.

SIN: HOW IS SIN DEFINED IN THE PARABLE?

The parable begins with the younger son wanting his father dead (11.1). This contrasts sharply with the saga because Jacob has no such wish. In the

---

[1] I will continue to use the number designations from the previous chapters to make it possible for the reader to check the fuller discussion if desired.

parable Jesus is turning a traditional account into a story that applies both to the nation and to the human predicament. This death wish is a critical element in that process. On the deepest level, sinners want God dead and out of their lives. By expressing such a desire, the prodigal causes a radical break in his relationship with his father (11.2). Sin, as here defined by Jesus, is primarily a broken relationship with a person and not merely a broken statute in a legal code. The prodigal burns his bridges (11.12). Jacob does not. Again, the radical nature of sin is set forth. Sinners move away from God with no thought of return.

The prodigal's journey into the far country widens the gap between him and his family. Jacob, even in the far country, is with his family (12.4). While in that distant land, the prodigal descends into the abyss of feeding pigs for Gentiles and even wishes he could become a pig so that he could eat their food (12.3). The utter revulsion in the Jewish mind of such a thought makes clear the seriousness with which Jesus views the problem of evil. The prodigal fails miserably at finding a paying job that will generate enough cash to make reconciliation with the family a possibility (12.5). After losing the money, but before going off to feed pigs, the prodigal was in the same financial position as Jacob when he arrived in Haran. That is, Jacob began poor, worked hard and became rich. The prodigal descended from wealth not only to poverty but to degradation. He was unable to succeed on his own. Sin, as defined by Jesus, is a problem sinners cannot solve alone.

In the final scene in the parable Jesus sets forth a second type of sin. The saga has a "good guy" (Jacob) and a "bad guy" (Esau), while the parable has two "bad guys." Lawbreakers (such as the prodigal) and lawkeepers (like the older brother) break their relationships with God their father. This severed relationship causes their continued "exile" from God (13.13). With these shifts of emphasis, Jesus reveals important aspects of his understanding of evil. What then of the nature of God?

THE NATURE OF GOD: WHAT IS JESUS SAYING ABOUT GOD?

The image of God as father is here depicted in its most compassionate life-giving and life-changing form. No sacred literature in any tradition known to me surpasses it (11.3).

We noted Islamic opposition to applying human metaphors to God. Addressing God as Father is to liken God to a human being, Islam insists, and in its view such a comparison will lead inevitably to idolatry. As Kenneth Cragg writes, "Islam here falls back upon a final agnosticism."[2] God's nature is unknown; only his will is revealed. By contrast, this parable gives rich meaning to an important part of the biblical affirmation "God is love." Only in God's actions in history, in the incarnation and the passion of Jesus, is the love of God given its fullest expression. Both those themes are embedded in the parable (13.15).

All through the parable the process of "upgrading" is evident. The inept Oriental patriarch (Isaac) is replaced by the compassionate father and his costly love—a love that includes the tender compassion of a mother (11.4). Both sons deeply offend the father, but their offense in no way lessens his love and faithfulness to them. As observed, the father in the parable evolves into a symbol for Jesus. What therefore is the Christology of the parable?

CHRISTOLOGY: WHAT IS JESUS SAYING ABOUT HIMSELF?
Each account contains a divine visitation and the contrasts between the two are outlined above (13.1). The father empties himself twice to offer costly love to his wayward sons (13.2; 14.5). No other possible action can achieve the goal of reconciliation with himself and reconciliation between the two brothers. Such reconciliation did not take place in the Jacob saga. The parable offers new options that can make such a reconciliation possible. Jesus is its agent (13.5). He is the one who eats with sinners (like the father plans to do) and in so doing affirms himself to be the divine presence in the community (14.10). When Esau runs, falls on the neck of Jacob and kisses him, threatened violence is avoided and a temporary truce is achieved, but permanent reconciliation eludes them. In the parable the father takes upon himself that critical role, and in the process Jesus tells us who he is (13.14). The little boy in the courtyard of the family home confirms that identification (14.11).

Indeed, this parable, with its comparisons with the Jacob saga, provides a clear picture of Jesus of Nazareth, the theologian. The brilliance, subtlety, insight and daring exhibited in this new story structured on the old saga quicken the mind and move the heart. This accomplishment sheds light on who Jesus was, the theology he developed and the task he accomplished.

The human and divine reconciliation that Jesus seeks is not merely for individuals and groups of people in the community but also for the nation as a whole. Jesus sees the nation (tax collectors as well as Pharisees) still in exile

---

[2]K. Cragg, *The Call of the Minaret*, p. 55.

from God. His goal includes a call to the nation (represented by the two sons) to accept being brought back from that exile. Both the lost sheep *and the lost flock* need to be brought home from the wilderness.

REPENTANCE/SALVATION

In the light of the Jacob saga, what is said in the parable about these two interrelated themes? Again, the flow of the story will guide this brief summary. Each of the following dramatic incidents has roots in the Jacob saga.

1. The great rebellion. The two sons in the parable are not historical figures and do not possess names. They are more than "Pharisees" and "sinners." They represent types of human beings and thereby portray the human predicament (11.6). This universalizing of the drama of "exile and return" is evident in the nature of the blessing/inheritance (11.2). The prodigal is given the father's "life" *(ton bion),* and the reader is called on to reflect on the life of God given to humans made in God's image (Gen 1:27). In both stories, on the eve of the younger son's departure the older son is quiet, and that silence reflects profound displeasure (11.11). Thus the "drama of salvation" opens with sinners radically estranged from God and the "righteous," who stand ominously aloof. These two kinds of people are found in every culture. They are also rooted in the "sinners" and the "scribes and Pharisees" that surrounded Jesus.

2. The far country. Going into self-imposed exile from God, the prodigal in the end is reconciled to him in the person of the father. The great drama of exile and return is presented as the potential journey of person, a party and a nation in spiritual exile, not the migration of a tribal leader (12.1; 12.7). The plot thickens dramatically when the prodigal (like Jacob) plans his return from the far country but evidences no remorse (12.8). He prepares a speech that is a quote from the mouth of Pharaoh trying to manipulate Moses (13.4). Jacob does not prepare a speech for his father or for Esau, but on meeting the latter the speech he delivers successfully manipulates Esau and achieves Jacob's purpose, which is survival.

Jacob expresses no need for repentance, but at the edge of the village, after accepting his father's love, the prodigal's speech shifts dramatically from a calculated attempt to manipulate his father into a sincere confession of sin and unworthiness (13.4). The prodigal's speech, as formulated in the far country, appears to fulfill the popular understanding of repentance as it was known in Jesus' day. He will confess sin *and make compensation for it* (13.4).

3. The edge of the village. Esau goes out to meet Jacob. In a similar yet radically different way the father does not wait for the prodigal to reach the house but also leaves home and runs out through the village to meet the prodigal (13.6). Seeing the prodigal "yet at a distance" (Lk 15:20), the father pays a high price in public humiliation to offer costly love to him (13.3) and to achieve reconciliation with him (13.5). The father wants this to take place in public so that the villagers will see his actions and themselves be reconciled to the prodigal (13.6). The father's servants follow him down the street and become agents of the larger plan of restoration (13.7). They are not a small army mustered to force the father's will as in the case of Esau. The kiss is no longer an act of deception, like Jacob's kiss on Isaac's cheek, but rather an act of compassionate love as the father kisses his lost, dead son (13.8). The prodigal receives gifts instead of giving them, as Jacob managed to do (13.9). The best robe of the house is not a stolen garment of deception but an offered robe of reconciliation and restoration (13.10). Body contact with a divine agent is not a wrestling match but an act of surrender (13.1) The prodigal returns to a restored relationship, not to a chieftain's inheritance of land (13.11). The role of hero (Jacob) is transferred to the self-giving father (13.12). Acceptance of being found becomes the model and meaning of the prodigal's authentic repentance (13.15). For him salvation is found in the freely offered, costly, self-emptying love of his compassionate father, who takes upon himself the role of a servant as he empties himself on the road before the village. The prodigal accepts the offered love, and the father orders a banquet to celebrate the success of his costly efforts (13.15). The banquet is to seal reconciliation, not separation as in the case of Jacob and Laban.

4. The older son. The older son (the "righteous") discovers that peace/ reconciliation has been offered to and accepted by his wayward brother (14.2). He becomes angry (14.4) at the "injustice" of grace (14.3). The father then offers that same grace to the older son, only at greater cost. (14.5). The reconciliation of the new Esau also has its price. Rather than accepting the love offered and evidencing comprehension of its cost, the older son delivers a bitter outburst, accusing and attacking his father (14.6; 14.7; 14.8). In the process he affirms a complete misunderstanding of the nature of the banquet (14.10). The father then offers love that is even more costly as he absorbs the public insult (14.9) and pleads for joy—a central part of the story (14.11). The two types of sinners are in need of the same freely offered, costly love in order to be saved. Will there be a "return from exile" for the older son? Will the older son "accept being found" by that costly love? Will he repent and accept being reconciled? Will the ninety-nine in the wilderness let the shepherd find them? The answer hangs in the balance as the listeners/readers are obliged to finish the play in the depths of their own hearts.

Individuals within Jesus' audience were related to identifiable parties. Those groups were part of a larger nation. Implications for both "sinners" and "the righteous" are clear for the individual listener, for the parties in that society and for the nation. In Jesus' eyes Israel was still in exile needing to be brought back to God her loving father. Armed conflict with Rome would bring death. Restoration from spiritual exile would bring resurrection.

Exile and return—Jacob's journey, the prodigal's journey and the hoped-for journey of the older son all resonate in the parable of the compassionate father.

Conclusions

Four early Jewish presentations of the saga of Jacob were examined above. The author of *Jubilees,* writing in Hebrew, rewrote the story giving it his own coloration. Philo, writing in Greek, found in it philosophical allegory. Josephus, also writing in Greek, tried to gain a sympathetic understanding of Jewish history and culture among Gentile readers. In the first century, and in the centuries immediately following, the rabbis reused older scriptural material for new purposes. To repeat Neusner's image, the Scriptures were paints on the palettes of the sages as they painted their own new pictures. What then does Jesus do with this tradition?

Within that world in general, and within the world of *Jubilees* and the sages of Israel in particular, Jesus tells a new story that follows the outline of the old. He creates the parable of the prodigal son following the story line of the saga of Jacob. Like the writer of *Jubilees,* he takes liberty with the old story, and like the sages he uses old paints to create a new picture. But what is truly startling is that, unlike the writer of *Jubilees* and the sages, Jesus writes himself into the drama as its hero and main character. Jesus is the good shepherd, the good woman and the good father. The good shepherd is built on Psalm 23, Jeremiah 23:1-8 and Ezekiel 34:1-31, as has been seen. The tale of the good woman mirrors the good shepherd and has behind it various texts in the Hebrew Scriptures where God is described in female terms. The parable of the good father and his two wayward sons borrows from and reshapes the saga of Jacob. Building on the past provides the potential for re-creation for the present and for the future.

It is possible to see Lincoln at Gettysburg doing the same kind of thing in a much lesser way. In his famous speech at the dedication of the cemetery in Gettysburg on November 19, 1863, Lincoln reshaped America's self-understanding. To do so, he opened with a selection out of the story of America's past. He did not begin with the Constitution—compromised as it was by its accommodation to slavery. Instead, he chose the Declaration of Independence with its ringing phrase "All men are created equal." Lincoln began, "Four score and seven years ago our fathers brought forth on this continent a new nation, dedicated to the proposition that all men are created equal."

Lincoln then took that carefully selected foundation stone embedded in American history and built on it. The new construction he placed on that foundation was a new story in which he was a major actor. He said, "We are now engaged in a great civil war, testing whether that nation, or any nation so conceived and so dedicated, can long endure."

He concluded by saying, "We here highly resolve that these dead shall not have died in vain—and that government of the people, by the people, for the people, shall not perish from the earth." Building on a selection out of the founding story of the nation, he created a new vision for the present and the future. The selection and the creation are critical for the finished reality, which, as Garry Wills affirms, "remade America."[1] Was Jesus not engaged in something somewhat similar?

It is easy to forget that the creator of a great story has the freedom to choose where to begin. Jesus sees himself as the divine presence in the community with the task of calling Israel back to God. Israel is *"lost in exile"* and needs to be *brought back*. To philosophize like Philo will not do. He must tell a story; and to be effective the new story must resonate with a time-honored tale out of the past. The story of Abraham will not do. Abraham migrated from Ur of the Chaldeans to the land of Canaan. The story of Isaac is also inappropriate. Isaac does not go anywhere. Joseph is born in Haran, on the Euphrates and dies in Egypt, and thus his story is also inadequate. Moses is born in Egypt and dies across the Jordan. Thus his pilgrimage does not mirror Israel's history. But Jacob's story is a tale of life at home followed by exile and finally return. The saga of Jacob has the necessary outline, and Jacob is Israel. Perfect! Jesus *deliberately chooses this story* out of all the other major stories available to him and reshapes it into an account of who he is, what Israel's

---

[1]G. Wills, *Lincoln at Gettysburg: The Words That Remade America.*

predicament has come to be, and how he has come to bring her exile to an end. The polished result is the story we have examined.

As Jesus re-creates the saga of Jacob/Israel in a parable, a few dramatic items are unique to one story or the other. The vast majority of the elements observed and discussed above first appear in the Jacob saga and are then *repeated, revised* or *reversed* as they appear in the second. There are too many of them for all of this to be an accident. The author of the parable is clearly creating a new story for a recognizable community that follows the outline of and builds upon the old story. With confidence we can affirm Jesus of Nazareth as the theologian who created these three sophisticated, intertextual and interlocking stories.

The issue is not a question of absolute proof but rather of overwhelming probability. The author of the lost sheep, the lost coin and the two lost sons must be a Jew steeped in the Hebrew Scriptures who is composing for a sophisticated Jewish audience. The author has so totally absorbed the three accounts of the good shepherd (Ps 23; Jer 23:1-8; Ezek 34:1-31) and the saga of Jacob (Gen 27:1—36:8) that they are a part of his bloodstream. There is no point in expending the enormous creative energy required to build a finely crafted new story with dozens of dramatic elements taken and reshaped from an old story, unless the audience for which this masterpiece is being fashioned is able to absorb and interact with what that author is doing. Theophilus, the recipient of Luke's Gospel (Lk 1:1-4), would catch little if any of this sophisticated intertextuality. The story applies to him in a broad sense but is not created for him in the rooted historical sense. In fact, the Gentile church did not see this deep interconnectedness with the story of Jacob. Yes, the story does have a universal appeal, and its impact can be felt in any culture, which is why it has had such enormous influence across the ages. But who is responsible for the counterpoint—the blending of two melodies, Jacob and the prodigal—this sacred dance that is so majestic to behold? The only reasonable conclusion is to affirm that Luke was given this material by the apostolic community and that it was composed by Jesus of Nazareth.

These three parables show Jesus responding to a challenge from his contemporaries. He takes a story about a particular tribe and its self-understanding and transforms it into a drama that relates both to the nation as a whole and to the human predicament. The heart of this new story, built on the old, climaxes on a particular divine intervention of costly love into that predicament. As seen, Jesus presents himself as the agent of that divine intervention:

as the good shepherd, the good women and the good father. To repeat N. T. Wright's choice phrase, Jesus offers "significant variations on the parent worldview."[2]

In short, in this great parable, Jesus presents a freshly created identity-forming story for his entire community knowing that it is also appropriate for all the sons and daughters of Adam, not merely for the children of Jacob.

"Rebellious sinners" become "Jacob," and "righteous sinners" are presented as the new "Esau." The father, a symbol for God, evolves into a symbol for Jesus, who at great cost offers reconciliation separately to each type of sinner. If accepted, this new identity-forming story will make irrelevant the politics of "fight to the death against Rome" espoused by the zealots of the day. Jesus is quite able to hear the rumbling of the approach of a great storm. His offered new story, if accepted, will disperse that storm, and the nation will be saved. When it becomes evident to him that only a few catch the vision of the new story, he weeps—over Jerusalem! Even on his way to the cross, his perceptions of the hard days ahead for the nation are still on his mind as he responds to the lament of the women (Lk 23:28-31).

As he creates the parable of the good shepherd Jesus rewrites Psalm 23. In the parable of the compassionate father and the two lost sons, he presents a new version of eight chapters of the Torah with himself at its center. The centuries-old Latin saying is correct—this parable contains the gospel within the gospel. It is indeed

Evangelium in Evangelio.

---

[2]N. T. Wright, *Jesus and the Victory of God*, p. 139.

APPENDIX

*Index of the Various Types of Contrasts and Comparisons
Between the Saga of Jacob (Gen 27—35) and the
Parable of the Prodigal Son (Lk 15:11-32)*

The fifty-one points of comparison and contrast noted in the above discussion can be classified into three types.

    A. Dramatic material that appears in each account in *nearly the same way*.

    B. Dramatic material that appears in each account where the reuse in the parable shows *some significant revision*.

    C. Dramatic material that appears in both stories but is *reversed* or *radically changed* as it reappears in the parable.

In both stories the younger son travels to a far country while the older son remains at home. Such dramatic elements appear in each account in roughly the same way and will appear in list "A." At the same time, Jacob receives a *blessing,* and the prodigal is given an *inheritance.* The two are similar, but there are important differences. These items will be labeled "B." Finally, Jacob begins his sojourn in the far country with *nothing* and becomes *rich.* The prodigal also travels to a far country but starts his time there as a *rich* man and descends into *abject poverty.* In this case the same theme of "riches/poverty" appears in each account, but the two uses are in sharp contrast. Such items will appear in list "C."

These are not clear-cut distinctions, and it has not always been easy to select the most apt category. The designations that appear below are suggestions for categories that the reader may find helpful. For cross-referencing purposes, the numbering system that appears in the above discussion is maintained here.

The three lists are as follows:

A. *Dramatic material that appears in each account with little change.*

11.5 A father and two sons

11.9 The need for haste

11.11 Estrangement

12.1 The rebellious younger son in the far country (exile and return)

12.2 The older son stays at home (off stage)

12.6 Fear on the eve of return

12.8 Lack of remorse

13.2 Run, fall on neck, kiss

13.13 Characteristics of the two sons

14.1 The older son comes in from the field

14.7 A young goat (kid) for a meal

14.16 The identity of the remembering community

B. *Dramatic material that appears in each account where the reuse in the parable shows some significant revision*

11.1 The death of the father

11.2 The younger son breaks relationship with his father

11.6 The identity of the two sons

11.7 The nature of the blessing/inheritance

11.8 The method of acquiring the inheritance

11.10. Deception and betrayal

12.3. Honorable versus dishonorable animal husbandry

12.7 Direction and purpose of return

13.4 The manipulative speech

13.6 The location of the meeting with the returning son

13.13 Salvation/repentance

14.2. The younger son's return and the question of safety/peace

14.3 On arrival at the house both older sons face "injustice"

14.4 The older son becomes angry

14.6 The angry, aggressive speech

14.9 Reconciliation with the older brother

C. *Dramatic material that appears in each account but with major dif-*
ferences

    11.3. The nature of the father

    11.4 The mother

    11.12 To burn or not to burn the bridges

    12.4 Community in the far country

    12.5 Success versus failure in the far country

    13.1 Divine visitation/incarnation

    13.3 The family agent

    13.5 Reconciliation with the father

    13.7 The retainers and the motive of the family agent

    13.8 The kiss

    13.9 Gifts on return

    13.10 Dressed in the best robe

    13.11 The promise of land

    13.12 The hero of the story

    13.14 Costly love

    14.5 The father responds to his angry son

    14.8. "All that you see is mine" versus "All that is mine is yours"

    14.10 A banquet celebration

    14.11 Joy

    14.12 The evolution of the symbol of the father to a symbol for Jesus

    14.13 The two sons and the intended listeners/readers

    14.14 The Gentiles

    14.15 The ending: present or missing?

BIBLIOGRAPHY

Abrahams, Israel. *Studies in Pharisaism and the Gospels.* 2 vols. 1917, 1924. Reprint, New York: Ktav, 1967.

Allison, Dale. "Books and the Book." An Installation Address Delivered May 9, 2000. Pittsburgh Theological Seminary (616 North Highland Avenue, Pittsburgh, PA 15206-2596), 2001.

The Anchor Bible Dictionary. Edited by David Noel Freedman. 6 vols. New York: Doubleday, 1992.

The Alternative Service Book 1980. Oxford: Oxford University Press, 1980.

Aristotle. *The Basic Works of Aristotle.* Edited by Richard McKeon. New York: Random House, 1941.

Bailey, Kenneth E. *The Cross and the Prodigal: The 15th Chapter of Luke, Seen Through the Eyes of Middle Eastern Peasants.* St. Louis: Concordia, 1973. Reprint, Acorn Press: Melbourne, 2000. Cited as *Cross.*

———. *Finding the Lost: Cultural Keys to Luke 15.* St. Louis: Concordia, 1992. Cited as *Finding.*

———. "The Historical Jesus: A Middle Eastern View." Four thirty-minute videocassette lectures. Crossways International (7930 Computer Avenue South, Minneapolis, MN 55435; phone: 800-257-7308), 2001.

———. "Informal Controlled Oral Tradition and the Synoptic Gospels." *Tamelos* 20 (1995): 4-11. Revised version of "Informal Controlled Oral Tradition and the Synoptic Gospels." *Asia Journal of Theology* 5 (1991): 34-54. Cited as "Informal."

———. "Jacob and the Prodigal: A New Identity and a New Vision of Atonement." *The Presbyterian Outlook,* April 24, 2000, pp. 23-24. Cited as "Jacob."

———. "Jacob and the Prodigal Son: A New Identity Story." *Theological Review* (Beirut) 18 (1997): 54-72. Cited as "A New Identity Story."

————. "Middle Eastern Oral Tradition and the Synoptic Gospels." *The Expository Times* 106 (1995): 363-67. Cited as "Oral Tradition."

————. *Poet and Peasant* and *Through Peasant Eyes.* 1976, 1980. Reprint (combined edition), Grand Rapids: Eerdmans, 1983. Cited as *Poet.*

————. "Psalm 23 and Luke 15: A Vision Expanded." *Irish Biblical Studies* 12 (1990): 54-71.

————. "The Pursuing Father." *Christianity Today* 42, no. 12 (1998): 34-40. Cited as "Pursuing."

————. "Recovering the Poetic Structure of I Corinthians i17-ii2: A Study in Text and Commentary." *Novum Testamentum* 17 (1975): 265-96. Cited as "Recovering."

————. "Women in Ben Sirach and in the New Testament." In *For Me to Live: Essays in Honor of James L. Kelso,* edited by Robert A. Coughenour. 56-73. Cleveland: Dillon/Leiderbach, 1972.

————. "Women in the New Testament: A Middle Eastern Cultural View." *Anvil* 11 (1994): 4-24. Also published in *Theology Matters* (Presbyterians for Faith, Family and Ministry, P.O. Box 10249, Blacksburg, VA 24062-0249) 6, no. 1 (Jan/Feb 2000): 1-11.

Batey, Richard A. *Jesus and the Forgotten City: New Light on Sepphoris and the Urban World of Jesus.* Grand Rapids: Baker, 1991.

Bauer, Walter, with William F. Arndt, F. Wilbur Gingrich, and Frederick W. Danker. *A Greek-English Lexicon of the New Testament.* 2d ed. Chicago: University of Chicago Press, 1979.

Blomberg, Craig L. *Interpreting the Parables.* Downers Grove, Ill.: InterVarsity Press, 1990.

Bonhoeffer, Dietrich. *Meditations on the Cross.* Louisville: Westminster John Knox, 1998.

Borgen, Peder. "Philo of Alexandria." In *The Anchor Bible Dictionary,* 5:333-42. Edited by David Noel Freedman. New York: Doubleday, 1992.

Corbo, Virgilio C. *The House of St. Peter at Capharnaum.* Translated by Sylvester Saller. Jerusalem: Franciscan, 1969.

Cragg, Kenneth. *The Call of the Minaret.* New York: Oxford University Press, 1956.

Danby, Herbert, trans. and ed. *The Mishnah.* 1933. Reprint, Oxford: Oxford University Press, 1980.

Derrett, J. Duncan M. "Law in the New Testament: The Parable of the Prodigal Son." *New Testament Studies* 14 (1967): 56-74.

Dodd, C. H. *The Founder of Christianity.* New York: Macmillan, 1970.

Dunn, James D. G. *The Parting of the Ways: Between Christianity and Judaism and Their Significance for the Character of Christianity.* Philadelphia: Trinity Press International, 1991.

————. *Romans.* Word Biblical Commentary 38-39. Dallas: Word, 1988.

Eisenmann, Robert H., and Michael Owen Wise, trans. and int. *The Dead Sea Scrolls Uncovered.* Rockport: Element, 1992.

Feldman, Louis H. "Josephus." In *The Anchor Bible Dictionary,* 3:981-98. Edited by David Noel Freedman. New York: Doubleday, 1992.

Fitzmyer, Joseph. *The Gospel According to Luke.* Anchor Bible 28B. New York: Doubleday, 1985.

————. *Luke the Theologian: Aspects of His Teaching.* London: Geoffrey Chapman, 1989.

Flusser, David. *Judaism and the Origins of Christianity.* Jerusalem: Magnes, 1988.

Flusser, David, with R. Steven Notley. *Jesus.* Rev. ed. Jerusalem: Magnes, 1997.

Ford, Richard Q. *The Parables of Jesus: Recovering the Art of Listening.* Minneapolis: Fortress Press, 1997.

Gerhardsson, Birger. *Memory and Manuscript: Oral Tradition and Written Transmission in Rabbinic Judaism and Early Christianity.* Translated by Eric J. Sharpe. Acta Seminarii Neotestamentici Upsaliensis 22. Lund: Gleerup, 1961.

Hatch, Edwin, and Henry A. Redpath. *A Concordance to the Septuagint and the Other Greek Versions of the Old Testament (Including the Apocryphal Books).* 2 vols. 1897. Reprint, Graz: Akademische Druck, 1954.

Hengel, Martin. *The Zealots.* Edinburgh: T & T Clark, 1989.

Holgate, David A. *Prodigality, Liberality and Meanness in the Parable of the Prodigal Son: A Greco-Roman Perspective on Luke 15:11-32.* Sheffield: Sheffield Academic Press, 1999.

Horowitz, George. *The Spirit of Jewish Law.* New York: Central Book, 1953.

Hultgren, Arland J. *The Parables of Jesus: A Commentary.* Grand Rapids: Eerdmans, 2000.

Jasper, R. C. D., and Paul F. Bradshaw. *A Companion to the Alternative Service Book.* London: SPCK, 1986.

Jeremias, Joachim. *The Parables of Jesus.* Rev. ed. London: SCM Press, 1963.

The Jerome Biblical Commentary. Edited by Raymond E. Brown, Joseph A. Fitzmyer, and Roland E. Murphy. Englewood Cliffs, N.J.: Prentice-Hall, 1968.

Jewett, Robert. *Dating Paul's Life.* London: SCM Press, 1979.

Josephus. *The Works of Josephus: Complete and Unabridged.* Translated by William Whiston. Peabody, Mass.: Hendrickson, 1987.

Jülicher, Adolf. *Die Gleichnisreden Jesu.* 2 vols. Tübingen: J. C. B. Mohr, 1899.

Kelber, Werner H. *The Oral and the Written Gospel.* Philadelphia: Fortress, 1983.

Kittel, Gerhard, and Gerhard Friedrich, eds. *Theological Dictionary of the New Testament.* 10 vols. Translated by Geoffrey W. Bromiley. Grand Rapids: Eerdmans, 1964-1976.

Klimkeit, Hans-Joachim, trans. and ed. *Gnosis on the Silk Road: Gnostic Texts from Central Asia.* San Francisco: Harper, 1993.

Lachs, Samuel Tobias. *A Rabbinic Commentary on the New Testament: The Gospels of Matthew, Mark and Luke.* Hoboken, N.J.: Ktav, 1987.

Levison, Nahum. *The Parables: Their Background and Local Setting.* Edinburgh: T & T Clark, 1926.

Maly, Eugene H. "Genesis." In *The Jerome Biblical Commentary,* pp. 7-46. Englewood Cliffs, N.J.: Prentice-Hall, 1968.

Marshall, I. Howard. *The Gospel of Luke: A Commentary on the Greek Text.* The New International Greek Testament Commentary. Exeter: Paternoster, 1978.

McLean, Bradley H. *Citations and Allusions to Jewish Scripture in early Christian and Jewish Writings Through 180 C.E.* Lewiston, N.Y.: Mellen, 1992.

Moore, George Foot. "The *Am Ha-aares* (the People of the Land) and the *Haberim* (Associates)." In *The Beginnings of Christianity,* 1:439-45. Edited by F. J. Foakes-Jackson and Kirshopp Lake. London: Macmillan, 1939.

———. *Judaism in the First Centuries of the Christian Era, the Age of the Tannaim.* 2 vols. 1927, 1930. Reprint, New York: Schocken, 1971.

Neusner, Jacob. *Genesis Rabbah: The Judaic Commentary to the Book of Genesis, A New American Translation.* Vols. 1-3. Atlanta: Scholars Press, 1985.

Neusner, Jacob, with William Scott Green. *Writing with Scripture: The Authority and Uses of the Hebrew Bible in the Torah of Formative Judaism.* Minneapolis: Fortress, 1989.

Newbigin, Lesslie. *The Gospel in a Pluralist Society.* Grand Rapids: Eerdmans, 1989.

———. *A Word in Season: Perspectives on Christian World Missions.* Grand Rapids: Eerdmans, 1994.

Nouwen, Henri J. M. *The Return of the Prodigal Son.* New York: Doubleday, 1992.

Perkins, Pheme. *Hearing the Parables of Jesus.* New York: Paulist, 1981.

Philo. *The Works of Philo: Complete and Unabridged.* Translated by C. D. Yonge. Peabody, Mass.: Hendrickson, 1993.

Plummer, Alfred. *A Critical and Exegetical Commentary on the Gospel According to S. Luke.* 5th ed. Edinburgh: T & T Clark, 1951.

Radzinsky, Edvard. *The Last Tsar.* London: Arrow Books, 1993.

Reisenfeld, Harald. *The Gospel Tradition.* Philadelphia: Fortress, 1970.

Safrai, Shemuel, and M. Stern with D. Flusser and W. C. van Unnick, eds. *The Jewish People in the First Century: Historical Geography, Political History, Social Cultural, and Religious Life and Institutions.* Vol. 2. Philadelphia: Fortress, 1976.

Sandys, Celia. *Churchill Wanted Dead or Alive.* New York: Carroll and Graf, 2000.

Scott, Bernard Brandon. *Hear Then the Parable: A Commentary on the Parables of Jesus.* Minneapolis: Fortress, 1989.

Temple, William. *Readings in St. John's Gospel.* 1945. Reprint, London: Macmillan, 1955.

Thoma, Clemens. "Literary and Theological Aspects of the Rabbinic Parables." In *Parable and Story in Judaism and Christianity,* ed. C. Thoma and M. Wyschogrod. Mahwah, N.J.: Paulist, 1989.

Urbach, Ephraim E. *The Sages: Their Concepts and Beliefs.* 2 vols. 1975. Reprint, Jerusalem: Magnes, 1987.

Walls, Andrew F. *The Missionary Movement in Christian History: Studies in the Transmission of Faith.* New York: Orbis, 1996.

Wansbrough, Henry, ed. *Jesus and the Oral Gospel Tradition.* Journal for the Study of the New Testament Supplement Series 64. Sheffield: JSOT Press, 1991.

Wills, Garry. *Lincoln at Gettysburg: The Words That Remade America.* New York: Simon & Schuster, 1992.

Wintermute, O. S. *"Jubilees:* A New Translation and Introduction." In *The Old Testament Pseudepigrapha,* 2:35-142. New York: Doubleday, 1985.

Wolfson, Harry Austryn. *Philo: Foundations of Religious Philosophy in Judaism, Christianity and Islam.* 2 vols. Cambridge: Harvard University Press, 1947.

Wright, N. T. *Jesus and the Victory of God, Christian Origins and the Question of God.* Vol. 2. Minneapolis: Fortress Press, 1996.

Arabic Christian Sources

Barsoum, I. Ephrem. *al-Lu'lu' al-Manthur* (History of Syriac Sciences and Literature [Arabic]). Baghdad: al-Sha'b, 1976.

Hibatallah ibn Al-Assal. *The Four Gospels (Arabic).* British Museum Oriental manuscript no. 3382. This critical edition of the four Gospels was composed by Hibatallah in Cairo in 1252. It contains more than ten thousand marginal notes.

Ibn al-Salibi, Diyunisiyus Ja'qub [d. 1171 A.D.]. *Kitab al-Durr al-Farid fi Tafsir al-'Ahd al-Jadid* (The Book of Unique Pearls of Interpretation of the New Testament [Arabic]). 2 vols. (Written in Syriac ca. 1150 A.D. Translated from Syriac into Arabic in the Syrian Orthodox monastery of al-Za'faran in 1729. The Arabic was edited and corrected by 'Abd al-Masih al-Dawalani and published in Arabic.) 2 vols. Cairo: n.p., 1914. Cited as *Durr.*

Ibn al-Tayyib, Abdallah [d. 1043]. *Diatessaron de Tatien* [Arabic and French]. Edited and translated by A. S. Marmardji. Beyrouth: Imprimerie Catholique, 1935.

———. *Tafsir al-Mishriqi* (The Interpretation of the Four Gospels by the Rev. Abu al-Faraj Abdallah Ibn al-Tayyib al-Mishriqi [Arabic]). 2 vols. Edited by Rev. Yousif Manqariyus. Cairo: al-Towfiq Press, 1908. Two manuscript copies of this work are held in Paris (Bibliotheque Nationale), Arabic 85 and 86. Cited as *Tafsir.*

Mount Sinai Arabic MSS #72 (Four Gospels). This manuscript, translated from the

Greek, is dated A.D. 897 and is the oldest of eight extant copies of the important early Arabic version.

Musa bar Kepha [d. 905]. *Commentary on St. Luke.* Unpublished Syriac. A microfilm of this manuscript is held in the Syriac Institute of the Lutheran School of Theology, 1100 E. 55th Street, Chicago, IL, 60615. A preliminary translation into English has been made by the director of the Syriac Institute, Dr. 'Abd al-Masih Saadi. All quotations of this work are based on the translation by Saadi. The folio references are to the original Syriac microfilm. Its shelf number in the Syriac Institute is Mardin 102. Cited as *Luke.*

Sa'id, Ebrahim. *Sharh Bisharat Luqa* (Commentary on the Gospel of Luke [Arabic]). 1935. Reprint, Beirut: Near East Council of Churches, 1970. Cited as *Luqa.*

Vatican Library Arabic manuscript no. 18. This copy of the Gospel of Luke was made in Egypt in 993.

Judaica

The Babylonian Talmud: Hebrew-English Edition. 32 vols. Translated into English with notes, glossary and indices by Maurice Simon. Edited by Isidore Epstein. New York: Soncino, 1960, 1965, 1972, 1980. Cited by tractate and folio.

The Dead Sea Scrolls in English. Translated by Géza Vermès. Baltimore: Penguin, 1973.

Genesis Rabbah, The Judaic Commentary to the Book of Genesis, A New American Translation. Translation and commentary by Jacob Neusner. 3 vols. Atlanta: Scholars Press, 1985.

Midrash Rabbah. Edited by H. Freedman and Maurice Simon. 3d ed. 10 vols. New York: Soncino, 1983. Cited by biblical book, chapter, and verse and by volume and page number in this edition.

The Mishnah. Translated from the Hebrew with introduction and brief explanatory notes by Herbert Danby. 1933. Reprint, Oxford: The University Press, 1980. Cited by tractate, chapter and, verse and by page number in Danby translation.

The Talmud of the Land of Israel. Translated by Jacob Neusner. 35 vols. Chicago: University of Chicago Press, 1982-1987. Quoted by tractate and folio.

The Tosefta. Edited by Jacob Neusner. 6 vols. Hoboken, N.J.: Ktav, 1986.

Index of Authors